The Congress Papers

Freiburg 1999

The Congress Papers

An Ongoing Discovery: Looking towards the 21st Century

From the 6th International Congress on the F. M. Alexander Technique 9–14 August 1999, Freiburg, Germany

edited by
Jean M. O. Fischer

STAT ❧ Books

Published January 2001 by

STAT Books Ltd.

The Books Division of
The Society of Teachers of the Alexander Technique
129 Camden Mews
London NW1 9AH
Great Britain

British Library Cataloguing-in-Publication Data
A catalogue record for this book is available from the British Library.

ISBN 0-9519304-8-6 (paperback)
The Congress Papers. An Ongoing Discovery:
Looking towards the 21st Century

Front cover typeset in Rotis Sans Serif.
Text in New Baskerville 10/12.
Front cover based on a design by Marcel Schmid.
Design, lay-out, and typesetting by Jean M. O. Fischer.
Printed on 80gsm High Opaque
and bound in the United Kingdom
by Redwood Books Limited, Trowbridge, Wiltshire.

Contents

Keynote Address, Topics, Evening Lectures, Senior Guest Teachers

Forum: Special Interest Classes

Photographs from the Congress (pp. 8, 16, 50, 53, 67, 121,148, 170, 172, and the back cover) were taken by Nicola Hahnefeld, Freiburg, and are reproduced with permission. All other illustrations supplied by the authors.

All lectures and presentations were recorded professionally and are available on CD. Contact Peter Ruhrberg, Columbusstr. 21, D-40549, Düsseldorf, Germany. Phone +49 211 572770. E-mail: p.ruhrberg@online-club.de

The Congress Directors, clockwise from top: Karoline Erdmann (Germany), Daniel Süsstrunk (Germany), Michael Fortwängler (Germany), and Doris Dietschy (Switzerland).

Foreword

Looking back to the 6.99 Congress, which took place in the summer of 1999, the planning and development up to the final form of this big event seems almost like a miracle to us now. When asked if we would accept the responsibility and the honour of organizing a world-wide Alexander Technique Congress in Germany we naturally had no idea of what to expect. But the wish to share our vision made us take on this big challenge. After some careful thought, we decided to increase the team to four and to include Doris Dietschy from Switzerland who had an invaluable amount of experience gained at three previous congresses.

As the theme of the prior congress in Jerusalem had been looking back to the past, it was clear to us from the beginning that we wanted to look ahead. We wanted to explore how the Technique might be viewed in the approaching millennium. We were certain that we wanted to be open to unknown possibilities. We were curious about what others had discovered as we wanted to learn from them for the benefit of our own work.

Three items appealed to us so much that they became the three main topics: emotions, concepts and communication.

Emotions are part of ourselves and occur in interaction with others, but where do they find their place in an Alexander lesson?

Regarding the topic of concepts, we first intended to explore Alexander's philosophical background, but it took a turn in the direction of neuroscience, the ability of the brain to learn.

The third of our interests was teaching and how important communication is in this process.

To develop these topics fully we needed just the right presenters. We found them in Mary Cox, who was a very excellent lecturer and engaged participant throughout the congress, in Kevan Martin and Lucia Walker, who developed their ideas together so admirably and, finally, in Cathy Madden and

Jeremy Chance, both of whom gave much thought to their subject and presented it in a very lively performance.

How could the ideas demonstrated be used in a practical situation? To answer this question we created the "Application-to-the-Technique" groups. Through the great efforts of the leaders and co-leaders the link to the theory was successfully made. We wish to thank Ann Battye, Bob Britton, Bruce Fertman, Michael Frederick, Joan Frost, Marie-Françoise Le Foll, David Garlick, Shmuel Nelken, Jane Saunderson, Susan Scott and Ken Thompson who undertook the great responsibility of coaching the participants.

An increasing interest in spiritual practise among Alexander colleagues caused us to devote one morning to spirituality. In Purna Steinitz and in the Zen monk Claude AnShin Thomas we were happy to have found two internationally well-known speakers. We thank them for their contribution.

There were many more people without whose help the Congress would not have been possible. Their commitment made it the success it was.

We would most particularly like to thank our senior guests Marjory Barlow, Anthony Spawforth, Elizabeth Walker and Erika Whittaker for taking the trouble to travel to Freiburg in order to greatly enrich the Congress through their participation and their classes.

We would also like to thank the facilitators guiding the practical work sessions: Alexander Bartmann, Rivka Cohen, Astrid Cox, Arie Hoorweg, Elizabeth Langford, Vivien Mackie, Robin Möckli, Hitomi Ono, Giora Pinchas, Irma Rellstab, Walter Tschaikowski.

We are also grateful to all the teachers who gave stimulating workshops, classes or talks.

We specially want to thank our secretary Sophie Josuttis who did a splendid and most efficient job managing the office. A big thank you to Peter and Irma Ruhrberg who were responsible for the superb sound and the recordings, and to all of the many helpers who took care of the registration, checking the rooms, locking buildings, and the many other small details which were so important.

We would like to thank the management of the Musikhochschule Freiburg and their most helpful team, the cleaning crew, the Tourist Office of Freiburg, all the Alexander societies for their help with addresses and advertising the Congress to their members, the translator who checked our English, the DJ of the farewell party, the video team, the catering service for their care and delicious food, and those we might have forgotten to name here.

We trust that the publication of this selection of papers reminding us of events that are full of good memories will continue the process of open-mindedness and willingness to learn from others that was started in Freiburg.

Doris Dietschy
Karoline Erdmann
Michael Fortwängler
Daniel Süsstrunk

Editor's note

All speakers and teachers who gave workshops at the Congress were invited to contribute to this volume. Some did so before the Congress, some after, but not everybody was able to contribute.

The two talks on spirituality and Marjory Barlow's Masterclass were transcribed from recordings and subsequently edited by myself.

Spelling and the use of capitals and italics have been standardised; grammar has been corrected and punctuation changed where necessary for greater clarity. Unless otherwise indicated, each contribution appears in full. All contributors were sent the edited versions of their papers for approval.

I am grateful to Seánan Forbes and Ian MacFadyen for their help and invaluable advice in editing the papers.

The views expressed in this volume are those of the authors and not necessarily those of STAT Books or of the Society of Teachers of the Alexander Technique.

Jean M. O. Fischer
London, October 2000

Preface

Michael D. Frederick

The 6th International Alexander Congress in Freiburg was tremendously stimulating and inspiring. My impression is that it was a profitable experience for all, both personally and professionally.

The Congress was an opportunity for us to learn from each other, to share our ideas, our feelings, and any new creativity we may have discovered in relationship to the work that we call the Alexander Technique. It gave us the chance to connect with old friends that we hadn't seen for years and to discover and make new friends.

A Congress can give one a sense of perspective on this important psychophysical work. It reminded me of a Sufi parable "The Great Namouss and the Elephant" from Idries Shah's *Tales of the Dervishes.* The story, I believe, goes like this:

> Once upon a time, a long, long time ago in a far off land, there was a gnat. His name was Namouss, and he was known as Perceptive Namouss. He decided, after careful reflection and thought, to move house. He wanted to live in the ear of a certain elephant. On the first day of moving in he paid his respects to the elephant according to established tradition and custom. He shouted, at the top of his tiny voice: "O Elephant! I, Narmouss the Gnat, known as Perceptive Namouss, hereby proclaim my decision to make this place my abode and give you notice of my intention!" To this the elephant did not answer, and Narmouss thought that the elephant had no objection. Narmouss did not know that the elephant had not heard him or felt him or his entry, and that he wouldn't feel any of Narmouss' family which was raised over the years. The elephant actually didn't realize the existence of the gnats at all.

> After some years, Narmouss decided, again after much consideration, taking into account many important pros and cons, to move house once again. Upon leaving, Narmouss again announced his intention to the elephant as his customs and traditions dictated. He shouted with all the strength of his tiny voice: "O Elephant! Know that I, the Gnat Perceptive Namouss, hereby leave my residence in this ear of yours for eminent and significant reasons." This time the elephant heard the gnat-cry. And Namouss continued: "O Elephant! Please tell me if you have anything to say about my departure!" The elephant hardly raised his head and trumpeted a little. This trumpeting meant nothing more, nothing less than: "Your going is of as much interest and significance to me as was your coming."

This tale of "Perceptive Namouss" might be taken at first glance as a sardonic illustration of the supposed useleness of life – from the viewpoint of a small gnat. Such an interpretation is limited. What is intended to be stressed here is the general lack of human judgement about the relative importance of things in life. The true perspective is that of the elephant, which is easily misunderstood. As our global society of Aleander teachers grows larger and larger there is a tendency to lose contact with the subtlety of Alexander's original discoveries. Not unlike the elephant in this parable, we can't quite hear the delicate voice of our collective internal consciousness. It whispers, "Don't get stuck in old thinking and teaching modalities . . . Keep the windows open so fresh air can come in."

How can we do this? Possibly by challenging and questioning our own assumptions relating to the Alexander Technique and our teaching of this work, and by reconnecting with the original discoveries of F. M. Alexander. This is a delicate balance due to the danger of getting stuck in dusty tradition. Albert Einstein said it most succintly: "The significant problems we face cannot be solved by the same level of thinking that created them."

I find each International Congress to be a breath of fresh air, and the 6th Congress did not disappoint. Many of the contributors to the Congress in Freiburg invited us to look at the Technique in new and different ways. It is wonderful to have the majority of contributions in this volume, and I hope you will find them as exciting as I have.

Michael D. Frederick
November 2000

Michael D. Frederick is a former chairman of the North American Society of Teachers of the Alexander Technique. He trained in England with Walter and Dilys Carrington and in America with Marjorie Barstow. Besides teaching the Technique in Santa Barbara and Los Angeles, Michael taught for over a decade at the Old Globe Theatre in San Diego. Michael was the originator and director of the first three International Congresses on the Alexander Technique held in the US, England, and Switzerland. He is a certified Feldenkrais Practitioner, having trained with Moshe Feldenkrais in the USA and Israel. He has also studied extensively in the US and India the Yoga tradition of T. K. V. Desikachar from Madras, India.

PO Box 408
Ojai, CA 93024
USA
Tel: +1 805 646 8902
Fax: +1 805 640 8776

KEYNOTE ADDRESS

TOPICS

EVENING LECTURES

SENIOR GUEST TEACHERS

The guests of honour: Anthony Spawforth, Erika Whittaker, Elisabeth Walker, and Marjory Barlow.

Keynote Address

Tony Spawforth

Friends and colleagues. I would first like to thank the convenors and organisers of this congress for inviting me to address you.

When asked to do so, I thought there must be teachers who are far better qualified than me to give such an address. Perhaps they had been offered the chance and turned it down!

I am not an experienced giver of keynote addresses, and as soon as I started work on this one, I realized what the definition of such an address was: something you agree to do and then wish you hadn't.

However, looking out at all you younger teachers, I am reminded of my beginnings. I began teaching in 1956 and then taught in Denmark for six years from 1958. I was for a few years the only teacher in the whole of continental Europe – quite a lonely path to tread.

Now, as this is the penultimate year of the century and millennium, I thought I would talk a little about Alexander and the two centuries in which the Technique has evolved and been taught, a period of extraordinary change in the way we live and in the development of our understanding of our world, ourselves, and the universe. I want to refer to some of the eminent men who lived during that period and particularly some of those who came to know Alexander and support his work.

But first, a little about the distant past. When Professor Sampson Wright, the anatomist and physiologist, gave evidence against Alexander in the famous libel action in South Africa, he said that if what Mr Alexander claimed in his books was true, it would be one of the most important discoveries in the history of mankind. Of course, since he had no personal experience of what the Technique was about, he dismissed it as worthless, but he had understood the implications of what Alexander was saying.

I realize that, in mentioning the history of mankind, I have gone back a little too far but I will make only one more reference to the distant past.

Recently the BBC conducted a poll among listeners to decide who was the greatest figure of this millennium. Charles Darwin, Sir Isaac Newton, and Shakespeare were in the first ten. As I had a somewhat curtailed scientific education, I voted for Newton as he had evolved his famous laws of motion and gravitation. However, Shakespeare was the winner. Alexander would have liked that.

I think it is of great interest that the eminent men who came to support Alexander's work in his lifetime were scientists of the best sort, that is to say scientists who were seekers after the truth in their own particular field but who were also aware of their own limitations and how little they knew. Socrates, the eminent Greek philosopher, said that he "knew very little and hardly that", which was why the oracle at Delphi proclaimed him to be the wisest of men. Great scientists are modest and not pompous; they solve problems by seeing what no-one has seen before and then putting forward testable theories or conjectures as to a possible solution for those problems.

The first two men I will mention are Darwin and Dart. Darwin was before Alexander's time; but he died in 1882, just as Alexander was approaching adulthood and before he evolved his technique. We know from Alexander's books that he was influenced by Darwin's theory of evolution as expressed in his *The Origin of Species by Natural Selection* and *The Descent of Man.* It is difficult for us now to understand what a terrible shock Darwin's theory of evolution was to Victorian and other Western societies, particularly among people with strong fundamental religious beliefs.

However, many educated people liked the idea that evolution was like a pyramid, with highly evolved, civilized people at the top, and more primitive, less evolved people, the animal kingdom, and other life forms lower down. Today's view of evolution is rather different. It is now considered to be a process more like the growth of a many-branched tree with humanity portrayed as one very successful branch with no guaranteed future. Alexander came to see that subconscious control, however well it had served us in the past, had to be replaced by conscious control. It would be the next vital step in humanity's evolution.

Raymond Dart was professor of anatomy and physiology at Witwatersrand University in South Africa. He was famous as a palaeontologist for his discovery of the fossil remains of *Australopithicus*, an extinct bipedal primate, which had ape-like and human characteristics. He became very interested in Alexander's work because he had children with developmental problems. Dart met Alexander only once, but he had lessons from Irene Tasker, one of the first teachers Alexander trained, when she taught the Technique in South Africa. Dart wrote three fascinating but fairly technical articles about the relationship between Alexander's work and different aspects of the evolutionary development of our upright stance. If you have not read them, please do; they are worth the trouble.[1]

On the present state of humanity, Dart stated (and it is even more true today than it was when he wrote it nearly half a century ago):

> Perhaps the richest comedy presented by the evolutionary process is that creatures nature designed to have perfect posture and vision should today present a picture of bespectacled decrepitude.

Next we come to Sir Charles Sherrington, a pioneer neurophysiologist, whose work *The Integrative Action of the Nervous System* (based on lectures given in 1904) was published in 1906 – the year that Alexander arrived in London. His work formulated the principles of reflex action. More than forty years later Sherrington supported Alexander in the South African libel action.

In another book, *The Endeavour of Jean Fernel*,[2] Sherrington wrote,

> Mr. Alexander has done a service to the subject by insistently treating each act as involving the whole integrated individual,

> the whole psychophysical man. To take a step is an affair not of this or that limb solely but of the whole neuromuscular activity of the moment – not least the head and neck.

This is a remarkable tribute from someone who had not had lessons.

George Coghill, who wrote the introduction to *The Universal Constant in Living,* is my final scientist. He came to see that what Alexander had discovered about the use of the self was related to the developmental, total and partial patterns of movement Coghill himself had observed in the growth, from the embryonic stage to adulthood, of a lowly vertebrate called amblystoma, a type of salamander. Coghill had lessons with Alexander very near the end of his life when he was a sick man. He said to Alexander words to the effect that "your life's work has made you into a healthy old man – my work has ruined my health!"

When, during his lessons, he first experienced the release of "going up", he is reported to have exclaimed excitedly, "It's the growth process" – a eureka moment for him.

A fascinating biography of Coghill by Judson Herrick is well worth reading – a demanding but profound work.[3] Coghill's own researches are related in his book *Anatomy and the Problem of Animal Behaviour.*[4]

Now a little about two men who were not scientists as such but who were very eminent in their own fields – John Dewey and Karl Popper.

Professor Dewey had a long association with both of the Alexander brothers. He was a philosopher and educationalist with an unswerving loyalty to scientific method. He opposed the traditional method of learning by memorisation under the authority of teachers. He thought that any sort of learning must begin with experience, hence the appeal for him of Alexander's work. Dewey's ideas contributed to the changes in primary education in our schools. However, he came to see that so-called "progressive education", which was the rather extreme opposite of authoritarian teaching, had great dangers. Alexander agreed with this from his own experience. Dewey was a pragmatist; pragmatism is an approach that evaluates assertions solely by their practical consequences and bearing on human interests. We heard some objections to Dewey's pragmatism in the 1998 F. M. Alexander Memorial Lecture but, having just re-read Dewey's introduction to *The Use of the Self*, I consider this introduction to be a remarkable tribute to Alexander and his work. Incidentally, it was Dewey who stimulated Frank Pierce Jones to carry out his in-depth experimental evaluation of the Technique as described in his book *Body Awareness in Action*[5], which I am sure many of you have read.

Finally, I come to Sir Karl Popper, again not a scientist as such but a philosopher of science; in my opinion his writings on the nature of scientific method were truly seminal. I am including him because Alexander's investigations described in *The Use of the Self* in the chapter "Evolution of a Technique" have been described as soundly "scientific".

Popper was concerned with our search for truth but saw very clearly that we can never finally prove anything. That we can is an illusion all too often seen in popular articles which begin "Science has now proven that ..."

Popper, who criticized the traditional view of science, where theories are tested by the repetition of confirming instances, said that all science begins with a problem, and the solution of the problem is attempted by putting forward a theory or conjecture for its solution. The theory is then put to the test by patient observation and experimentation. If you find experimental evidence as to the truth of your theory, you regard that as only provisional. Someone can come along with evidence that your theory has holes in it, and this should be welcomed, as now a better theory can be produced and put to the test, and so on. There is no final truth. Quite a few scientists have defended their theories almost to the death. They did not welcome evidence showing they were wrong.

Alexander's own problem was his loss of voice when reciting. His theory or conjecture was that what he did himself was causing the loss of his voice. That is to say, his use or misuse of himself as a whole was affecting part of his general functioning. He found a solution to that problem by evolving his technique, and he put his theory and technique to the test in himself and in his pupils for the rest of his life. Alexander echoed Popper when he said, "We can only be certain of one thing in this world and that is when we are wrong." Dewey had noted in his long association with F. M. and A. R. Alexander that they modified their teaching of the Technique over the years in accordance with their experience and increased understanding. The teaching of the Technique was never set in stone.

I was very intrigued to hear from Marjory Barlow that near the end of his life Popper had lessons from Dr Barlow. Alexander would have liked Popper's way of thinking. There is an excellent summary of Popper's works in Brian Magee's book *Popper.*[6]

Now, you can rightly argue that I have so far been overly academic in my address and I apologize for this. I can assure you that I am not an academic, an ex-intellectual perhaps, but definitely not an academic. The Alexander Technique is about day-to-day practical matters and is about experience and what we make of our experience.

I have made no mention of the many scientific discoveries, events, and people that have affected all our lives either directly or indirectly. I have said nothing about all the idealistic attempts to create solutions for the ills of mankind by cults, political systems, and religious revivals that have been current this century, and I have made no mention of Freud or Jung or any of the proponents of psychological theories that have attempted to explain human behaviour and conduct. Alexander was not an "ideas man" and I suppose that was what impressed me most about him. It should always be remembered that conscious inhibition and direction are potentially natural accomplishments. The Technique is a process that we can use if we put ourselves to the task, but as Alexander used to say of some of his pupils, "They forget to remember". We all know about that.

Alexander was not a religious man, but he was a great believer in what he called the life force. We all have that in us whether we have strong religious beliefs or none. The Technique can help us to channel this force for our great benefit.

Currently the Technique is being applied to a wide variety of activities and conditions – too numerous to mention. To organize whatever energies one has in a cost-effective way is important for any activity. It has been shown to be of value in medical conditions such as Parkinson's Disease, but it is terribly important that we are seen to be, as Walter Carrington put it, "specialists in the field of health education" and not as therapists, however therapeutic in effect the Technique can be. Different therapies, orthodox or unorthodox, and drugs can be evaluated by tests such as double-blind trials, but I think that such trials can fail to treat people as individuals; they can become just statistical units.

Now what of the future? I am afraid I have no idea what the future holds for the development of the Technique.

Alexander was adamant that its future lay in the education of children and that teaching adults would one day become redundant – but that is a long way off. The present day state of education in Britain – in the public sector at least – is all about results and ends, and not much about helping children to acquire the ability to help themselves. I was reading in a physical fitness report only the other day that quite a number of normal ten-year-olds are no longer able to get out of a chair without using their arms to help push themselves up. More and more young children are suffering from asthma. All get far less exercise than they did earlier in this century. Over fifty years ago, Sherrington was agreeing with Alexander about the poor breathing standards in young and older children and in very many adults – the situation is far worse today.

Walter Carrington said to me the other day that he thought that the core teaching of the Technique was secure for the future and that future is in the hands of young teachers such as yourselves for the new century. I think one of the dangers is that the Technique will become diluted by sloppy writing about it and by the increasing proliferation of group classes for beginners with far too little hands-on experience of the basics of the Technique. It is absolutely fine to be taught the Technique in relation to improving your riding, cycling, swimming, dancing, acting, instrumental playing, or whatever, but it is important that we see clearly that the Technique is generalist in the art of living and not specific. Also, please don't mix the Technique with other things, however valuable they may be in themselves.

Now, I have gone on long enough and I will finish by reading a short passage from the 1941 edition of *Man's Supreme Inheritance*:[7]

> The physical, mental, and spiritual potentialities of the human being are greater than we have ever realized, greater, perhaps, than the human mind in its present evolutionary stage is capable of realizing. And the present world crisis surely furnishes us with sufficient evidence that the familiar processes we call civilization and education are not, alone, such as will enable us to come into that supreme inheritance which is the complete control of our own potentialities. One of the most startling fallacies of human thought has been the attempt to inaugurate rapid and far-reaching reforms in the religious, moral, social, political, educational, and industrial spheres of human activity, whilst the individuals by whose aid these reforms can be made practical and effective, have remained dependent upon subconscious guidance with all that it connotes. Such attempts have always been made by men or women who were almost completely ignorant of the one fundamental principle which would so have raised the standard of evolution, that the people upon whom they sought to impose these reforms might have passed from one stage of development to another without risk of losing their mental, spiritual, or physical balance.

Remember that Marshall McLuhan said famously, "The medium is the message". For the Alexander Technique I would prefer, "The experience is the message".

Thank you – have a good congress.

References

1. Raymond Dart *Skill and Poise* (London, STAT Books, 1996).
2. Charles Sherrington *The Endeavour of Jean Fernel* (Cambridge University Press, 1946).
3. Judson Herrick *George Elliott Coghill* (Chicago, University of Chicago Press, 1948).
4. George E. Coghill *Anatomy and the Problem of Animal Behaviour* (Cambridge University Press, 1929).
5. Frank Pierce Jones *Body Awareness in Action* (New York, Schocken Books Inc. 1976).
6. Brian Magee *Popper* – Fontana Modern Masters series (London, Fontana, 1973).
7. F. Matthias Alexander *Man's Supreme Inheritance* (1946), p. 5.

Tony Spawforth joined Alexander's training course in February 1951 and, after Alexander died in 1955, qualified with Walter Carrington in April 1956. Spawforth assisted on Carrington's training course from 1956 to 1965. From 1958 until 1964 he taught in Denmark for three months every year. Since 1966 he has taught in Bournemouth. He was a visiting teacher on Aksel and Jeanne Haahr's training course in Totnes. He is married with two daughters; the elder daughter, Penny, is also a teacher of the Technique.

Alexander House
12c Richmond Wood Road
Bournemouth
Dorset BH8 9DB
England
+44 1202 526297

Alexander and Emotion

Walter Carrington

What did F. M. think about emotion? How did he deal with it in his teaching?

From an early age, F. M. wanted to be an actor; and the essence of acting is the expression of emotion. He was familiar with all the problems that this entailed and he studied long and painstakingly to equip himself as completely as possible for the task.

In the course of self-experimentation, and as he gradually evolved his technique, he came to recognize the reality of psychophysical unity, the impossibility of separating mind and body, and the necessity for what he called "conscious control", the "constructive conscious control of the individual". This was control of a positive kind, obtained, as he said, by "the employment of the processes of reasoning in all the activities of life". It involved the constant practice of conscious inhibition and direction in the use of the self.

This concept of inhibition, the withholding of consent to "a too quick and unthinking reaction", might appear to negate spontaneity and hence the free expression of emotion that acting demands. However, his objective was what he called true spontaneity, a response generated by reason, but also validated by the senses and by a realistic appraisal of the requirements of a situation. He had discovered that our habitual sensory appreciation is apt to be highly untrustworthy and unreliable and that our emotional reactions are therefore frequently at variance with our true wishes and intentions.

When people express negative emotions, they frequently disable the whole working of their postural mechanisms. They stiffen their necks and pull their heads back, incurring imbalance throughout the body, and causing harmful tension which affects the vocal mechanism, the breathing, and the totality of movement and gesture. This pattern of response clearly needs to be prevented. On the other hand, the freedom and release, the lightness of body as well as of heart, that results from joy and laughter and happiness should be sought.

During F. M.'s lessons, it was not uncommon for people to manifest all sorts of emotional reactions. Tears, he would ignore; he would continue to work quietly with his hands without making any comment. Depression and unhappiness, he would try to alleviate with both his voice and his hands. Anger, he would challenge.

I remember his story of an elderly man who grew more angry and resentful as the lesson progressed. At a certain point F. M. said mildly, "Mr So-and-so, you behave as if I were an enemy of yours;" whereupon the pupil burst out, "Yes, you are my enemy! You are my enemy!" half-rising from the chair and waving his fists in the air. Then he collapsed into the chair and sat sobbing. Eventually, he regained his composure. He became entirely calm and quiet, and the lesson proceeded as if nothing had happened. There was no further incident, and he became a good pupil thereafter.

On another occasion, an elderly lady, a former pupil, came for her lesson in a state of deep depression. Without saying a word, F. M. went to the corner cupboard, took out a bottle and a glass, and poured her a glass of sherry.

I never knew him to discuss their emotional states with his pupils and only very exceptionally would he discuss their personal affairs or anything apart from how they were responding in the lesson. For instance he would say, "you are stiffening your neck" or "you are pulling your head back" or "you are using your legs". But he *would* speak of general matters such as current news in the papers, the latest score in the Test Match or whatever. Often, particularly in the last years, I have watched him giving a lesson and he was talking earnestly to the pupil, but what he was saying even I could not understand. After a while it dawned on me that he did this deliberately, to both soothe and distract the pupil's attention from what he was doing with his hands, thus promoting inhibition or "leaving alone". He had remarkably powerful and sensitive hands, and his touch conveyed a sense of both strength and reassurance. You felt that here was a true friend, someone who was on your side.

He was obviously well aware of pupils' emotional states, as he was observant of everything else about them; but in his manner he usually sought to promote quietness and calmness, to discourage any physical effort to do something, and to persuade them to leave themselves alone. Occasionally, however, he would appear to be angry and would adopt an hectoring or bullying tone which some pupils could find quite daunting. On one celebrated occasion, after a lesson, his pupil walked into the street and turned past the windows of his teaching room. There was the sound of a sash-window opening and the next moment a book hit him on the side of the head. Looking round, he saw F. M. glowering at him and called out, "Why did you do that?", to receive the reply, "You know perfectly well why I did it!" It was clear that his anger was deliberately assumed in order, as he used to quote Emerson, "to administer sharp electric shocks to bring [people] into communication with their reason."

In his personal life he certainly got angry on occasion; however, his anger did not lead to irrational behaviour, but seemed to be the outcome of a process of reasoning and a considered judgement of the situation. He did not suffer fools gladly and if anyone appeared to be trying to take advantage of him he would soon let them know that they had chosen the wrong person to deal with.

Although he constantly pointed out the unreliability of our sensory appreciation and required us to be at all times on our guard in this respect, he also frequently pointed out that it was *feeling* that made life worthwhile. He had a great sense of fun, and his sense of humour might have been described as child-like, rather than childish. He enjoyed the good things in life, and he had high standards of taste in clothes, food, wine, and cigars. His choices were scrupulously reasoned and discerning. Of course he enjoyed the thrill and excitement of the racecourse, but he was a serious judge of a horse and of all aspects of breeding and form. If he could be described as a gambler, he was a thoughtful gambler and not a careless one.

It could truly be said that he lived his own technique. Through personal experience he had discovered a new way of living in the fundamental sense, a new way of solving many of the problems of everyday life. People often fail to realize the full significance of his work, because of our human mania for "separation" in our thinking. It is not just a matter of the use of the body, but of the whole of the self. It is not a technique to be used only on occasion, as circumstances require. It is a technique to be practised and put into practice, to be lived. But this is something that must be experienced before it can be properly understood.

18 February 1998

Walter Carrington trained with F. M. Alexander from 1936 to 1939. He served in the Royal Air Force 1941–46. He taught at Alexander's teachers' training course 1946–55 and carried on the training course after Alexander's death. Carrington is past chairman of STAT and has written and lectured extensively on the Technique.

18 Lansdowne Road
London W11 3LL
England
+44 20 7727 7222

Emotions

Mary Cox

First, I would like to say how honoured I feel to be asked to give this address, and I feel nervous about my responsibility since this is the second time I have been given this privilege, and I ask myself whether I can live up to my own standards.

Second, I want to say how sorry I am that Walter Carrington is not with us today to give his talk himself. I was given a copy of his material and I found it very useful.

I would like to acknowledge and thank all the people from the Alexander teaching profession who have helped me personally. In particular, I want to mention Jamie McDowell who has lent me books, made many discussions with me, worked with me, co-worked with me, and given generously of his time, energy, and creativity.

There is one other person I would like to appreciate, for without him I never would have got all this material into and out of computer, or have created the transparencies for the OHP and diagrams for the publication. Thank you to my technical right hand, my patient and impatient support team – my husband, Ron Thompson.

Introduction

I would like to begin by being very personal. I was born into a family where feelings were the currency of communication. Everyone had strong feelings, and lots of them. They were not reluctant to express them or act them out. Sometimes they would all have feelings together, which resulted in the most tremendous noise and confusion. Sometimes one member would have lots of feelings all alone, but would reappear showing the trace marks of this emotional upheaval.

When I look back now I see that many of these emotional outbursts were not an accurate or reliable representation of what anyone was actually experiencing. For example, my mother was often angry, showed it, and expressed it vociferously. I know now, as an adult, that at those times she was almost certainly very anxious and afraid. But she was a lone parent much of the time and could not afford to be afraid.

Both of my parents were talented and creative, charming and attractive. They were also volatile, loud, and dangerously unstable. Despite being so emotionally charged, they rarely dealt with their underlying emotional needs. Most of us children grew up rather the same. We learned early to feel and show guilt and shame, deeming this to be the most appropriate response to mother's anger, anxiety, and sadness. Coping with this continual emotional maelstrom did not leave much time and space for consideration of one's own feelings, those true feelings coming from one's own heart, stomach, or soul. We learned to use the currency of emotion whilst at the same time becoming curiously concealed about our own real feelings.

There are two things about this personal story. First, I see that the family is a powerful educational force and showroom, in the field of emotions no less than in the fields of morals, religion, and social behaviour. Second, it became clear to me early on in life that I could experience feelings which were my own, but that, even if they had been noticed, any display of real emotion was not welcomed. I began to experience a puzzling, and occasionally de-stabilising, conflict. On the one hand, I appeared to be a very emotional person; on the other hand I felt emotionally constricted and concealed, afraid to show what I called my "real" feelings. I became an expert emotional dissembler, if not an actual liar – a performer in the art of emotional display.

It was this conflict that pushed me into personal therapy, interfered with my parenting of my children, made me physically ill sometimes, and drove me as a therapist myself to learn what I could about emotions. What are they? How do they work? Could I have done things differently? If so, how? Could I learn to be in a different way? From whom? Could I help myself to be in charge of my emotional life, rather than being controlled by it? Could I learn to distinguish between emotional performance and expression of my true feelings?

As I worked with clients, I saw that the problems I had experienced were, in fact, rather common. Many people seemed not to know about or understand feelings and emotional life, and yet, so often, it was this very aspect of their lives that prompted them to seek help.

Out of all my studying, my striving to help my clients, my almost obsessive need to understand myself, it has become clear to me that emotions are a natural and normal part of being human. A person cannot not have feelings. We can repress them, suppress them, refuse to show them, cut off our awareness of them. We can act them out instead of experiencing them, dilute them, turn them into thoughts before experiencing the impact of them. We can somaticize them, spiritualize them, sexualize them. We can fake them, hide them, lie about them, but we cannot not have them. They simply occur involuntarily, as easily and regularly as breathing. And, like the breath, when not interfered with, they come and they go.

I would like, at this point, to say a few words more about my contact and experience with the Alexander Technique. From the moment I had my first short lesson as part of a conference presentation, I knew I had been introduced to a way of working that I needed more of. Each subsequent encounter, including taking regular lessons for a year, has deepened my insights into myself, my way of being and doing, and has excited me. It used to frustrate me too. I, like most pupils, thought there was something I had to learn to do, something I was doing wrong (which was true) and which I could correct by finding out what was the right thing to do. Then one day I read that famous quote from F. M. Alexander,

> You are not here to do exercises, or to learn to do something right, but to get able to meet a stimulus that always puts you wrong and to learn to deal with it.

When I read this and understood it, my whole vision and understanding shifted. Not just my understanding of myself and my way of being, but my entire understanding of psychotherapy. The shift was one of only a few degrees, but those few degrees enabled me to let go and leave the empty space. From that day on I began to see to how to work in a different way, also well encapsulated by F. M.:

> The experience you want is in the process of getting it. If you have something, give it up. Getting it, not having it, is what you want.

Here today, and all this week, I invite us all to remember that getting something from this Congress, from teachers and presenters, and from each other, is not about getting something to have. The getting will be in the process.

Now I shall address the following four questions:

- What do we mean by "self", in psychotherapy and in the Alexander Technique phrase "the use of the self"?
- How do we conceptualize "health" in a way that allows us as practitioners, to work with, and respect, the choices of our pupils or clients, particularly when we can see that sometimes those choices are "faulty"?
- What are emotions, and how do they function as part of everyday personal life?
- Are all feelings "just feelings", or are there categories/types of feeling that would be helpful to know and use?

The concept of self

Since Alexander teachers refer to "the use of the self", I would like to define and illustrate how I use the term. To do this I am going to show you a simple model I made some years ago (Diagram 1). It is derived from many theories, models, and researches, but is based primarily on the work of James Masterson (1985), a master psychotherapist from the USA; Heinz Kohut (1977), a psychoanalyst from Austria, and later

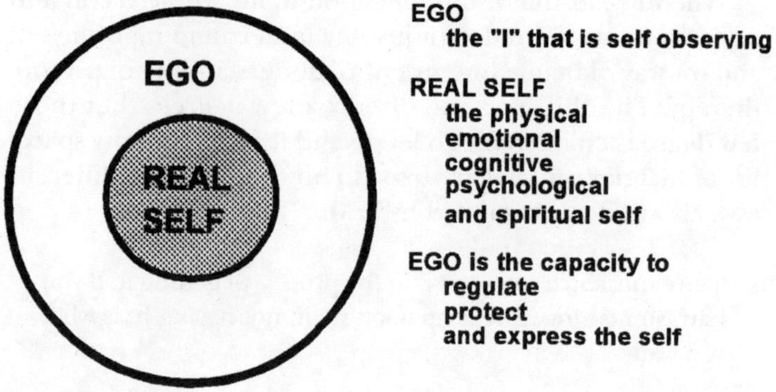

Diagram 1: The ego and the real self.

the USA, who created the school of "self-psychology"; and the work of Ronald Fairbairn (1952/1984), a British psychoanalyst.

You will see from the diagram that the "real self" is shown at the core and, in my view, has the following characteristics:

- physical – the body and its physiology, neurology, electrochemistry etc. We are real, we are blood, bones, and guts. As Shylock says, "If you prick us we bleed."
- emotional – feelings of sadness, fear, anger, joy, which constitute a subjective knowing of one's aliveness;
- cognitive – the functioning of the brain, articulated in language and symbols;
- psychological – the sense of identity – "me-ness';
- spiritual – a sense of "being-ness" which is somehow more than the list given above, a transpersonal self, a soul.

I have diagrammed the "ego" as the surround to the "real self". In this model it represents a capacity rather than a tangible entity. It represents the capacity that human beings have for self-observation, and self-reflection. We hear (in the English language) sentences such as, "I know things about myself that I never tell anyone else," or, "If I showed you my real self you might not love me," "He never tells you what he really thinks," and, from some therapy clients, "I don't who I really am."

The ego is capable of constructing a sense of self – a self-image. But these constructions are personas, images, representations. They are not real, they have no substance – they are pictures of the mind that are intended to influence other people's minds.

The function of the ego is to mediate between the "real self", others, and the environment. It serves to regulate, protect, and give variety of expression to the "real self".

I will be using this model later to describe and explain some ideas about emotions.

What is "health"?

Part of how I see "health" is as the development and maintenance of a harmonious and effective partnership between "ego" and "real self".

F. M. had a concept of health. It was one that included emotions, liveliness, and as Carrington referred to, "true spontaneity". I quote Walter Carrington's words, for I cannot better them,

> [F. M.'s] objective was what he called true spontaneity, a response generated by reason, but also validated by the senses and a realistic appraisal of the requirements of a situation.

In Transactional Analysis we use the concept of personal autonomy as a measure of health. Eric Berne (1964) defined "autonomy" as the demonstration of three capacities:

- awareness – an uncensored appraisal of internal and external stimuli;
- spontaneity – a choiceful response based on a sense of options and related to here and now reality;

- intimacy – a candid "game-free" relationship in which there is no pretending, no lying, and no exploitation.

Relating this to my model of the "real self" and "ego", I have shown, in Diagrams 2 and 3, how I understand the concepts of "awareness", "spontaneity" and "intimacy".

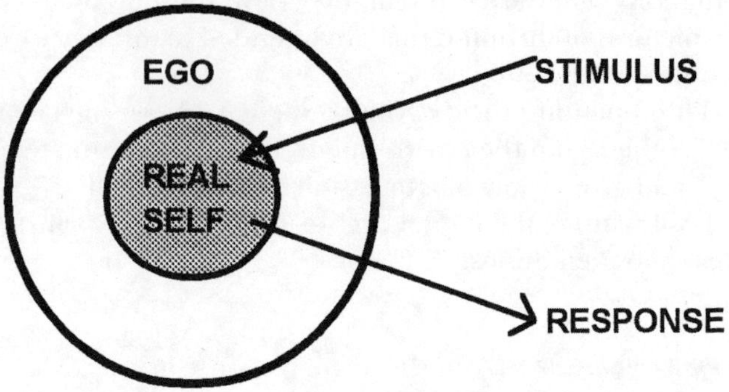

Diagram 2: Awareness and spontaneity

"Awareness" is when the person allows a stimulus to be experienced at the "real self" level, not blocked or deflected or redefined by ego. "Spontaneity" happens when the response comes from the "real self" outwards into the world, and is not blocked, limited, or redefined by ego. In Diagram 3, I have shown how I understand "intimacy", which is as "real self" to "real self" communication.

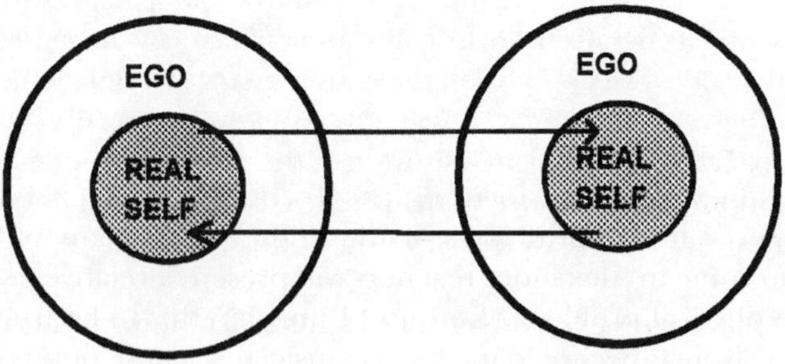

Diagram 3: Intimacy

Carl Rogers called this kind of contact and communication "authentic encounter", or relationship that is characterized by positive unconditional acceptance, congruence (between "ego" and "real self"), and genuineness.

When "ego" and "real self" function independently, or out of balance, problems occur. Ego domination leads to robotic rigidity. Lack of ego regulation leads to "a too quick and unthinking reaction". In either case, ego domination or impulsiveness, the person lacks "true spontaneity".

With regard to the Alexander Technique, I would suggest that the accomplishment of a healthy relationship between ego and real self is manifested in effective "primary control" (Alexander 1932/1985 pp. 49-51). I think that in Transactional Analysis we have the same idea as you have in the Technique, i.e. the responsive behaviour is said to be spontaneous when it is the result of conscious control, i.e. ego mediation of real-self impulses, otherwise the response may be described as "impulsive" or re-active.

If people become over-identified with ego then they are likely to develop a "false self", which usually is designed to hide the "true self".

> You are telling me about this deep split in your nature, so that your impulses make no contact, but your acceptance of reality is with a false self that does not feel real.
>
> *Winnicott 1972/1986 p.158.*

This kind of "splitting" between a false self created by "ego" and a true or "real" self leads to the development and use of defences which may seriously interrupt contact with others, and inhibit personal autonomy.

Now I want to re-focus on the Technique and relate this material to the principles of Alexander work. Many pupils who come to Alexander teachers will present a relatively simple physical problem of misuse. I imagine this to be true of many sports people, dancers, or musicians. These pupils will benefit enormously from re-education of their use. They may or may not feel a rather greater and deeper benefit, but that is a bonus.

However, a proportion of the people who come may be seeking relief for physical symptoms that have another kind of cause (rather than direct physical misuse). Wilfred Barlow includes some very useful material with regard to medical conditions in his books, *The Alexander Principle* (1973) and *More Talk of Alexander* (1978). Increasingly, people are approaching Alexander teachers for help with less well defined problems, such as stress, depression, inexplicable physical discomfort, and so on. There is also a small, but increasing, number of clients who, through psychotherapy, have realized that they need the help of a body-work specialist to deal with psychological and emotional issues that have their origins in somatic trauma: early childhood abuse or neglect, for example.

However, I also want us to keep in awareness those pupils who come for Alexander re-education, and "run into" emotional turbulence. In this group may be trainee teachers of the Technique, who often work persistently, diligently, and more deeply than a member of the public coming for help with a specific physical problem.

Those people who come primarily for re-education of their use may neither demonstrate any emotional disturbance, nor respond to the Alexander work with any emotional turbulence. And if momentarily they do, Alexander himself gave a good model to following generations of teachers: for example the case of the angry man, and that of the woman who arrived feeling rather depressed.

However, is there something more or different a teacher could, or even should, do when emotional turbulence arises? In order to formulate an answer to this, some model of emotions is needed, some way to think about feelings.

What are emotions?

I am deliberately going to avoid any definitions. Instead, I offer here an operational model of how I understand "emotion" to be part of the human way of being. This rather simplified schema is shown below.

STIMULUS
excites a
SENSATION
producing an
EMOTION
involving
THINKING
before choosing a course of
ACTION
which stimulates further exchanges and feedback
on the appropriateness and effectiveness of the action.

Fig. 1: SSETA Sequence.

When I am working as a therapist, I work as if there is a sequence of happenings, as a person receives a stimulus and makes a response. The first step is a *stimulus*: something occurs internally or externally and this excites a *sensation*: this is the physical registering of the stimulus. The sensation may be noticed, or not, but it will be evaluated for significance, which process in turn produces an *emotion*: a feeling – note that all emotions have physical concomitants, i.e. they are "real", not just mental, events. The mental registration and interpretation of the sensation produces the emotion/feeling. For example, pain (which is a sensory experience) may produce fear, or it may produce anger, and so on. It depends on the interpretation and significance placed on the painful sensation.

The evaluation and interpretation of the sensation as a feeling will involve *thinking*: which may take place in representations (e.g. pictures, sounds) or in words only (digital). The representations of the stimulus, its actual effect, and its experienced and fantasized significance, may be re-interpreted and manipulated through many possible scenarios before the person chooses a course of *action*: this action is the response to the original stimulus, and in turn becomes itself a stimulus in the interpersonal field for further exchanges. These consequential exchanges act as feedback on the level of appropriateness and effectiveness of the chosen action.

Note: There may be interaction between, and re-cycling through, "sensation", "feeling", and "thinking", before an action is decided upon and enacted.

This schema defines a response to a stimulus as the result of a definite, if complex, sequence of steps, all of which usually take place so fast that a person is not consciously aware of the intermediate stages of the process unless attention is drawn to self-examination. However, it is possible to slow down the process, support awareness, and therefore increase choice at every step. A major part of Alexander work involves bringing about this conscious awareness.

I invite you to try a small exercise. Read through the following list of situations and write down what would be your first feelings and reactions in each one. Just make a brief response of two or three words only.

1. You reach the checkout at the supermarket with a full trolley and discover you have left your purse at home.
2. You are already tight for time driving to an important appointment and you run into a traffic jam.
3. You suddenly realize you have forgotten to send a birthday card to someone important to you, and at that moment they call you on the phone.
4. A visitor does not give you sufficient appreciation or thanks for your hospitality.
5. Your best friend chooses to do something else, instead of coming to your birthday party.
6. A friend across the road does not see you or respond to you when you call out "hello".
7. You come out of your house to find that someone has stolen the windscreen wipers from your car.

8. You discover you have made a mistake that a) only you will ever know about, or b) someone else is bound to discover.
9. You are in an unfamiliar place or with an unfamiliar group of people and you do not know how to do the next thing.

When you have completed the list, reflect on your responses for a moment. Ask yourself if it could be possible for you, or for another person, to experience quite different emotional reactions to each situation. Perhaps what makes you feel angry makes someone else feel anxious, or guilty, or impatient . . .

Historically there has been considerable debate about what should guide a person's choices of action. Should choice be based upon rational consideration and objective appraisal, as Alexander himself proposed? On the other hand, feelings are thought of by many as yielding the most personal and truest choice of action. And in yet another way, there is a school of thought that says simply just "do what comes naturally", follow your impulse . . . In my view, these debates are flawed because they make false polarization of feeling or thinking, thinking or behaviour. Alexander understood very well the psychophysical unity of the human being. Responding to a stimulus is a flowing and integrated process that needs to take into account sensation, emotion, and thinking in coming to a decision and choosing an action.

As I see it, problems are symptoms, and symptoms are communications that something is wrong. We can go back now to the model of "real self", and to Berne's notion of personal autonomy as health. We can then ask some useful questions. In what ways, and why, is this person impeding their awareness, spontaneity, and their enjoyment of intimacy? How are they stopping themselves from being real, and where in the sequence of stimulus and response is this person blocking or skipping over stages? Is the person interfering with sensation, emotion, thinking, or, indeed, with action itself? And what happens to the energy flow as it becomes blocked by this interference?

F. M. said, "You translate everything, whether physical or mental or spiritual, into muscular tension." We might justifiably add "emotion" to the list he gives. I think it is the physical discomfort caused by this muscular tension, which is caused in turn by interference with awareness, spontaneity, and intimate contact, that brings your pupils to you for help.

F. M. also said,

> Link up your message and the feeling of it now. When you have learnt that you have learnt the thing by means of which you do any exercise.

> As a matter of fact, feeling is much more use than what they call "mind" when it's right.

> But how do you know when a feeling is "right"?

Different kinds of feelings

If it is at all meaningful and useful to speak of feelings being "right", does that mean there are feelings that are not right? I think Alexander would have said a definite "yes", and moreover I think that he would mean by this that we can develop faulty emotional habits, just as we can create faulty physical habits. We can distort, even corrupt, our sensory appreciations, which in turn means that the emotions we generate are unreliable, and our consequent interpretations then also become erroneous, leading to "faulty" action.

I think there is a useful and usable distinction to be made between different kinds of feelings, and this distinction could be said to apply to the notion of "right" and "not right". In Transactional Analysis we make this distinction through the concept of "racket" feelings (English 1971, 1972) versus "real" or authentic feelings. Racket feelings have certain observable characteristics and these are listed in Figure 2, opposite.

Racket feelings are

- *learned:* the feeling and its expression was learned or copied in childhood and positively reinforced.
- *substitutive:* the feeling "covers", or is displayed instead of, another, authentic, feeling.
- *repetitive:* the feeling is produced over and over again, even when the stimulus varies.
- *inappropriate:* the feeling goes on too long, is too strong, in rational relation to the stimulus.
- *manipulative:* the display of this feeling affects other people in a certain way that brings some pay-off to the person. The manipulation is unconscious or, at best, semi-conscious.

Racket feelings

- *do not serve toward problem-solving.*
- *are never resolved in a way that they are worked through naturally and finished.*
- *rarely induce in others a genuine sense of empathy and compassion.*

Fig. 2: Characteristics of racket feelings.

Racket feelings are a response to an internally generated stimulus, for example fantasy, imagination, memory, or beliefs. These feelings are generated by the ego and serve as defences against real feelings. The real feelings are feared as painful or difficult to manage. Because these real feelings were experienced at the time of the original stimulus as "too" painful, or as "overwhelming and inexplicable" they are repressed and remain "buried" out of awareness.

Here are some examples of possible displays of "racket" feelings. An amusing one first. A man is having his teeth fixed. The dentist approaches, drill in hand. The man gives a yelp of pain. Surprised, the dentist steps back, "Did I hurt you?" "Oh no," says the man "I thought you were going to!"

A rather more serious one now. Imagine a man who is privately ashamed of his emotional and physical vulnerability. He sees this vulnerability as weakness. He generates (at an ego level) feelings of superiority and boredom which he uses to keep himself distanced from real relationship with others, for fear they might see "how weak he really is".

And lastly, reflect on a woman who is angry and aggressive in her behaviour toward men, because she is afraid of them.

In Figure 3, I have listed the characteristic of "real" or authentic feelings.

They are an appropriate and direct response to a here-and-now stimulus. They are expressed, worked through, and finished. They have a functional part in resolving a problem or a problematic situation The expression of authentic feeling usually touches and moves others present, engendering compassion, whether the feelings are current or the return of archaic feelings.

Fig. 3: Characteristics of authentic "real" feelings.

Real, authentic emotions are "right" in the Alexander sense. They are generated out of direct sensory experience resulting from a here-and-now stimulus and, as such, form part of the stimulus response sequence shown above. Real feelings serve to inform and support problem-solving and the process of spontaneous choice of action. They are "validated by the senses, regulated by reason, and based on a realistic appraisal of the stimulus and the environment."

I would like now to refer to Walter Carrington's account in which F. M. says to the angry pupil, "You behave as though I were your enemy!" and the man replies "Yes, yes! You are my enemy!" Since Alexander knew this was not true and knew there was no present or rational reason for this man to feel angry, he did not respond to what we can now hypothesize was a racket feeling. Alexander gives no reinforcement to the man's racket anger, and the man then suddenly cries. These tears might have been an escalation of the racket but I think it more likely to have been the expression of a previously repressed real feeling. We do not know what past incident had occurred during which this man might have felt sad or vulnerable but had decided not to show his real feeling, to cover it instead with outbursts of anger which would drive others away from him. In this one reparative moment, F. M. confronted the man's racket and refused to be driven away. The man was enabled to release a deeper feeling (sorrow shown by the tears) and "finish" the incident instead of repeating and repeating it. The fact that the angry outburst was never repeated, nor the crying for that matter, suggests that the crying was the release of a real feeling which then was "finished".

The sudden emergence and expression of long held authentic feelings is called in Transactional Analysis "rubber-banding" (Kupfer & Haimowitz 1971). These "rubber-band" feelings have all the characteristics of authentic feelings, and none of the characteristic of racket feelings, but the here and now stimulus is not directly the cause of the feeling. The stimulus is, however, sufficiently similar to the original stimulus that it triggers a previous repressed experience. When this earlier and repressed experience is stimulated, the person "rubber-bands" back in time and re-lives, at least in part, the long held, unworked through, original experience, including its emotional component.

We might guess that something about Alexander or his actions was a sufficiently similar stimulus to a previous incident in the angry man's life that it triggered a "rubber-band". The racket anger served as a patterned defensive response. Alexander (quite correctly in my opinion) calmly waited for the man to come past this habitual defence, and waited again quietly while the man released the deeper feeling and naturally calmed down by himself.

So what about when Alexander work stimulates deep or strong emotions in a pupil? Very often the nature of Alexander work is therapeutic in the reparative sense, whether teachers mean it to be so or not. The relationship established between an Alexander teacher and pupil is often experienced by the pupil as tender, calming, understanding, instinctive, insightful, empathic, helpful, and beneficial. Are not most of us hoping for many of these qualities in all our primary relationships, and did not many of us miss them in some of our key childhood relationships?

There is a story recounted that Donald Winnicott, a leading British psychoanalyst, once behaved very uncharacteristically for a psychoanalyst. His patient became distressed and agitated and threw up his arms in a way reminiscent of a baby in alarm. Winnicott leaned forward and gently touched the patient, who immediately broke down into sobbing. On another occasion Winnicott quietly offered to a patient the following interpretation:

> There are two things I do. One is when I am good enough I displace your mother and others who failed you. When I am bad I reactivate the bad past and it comes into the present.

Pupils, patients, and clients, when faced with an experience of the "good parent who was not" may suddenly release deep sorrow with regard to all the love and tenderness missed as a small child. This may have some bearing on the story of F. M. and the angry pupil, and, indeed, on the account of F. M.'s kindly response to the depressed woman pupil.

Sometimes Alexander work unintentionally evokes specific, previously unconscious emotional memories, especially unfinished experiences of trauma. Then both defensive racket feelings and, later, deeply repressed real feelings may surge up in the pupil. Sometimes, as with the angry man, a momentary holding space is enough for the pupil to "work through". But sometimes this upsurge is the beginning of the emergence of a great well of repressed archaic painful experiences with their accompanying emotions. The teacher may choose to refer the pupil to a psychotherapist to do the working through, or keep working gently and with respect, waiting as Alexander did. The main thing is not to lose the relationship through becoming anxious, angry, or confused, or by becoming either ego-dominated or impulsive. To this extent, the Alexander teacher does need some education in the field of emotional experience and expression: enough so as not to become frightened or irritated by sudden outbursts or collapses, sufficient to know when to keep working quietly, or to be able to sense when to stop and recommend psychotherapy. But, in many ways, Alexander training is in itself sufficient to enable a teacher to stay present and grounded during an experience of turbulence and distress. Either way, it never is the job of the teacher to do therapy, any more than it is the job of the psychotherapist to do re-educative bodywork.

However, there is a rich opportunity here for psychotherapists and Alexander teachers to work together when a pupil/client needs the help of both. In the Transactional Analysis literature, there is just such a case history (Ruppert and Ziff, 1994), in which the client, Shari, was treated conjointly and simultaneously by a psychotherapist and a body therapist. The body therapist (Ziff) was trained in Alexander work. Shari had been seriously abused in childhood. You can easily imagine how hard it was for this client to let anyone, especially a male person, touch her. The female psychotherapist, Emily, had worked as sole therapist prior to the final stage: that of doing the bodywork. Emily then accompanied Shari through the beginning stages of the re-education of her body as she learned to accept touch without regressing into terror, rage, and disgust.

But it was not simply a matter of Shari getting used to touch that is health-giving and caring. It was essential for her to come in touch with and release long held, deeply split off, feelings. Feelings held since childhood in her body, in her musculature, maybe even at a cellular level. She needed to unlearn strong defensive habits, and needed a sensitive and experienced body worker to help her to do that. Shari needed someone who knew how to recognize these habits and help her to release herself from them; someone who could speak with their hands, and actively help her to free not just her neck, but her whole real self from years of terrified imprisonment by an inadequately and inappropriately informed ego. This ego was a "child ego" that had interpreted abusive experiences and made the best decisions she could under the circumstances, but in so doing had opened a deep split between ego and body self. Due to this split Shari had lost touch with, and access to, her own primary control, and to intuitive body and emotional information that she might have been able to use to forewarn herself of future risks.

An Alexander teacher is likely to draw the pupil nearer to, and sometimes right into, a more authentic kind of emotional experience, simply because the Alexander work is aimed at bringing a pupil away from habit and into the free space of the "right frame of mind". Not that there is one right thing or right way a person should be doing. The problem, almost entirely, is that the person believes that there is. For Alexander teachers and for psychotherapists, it is not a question of finding the right thing to do with emotions, but rather of getting into the right frame of mind in order to meet the stimulus which otherwise might put you wrong.

In terms of distinguishing between an emotional outburst that is a sudden release of authentic feeling, and an outburst which is a destructive racket display, simple observation and practice will enable the Alexander teacher to recognize a racket, in the same way that a Transactional Analysis therapist learns. There is nothing magical about it. The main characteristics have been listed. In addition, learn to use your own emotional response. Remember that the effect of racket feelings is deadening to the observer, and to relationship. Very little compassion or empathy is engendered.

Alexander teachers cannot expect not to have feelings. Your pupils will have an emotional impact upon you. You may feel anxious, comfortable, or uncomfortable, afraid with some pupils, caring toward others. You are a real human being. When you are teaching, you are entering into a relationship, and that in itself will evoke changes in your pupil, just as it will in you, and each of you becomes more than you were before because of that.

As a way of closing, I quote from the Ruppert and Ziff article, as they speak about their work with Shari...

> . . . here we advocate personal involvement and physical contact. We have outlined a course of treatment which we believe speaks to serious consideration of ways to protect the

client from unwanted invasion or careless contact by professional psychotherapists.

... healing (is) accompanied by principles of mutual respect and appropriate sharing of power. ... Ethics and dialogue are the foundation of trust. Humour, honesty, contact, and warmth are the context of healing. We believe that healing is mutual and that, in the process, we, as therapists, must look honestly at the price and the rewards of entering into such a relationship with someone. ... Through ... respect for the function of behavioural roles, we arrive at a method of changing the underlying structure and arrangement of beliefs and emotions that defend the fragile self. The body as well as the mind must be touched to allow healing.

References

Alexander, F. M. (1932/1985) *The Use of the Self* (London: Gollancz).

Barlow, W. (1973) *The Alexander Principle* (London: Gollancz).

Barlow, W. (1978) *More talk of Alexander* (London: Gollancz).

Berne, E. (1964) *Games People Play* (Penguin).

English, F. (1971) "The substitution factor: rackets and real feelings." *Transactional Analysis Journal,* 1(4), 225-230.

English, F. (1972) "Rackets and real feelings. Part II." *Transactional Analysis Journal* 2(1) 23-25.

Fairbairn, W.R.D. (1952/1985) *Psychoanalytic studies of the personality* (London, Routledge and Kegan Paul).

Kohut, H. (1977) *The Restoration of the Self* (Madison, Connecticut, International Universities Press).

Kupfer, D., & Haimowitz, M. (1971) "Therapeutic interventions. Part 1, Rubber bands now." *Transactional Analysis Journal,* 1(1), 10-16.

Masterson, J. (1985) *The Real Self: a developmental, self, and object relations approach* (New York, Bruner Mazel).

Ruppert, E., & Ziff, J. (1994) "The mind, body, and soul of violence." *Transactional Analysis Journal* 24(3), 161-177.

Winnicott, D.W. (1986) *Holding and Interpretation: Fragment of an Analysis* (London: Hogarth).

Bibliography

Gelb, M. (1981) *Body Learning* (London, Aurum).

Jones, F. Pierce (1976/79) *Body Awareness in Action* (New York, Schocken).
Maisel, E. (1967/1989) ed. *The Essential Writings of F. Matthias Alexander* (New York, Carol Communications).
Park, G. (1989) *The Art of Changing: A New Approach to the Alexander Technique* (Bath, Ashgrove Press).

Mary Cox M.Ed. is a UKCP registered psychotherapist and a Teaching and Supervising Transactional Analyst (Clinical) in private practice in Cumbria, England, where she trains and supervises psychotherapists. She has more than 30 years' experience of working with individuals and groups, both privately and within organizations.

Cambrai House
Calderbridge
Cumbria CA20 1DH
England
+ 44 1946 841 239
e-mail: marycox@cambraihouse.demon.co.uk.

Mary Cox (right), Transactional Analysis, presenter of the topic "Emotion", listening to Elisabeth Walker after her Masterclass.

Spirituality

Part One

Claude AnShin Thomas

I am invited to talk about spiritual realities. What is spirituality? If we think we know, it is probably not spirituality. You see, there is no fixed point. There is nothing to attach to. The moment we think we know, we are filled with concepts and ideas which prevent us from experiencing spirituality, the spiritual reality of life.

I talk from the perspective of Buddha's teaching, not from the perspective of Buddhism. Because in Buddhism – like in any -ism when any school develops – there are many interpretations of the founding teacher's teaching.

Of course, everyone claims to know exactly what the teacher meant. Everyone claims to know the way. Well, there isn't any one way. This is what the Buddha taught. We have to find our own way. The teaching is not meant to be something held rigidly, it is not a fixed point. The teaching is a guide, a guide to help us to wake up.

What does it mean to wake up? To wake up in a Buddhist understanding – it is not just Buddhist, but this is the language I use – is to become aware of those points that keep us from waking up, of the nature of our resistance. The moment I look at someone as different from me or perceive them as different from me I create separation. This is not spiritual practice. To become aware that this is happening is spiritual practice.

There isn't a spiritual part of life. Life is in fact a spiritual reality.

Sometimes people will come and ask to study with me because they are interested or stimulated in some way, but they also have expectations of what they are coming to. Most of them become disappointed because the reality they experience doesn't measure up to the expectation. And then I am held responsible, because I didn't satisfy their expectation.

What I teach – actually I can't teach anything – what I do is live life, really fully, as fully as possible, so that I make every moment a moment of spiritual practice. Spiritual practice is not meant for one and a half hours in the morning where you do service, or sitting meditation; it is not meant for the one day a week you go to church; it is not meant for that time you set aside; that is only an aspect of spiritual practice. Spiritual practice is how I wash the dishes, how I put on my shoes, how I care for my body, how I sit in a chair, how I stand up, how I open a door. I mean really, if I open a door just to open a door, then it becomes a possibility or a tool for awakening to the spiritual reality of life – which is nothing other than the interconnectedness of all things. You see, there is no separate self, there is no fixed point.

That we strive to grasp some fixed point prevents us from waking up, from living fully in life. It creates suffering. Because each time we grasp for a fixed point, it moves.

If I am uncomfortable, and it is discovered that I have an ache because I don't move quite right, then if just stop fighting with my body and move quite right, the ache will go away. Maybe. What if it has nothing to do with the way I move?

What I have come to understand is that all that I am is influenced by all past generations. All past generations live in me. All that I am is a result of my own actions, of what I create. In the Buddhist language this is called karma. This is not some mystical concept, some philosophical notion, or metaphysical idea. Karma is very real. It is already defined through the laws of physics. The laws of physics state that for every action there is a reaction. It has been proven. What has also been discovered in physics is that where it is true that for every action there is a reaction, it is also true that we cannot know what the reaction will be. This is the law of karma. When I commit an action, this action has consequences. There is a reaction. If I am not aware it doesn't mean that this doesn't happen. There is a saying: "If someone drops a bag of rice in China, it doesn't have any effect on me." This is not true.

Claude AnShin Thomas giving his talk.

Because I don't see with my eyes, feel with my skin, hear with my ears, taste with my mouth or smell with my nose the consequences of such an action, it doesn't mean it doesn't have an effect.

My father was a soldier in the Second World War. My grandfather was a soldier in the First War. My great-grandfather was a soldier in the Spanish-American War. I was a soldier in the Vietnam War. I went because I thought I was making a choice to go – I volunteered. What I have since discovered was how unawake I was. I went not because I thought it was the right thing to do, but because I had no choice. Each moment then is decided for me by the karma that I inherit when not living consciously or present in the moment.

To wake up. This is the invitation of spiritual practice. There are many expressions of it. There is not one. There is not one way. That we think there is one way: this is suffering. This is our grasping for a fixed point, grasping for something outside of us to give us meaning. In the Middle Ages the castles and the churches were huge structures with very thick walls. Why? To protect people, to keep evil out, or someone's perception of evil. I do the same thing. I create very thick walls inside myself to protect me from what I think is evil. This is the nature of my suffering: that I do not want to be present in the moment, aware of all that is. But I am not really keeping evil out. I am simply keeping this suffering that is sometimes described as evil trapped inside. So I have no freedom.

I arrived in Vietnam at the end of September or beginning of October 1966. My birthday is in November. By the time I became 18 years old, I had already been directly responsible for the deaths of hundreds of people. This finger, the index finger on my right hand, pulled the trigger. This body committed the actions. In the process I am creating karma. What happens to me is a direct result of how I am in the world although I may want to see myself somehow as an innocent victim. It is much easier to present responsibility to another person. While it is true that the actions of an another person have an effect on me, it is also true that the actions I committed I am responsible for. That I killed I am responsible for.

That I killed is not a good thing or a bad thing. If I hold it as a good thing or a bad thing there is no possibility to heal. Healing being the ability to live now, in the present moment. Healing is not the absence of pain and suffering. Healing is learning to live in harmony with the nature of all that is. It is true that if I have a headache I can take an aspirin. And the headache appears to go away. In fact, it's just the symptoms which are met. What is the source of the headache? Where does it lie? Where does it rest? It may be physical, psychological, or emotional. It is at its root spiritual. Mark Twain, an American writer, had a cure for headaches. He said, "If you have a headache, get a hammer and smash your thumb. Your thumb will hurt so badly you'll forget about the headache." Most of us live life in this way. We are constantly smashing our thumbs in an effort not to look directly at the nature of our suffering. We engage in the process of healing others in an effort to heal ourselves. But it doesn't work. It never works. If we are not awake, if we are not committed to our own awakening, we are perpetuating suffering, violence, and war.

I went to Vietnam to fight for peace, to assist the South-Vietnamese who were fighting for independence against the North-Vietnamese. I went to fight for an ideology in the name of democracy and freedom. If fighting, if war were the solution, if war had helped us to find peace, then by now we would all live in a state of bliss. Are we blind that we cannot see? War is not the solution. Violence is not the answer, never the answer. It is simply the law of karma. When I commit an act of aggression then I am going to perpetuate that cycle. Where is the responsibility for healing? Here with myself. Who is responsible for healing? I am. No one can do it for me.

When I look at my life I see the war before the war. Then I see the war and I see the war after the war. To see war in this way is to expand my whole concept. What is war? Who is immune from the effects of war? Who has lived in an environment in which there has been no war? None of us. We are all directly affected. To wake up to the war in us. To wake up to how we perpetuate the cycles of suffering. To see, to experience the interconnectedness of all things.

My left hand is different from my right, but they don't fight against each other. They work in harmony – most of the time. Could you imagine sitting down at your table to eat and suddenly your left hand decides it doesn't want to eat the way your right hand does? And so they fight with each other. That the left hand is going to convince the right hand to eat in the way in which the left hand thinks it should. It's crazy. Yet, we are constantly doing this. This is the nature of suffering. I mentioned the word "crazy." It is insanity.

I would like to offer a definition of insanity. *Insanity is continuing to do the same things expecting the results to be different.* It has nothing to do with our state of mind, but with our state of being.

The teaching of the Buddha simply invites us to know ourselves intimately. To live in an integrated way. I am not my mind; I am more than my mind. I am not my emotions; I am more than my emotions. I am not my senses; I am more than my senses. I am not my thoughts; I am more than my thoughts.

Most of my practice is outside. People who want to come to my monastery have to find me. Part of my practice is pilgrimage. I walk. I don't like walking very much so it is quite interesting. I much prefer riding or driving. But since 1994 I have walked about 9,000 miles – 15,000 km. The last walk that I did was from the eastern part of the US to the western part. I walked pretty much as I am dressed here. I walked without money because I've made a commitment to live this way. I carry everything on my back. I walk from one small town to the next. 20-40 kms each day. When I arrive in a small town we knock on the door of a religious institution. I explain who I am, what I am doing, and ask them if they can support me with a simple place to stay and simple food to eat. Accepting that if they say no, I will sleep outside and I won't eat. And I walk to the next place. I've slept in pig barns, in garages, in fields. I've slept in all sorts of places, under trees, in parks. I've spent many days without eating. Why? Because the other perceives me as different, as separate. What I discover is that my presence challenges the artificial walls of protection that the others have created. Suddenly they are brought directly in touch with their fears, doubts, insecurities, and suffering. Exactly in that moment I, or that which is different, is the reason that they are afraid. So if they eliminate me, or that which is different, then their fear is gone – until the next time. And the next time. Because there will always be a next time.

When I am hosted in a Church or they provide me with a place, I always ask if I can set up an altar, because I begin each day with a spiritual service and I end each day with a service. I explain what the altar is. I have a Buddha, a cup of water, a container for incense, a flower, and candle. It is quite standard in the tradition in which I am ordained. It represents the five elements: the flower represents the earth, the water is water, the incense represents air, fire represents fire, and the Buddha represents space or consciousness – it is not an icon that we worship. In some instances they say, "No altars here." I remember one place that didn't want us to put up an altar. We were sleeping in the children's nursery. I found a plant, a light, there was a glass of water, a bowl with some dirt in it, and a stuffed bird from Sesame Street. It is not the objects. It is the point of concentration. What does the object represent. Space and consciousness. [Rings a bell]. It is just like the sound of this bell. The sound of the bell is an invitation to stop, to sit still, and to breathe. To breathe in and to breath out and know that I am breathing in and breathing out. What is the most important thing in life? Many people would have many different ideas, but I'd tell you a little secret. The most important thing in life is your breath. If you don't have your breath, you have nothing else. To breath in awareness, to breath in and out, to live intensely in this moment, to live in mindfulness. This is not about Buddhism. I am not attempting to convert people. If we live intensely in the present moment then – whatever the nature of our spiritual practice – it will help us to look more deeply into the nature of this practice.

I put on robes to be of service. Putting on the robes reminds me of my responsibility to be of service, of service to others, and to get out of my skin. This doesn't mean that the nature of this suffering, of my suffering, goes away. It means that I learn a better relationship with it.

I carry this practice to the homeless, to the evicted, to the people trapped in the cycles of prostitution, to prisons, to war zones. I go to the places where people don't commonly go. There I practice. There is the Zendo. There is my monastery. I also practice in some pretty nice places too. This is a nice place. I had warm tea to drink. I had a wonderful bed to rest in. I had nice, hot water to take a shower in. I am thankful for those things as much as I am thankful for the other opportunities. This has been an opportunity for me. To meet people that I don't know. To not be stingy with the teachings, to not keep them to myself but to share them. I can't keep what I have unless I give it away. Nothing can be held. If I try to hold it too tightly, it will die.

I'll end here because there is another speaker. I want to thank you for your attention, because in this moment I've been given such a gift: you have been my teachers in this moment whether you know it or not. I am thankful for that. I thank you all and I bow to you. I bow for my chair because I am not different from this chair. I am not separate from it. I am thankful for the support that this chair has given. It has enabled me to sit in comfort. The interconnectedness of all things. Not to take anything for granted in my universe.

Claude AnShin Thomas served in the US Army in the Vietnam War 1966–67. He became a member of the Vietnamese monastery and retreat centre Plum Village, founded and guided by Thich Nhat Hanh. Claude was ordained a Soto Zen Priest in 1995 by Roshi Bernie Glassmann. He travels and speaks internationally, and facilitates retreats in mindfulness, especially for war veterans.

c/o Zaltho Foundation
9 Magnolia Drive
Mary Esther
Florida 32569
+1 850 243 8169
fax: +1 850 243 1167
e-mail: anshin@sprynet.com

Part Two
Purna Steinitz

I usually do not speak to groups this large. I am not sure exactly what to do here today. I've been thinking a lot the last few days about this talk. I am grateful to be here and to have an opportunity to share with you my experience of my path.

I don't know a lot about the Alexander Technique, but we have an office in Little Rock, Arkansas. It turns out that the man who rents us the office is an Alexander teacher. I didn't know this until two weeks after I was asked to speak here. I told him I was coming here, and he said, "Come on over to my office. . ." and I learned what to do with my neck. I love the work. I had three sessions with him, and I intend to continue the work when I go back.

When Claude was up here he spoke about lineage. He said that his tradition dates back to the Buddha. I am not a Buddhist, but from what I have studied there has been an unbroken chain in the Buddhist teaching, passed down from person to person. And he spoke about his great-grandfather, his grandfather, and his father, and he said there was also a lineage: this idea of being a warrior and going to war was passed down to him. I have been a student of a man named Mr Lee Lozowick for 24 years, and I am still his student. His teacher is a man in India whose name is Yogi Ramsuratkumar. And Yogi Ramsuratkumar's teacher was a man named Papa Ramdas. And Papa Ramdas' teacher was his father. The teaching is passed down.

In a sense you are all children of Mr Alexander – not in a co-dependent sense. You are all children of his work. Gurdjieff talked about the stink of enlightenment. He said that you can smell when someone has accumulated something spiritually important within them. He said that you can really smell that. I have learned over the past 24 years, in travelling with my teacher, to smell when something is real, and to smell when something is not real. In reading about Mr Alexander my nose smelled something very fine, very wonderful, and something very, very real. I smelled a human being who dedicated his life to the work that we have dedicated our life to. I smelled somebody who taught until five days before he died. I smelled somebody who was completely dedicated to the work. It was inspiring for me.

Claude spoke about his walking and knocking on doors of churches and religious institutions, and sleeping in barns and not having anything to eat. I come from the same kind of tradition except that I don't walk around, I ride in a car. But I am jealous of Claude in a certain way. My teacher's teacher, Yogi Ramsuratkumar, has been a beggar for the last 50 years. He dresses in rags, in Southern India, in the hot, hot summer. He wears five layers of clothes, and he bathes once or twice a year. He is very dirty. He travelled in India for probably 30 years. People threw rocks at him, and they spit on him, and they told him to go away. When we think what kind of thing Claude is doing and Yogi Ramsuratkumar did, we think of it very romantically sometimes.

The training that I went through was very unromantic. I met my teacher when I was 22 years old. I spent at least ten years being very, very angry at him, and very jealous and competitive, and always feeling agitated inside. Part of the work – from what I read about the Alexander Technique – is to help people find balance. The work that was done with me was to push me off balance as much as possible; so that I had to find a way to find true balance in my life. My teacher made it difficult. He didn't do me a lot of favours. He did do me favours, but he didn't do my ego a lot of favours. There was a period of one year in which he wouldn't talk to me or look at me. And I travelled with him all the time. Then one day something shifted in me; and he came down to breakfast and he said, "Good morning."

When my teacher met his teacher, he had a number of students. They went to India in 1976, and they were walking down the street in this little town which was dirty and where you couldn't even get Coca-Cola. Can you imagine that? In India now you can get Coca-Cola everywhere. They were walking down the street and this little man came out and said "come here," and they followed him down this alley, and there were six teacups. There was a beggar sitting there, and there were six of us. He was waiting. He gave my teacher a lot of attention. Then we went back a couple of years later and again he gave my teacher a lot of attention. Then we went back four or five years later and my teacher went with 20 students to see his teacher. At that period in time some people had bought Yogi Ramsuratkumar a little house. He lived in the house, but the house had nothing in it except piles of dirt. Just little piles of dirt and garbage. He collected garbage his whole life. We walked in, and Ramsuratkumar looked at my teacher and he said, "Who are you?" My teacher said, "I am Lee. I write to you. I am your student. Here are my students." And Ramsuratkumar said, "Who are you? I've never heard of you." He was very serious. Lee said, "I am Lee. I am a spiritual master." We were there for a week, and Ramsurat-kumar would not even acknowledge him. He said to us, "You are very nice people. You can come and see me again." But he looked at Lee and said: " You go away." So Mr Lee sat outside in the hot sun for a week. And Ramsuratkumar would not even look at him. Then he got a letter about a year later, from a student of Ramsuratkumar, saying please come to India. He came and there were all these signs in the town welcoming him, and he spoke at this big conference for Yogi Ramsuratkumar and so on.

So the spiritual process is a process in which our ego is ground down and made nothing. It is what Claude was saying when he said that Buddha represents space. We identify ourselves with our personality. "I am man. I am a teacher. I have a wife. I have students." Or "I am an Alexander teacher. I know this and this, and I am better than people who don't know how to eat, sitting straight." This is what ego does. One of the traps of the spiritual path is, as we begin to examine ego, to see how separate we are from other people, we judge that, and we make it bad. "This is terrible. This is very, very bad." But in our tradition we learn to say yes to everything which we don't like about ourselves. We learn to say to yes to the hate. I was very impressed in meeting Claude. He is a man who before his eighteenth birthday had killed hundreds of people. When I met him I knew that about him. I didn't feel a trace of that. I didn't feel any of that left in him. And I have a pretty good nose. The point is that in order to transcend that which we don't like about ourselves we learn – in the tradition that I come from – to welcome those things. We learn to welcome the hate, the anger, the fear, the terror, the sadness, and to just let it be as a way of dissolving it all.

You work with the body. In my tradition we use the phrase "the intelligence of the body." We say the body knows. The body knows so much; when we get cut there is a process called phagocytosis in which the immune system is mobilized. It goes to that cut and healing takes place through the natural intelligence of the body. The work which we do in the Baul tradition we call "surrender to the will of God." The tradition that I come from is a theistic tradition, a devotional tradition. I have many friends who are Buddhists, and we always tease each other. They always say there is no such thing as God. The Buddhists have a very different relationship to the absolute. We joke about that. My tradition is a devotional tradition, and we say that if the path has to have a goal, the goal is to surrender to the will of God. It is not a God in the sky – we say he does not live in the sky. We say God is life itself, but how do we surrender to life? We say our work is about learning to trust the intelligence of life. Just like the body has an intelligence of its own life has an intelligence of its own. When we trust life and surrender to that intelligence of life, when we say yes to life, then separation disappears. The wall that we've constructed to keep other people out, to keep life from coming in, disappears. How do we surrender to life? How do we say yes? In our tradition the process is one of grinding down that which separates me from you. In the process of grinding down what comes up is my resistance. The degree to which I can say yes to my resistance, rather than pretending it is not existing, pushing it down, suppressing it, and substituting some kind of addiction – for example to food, drugs, alcohol, talking, work, or movies. The degree to which I can face and say yes to every part of myself is the degree to which I am free in the moment. Nothing determines who I am as much as that which I chose to ignore and resist.

I remember reading a quote – I think from Alexander – about what a sensitive instrument the body is. The body is a very sensitive instrument and feelings and thoughts and higher and lower emotions are constantly rising in the body. My teacher took a stand for me, he said "Purna, you're going to look at it all. And I am going support you in that." Although much of the time it didn't look like I was being supported in that. I love attention, which is pretty obvious. So he didn't give me attention. It took me about a year to be able to not get any attention and let that be sort of okay.

Our animal nature makes us seek pleasure. When I am tired I want to sleep. When I am angry I want my anger to go away. "Relieve me of my suffering." I imagine that is why people come to you. I don't notice a lot of people coming to the work and just saying, "My life is working, everything is wonderful and working out great. I have no problems. I just want to grow." Mostly we come to the work of self in order to find relief for our suffering. The thing that I like about the Alexander Technique is that it is a way to become more deeply connected to reality, not to run away from it.

The subject that I was given, when I was invited to give this talk, was the distinction between the Alexander Technique and spiritual work. I had a really difficult time with that. Not because I don't think there is a distinction. I think that there is a distinction. I don't think the Alexander Technique is about grinding down people's egos. I don't think it is necessarily about finding equality between pleasure and pain. I don't think it is necessarily about living one's life saying yes to pain when every ounce of flesh inside you wants to say no, to say I just want relief from my suffering, any way, any how. I don't think it is about that. But I had a difficult time in thinking about that because I didn't want to separate myself from you. I didn't want to get up and say "I teach people about spirituality and Alexander Technique doesn't do that." I am really glad that that didn't happen today.

My experience is that we are all part of a whole. Each one of us is a part of a whole. As Claude said, when a bag of rice drops in China it affects us. It is part of a whole. It is the responsibility of the part to participate in the whole. We each have some role in the whole, thereby giving something back to the whole. Claude spoke about how he walks. He told me he goes to concentration camps and leads retreats. And Yogi Ramsuratkumar sits in Southern India 22 hours a day, just sits there and prays. I don't want to sit 22 hours a day. I have a community in Arkansas, and that is my way of contributing to the whole. You have your way. I am sure many of you have your spiritual practices. You have this wonderful gift in the Alexander Technique. I am very critical of most forms of healing. I think there is a lot of garbage out there that doesn't really provide lasting change for people. I want to end by saying that I think that the contribution you make to the whole is one that is quite profound and greatly needed.

Purna Steinitz has been a student of Lee Lozowick, a western Baul Master, for the past 24 years. Baul is a 500-year old tradition from Western Bengal: followers of this tradition are beggars and poets, who wander from village to village, singing and praising God. In 1998 Purna founded a small community, Trimurti, in Little Rock, USA. Purna was a trainer in transpersonal psychology methods for 12 years and has founded the Berstein Trainings and Heart Stream Education which provide training in relationship for individuals and couples in prison.

Trimurti
PO Box 17091
Little Rock, AR 72222
USA
e-mail: pau@aristotle.net

Communication[1]

Cathy Madden and Jeremy Chance

After Jeremy and Cathy are introduced on the platform, Jeremy runs off the side of the stage with Cathy chasing him. Jeremy first trips and falls over the balcony into the auditorium. Cathy keeps up the chase as he then charges across the front of the audience, heading for the exit doors opposite while both yell at each other in a German, French, Japanese and English clown act – the gist of which is that Jeremy is afraid to go onstage and Cathy bullies him into it . . .

Cathy: Jeremy, jetzt, jetzt. [Jeremy, now, now]

Jeremy: Nai , Nai. [No, no]

(Both entering auditorium:)

Cathy: Jeremy, Hals frei, hals frei. [Jeremy, neck free, neck free] Vo ist ihre hals? [Where is your neck?] Vo ist it? [Where is it?]

Jeremy: Hir. [Here]

Cathy: Ja, und ist ihre hals frei? [Yes, and is it free?]

Jeremy: Ich habe angst, Ich habe angst. [I have fear, I have fear]

Cathy: Nein, sie habe nicht angst. dinke dinke. [You aren't afraid. Think. Think.] Hals frei. [Neck free] Sie habe nicht angst, nicht stress. [No stress] Hals Frei!!!! [Neck free!!!!]

Cathy: Jeremy, get up off the floor now.

(He gets up.)

Jeremy: I'm leaving. . .

(Starts running up stairs.)

Cathy (*stopping him*): Stay here!

Jeremy: OK.

Cathy (as drill sergeant): Give your orders. Free your neck.

Jeremy (looking up to the ceiling): Free my neck?

Cathy: Free your neck. So your head can go forward and up . . .

Jeremy (looking up in wonder): . . . so my head can go forward and up?

Cathy: . . . so my body can follow . . .

Jeremy (*getting big idea)*: . . . so my back can lengthen and widen!

Cathy: . . . so I can march up on that stage and speak . . .

Jeremy: . . . so I can march right out the door!

(Starts to run out.)

Cathy (stopping Jeremy with her words): Arret! Jeremy, qu'est-ce que tu fais? Tous les personnes ici nous attendent. [Stop! Jeremy, what are you doing? All these people are waiting for us]

Jeremy (confident): J'ai changé d'avis; Je ne veux pas faire ça. [I have changed my mind. I don't want to do this.]

Jeremy Chance (Australia) and Cathy Madden (USA) during their presentation of "Communication."

Cathy: Mais, Ce n'est pas possible de changer d'avis. [But it is not possible to change your mind.]

Jeremy: Au contraire, M. Alexander disaient que c'est toujours possible. [On the contrary, Mr Alexander said that it is always possible]

Cathy: Silence!! Maintenant inhibe tes reactions! [Quiet!! Now inhibit your reaction!]

Jeremy: D'accord. [OK]

Cathy: Allons sur scéne. [Go on stage]

Jeremy: C'est n'est pas possible, je suis en train d'inhiber mes reactions! [It isn't possible, I am inhibiting my reactions!]

Cathy: Mon dieu j'abandonne! [My God! I give up]

(Cathy starts toward the stage. Jeremy, feeling left alone, starts to follow her.)

Jeremy: Cathy-san, Onegai dakara. Oite ika naide kudesai! [Cathy, don't leave me here, please, please, please]

Cathy: Jaa, watashito issho ni ikimaska? [So now you want to come?] Ii des. [Good]
Eigo-ga wakarimaska? [Do you understand English?]

Jeremy: Hai, eigo-ga wakari masu. [Yes, I understand]

(They finally reach the stage and create the first doorway.)

Introduction

Cathy: Hello, Gruezi, and Gruss Gott.

Jeremy: Ohio Gozimasu, and g'day.

Cathy: We are glad you are here.

Jeremy: And we are grateful for the opportunity to speak with you.

Cathy: Our topic today is communication. And our clown act is obviously an example of communication that isn't working. I, as the teacher, was not listening to or seeing my student in any ways that would help him learn.

Jeremy: And I as a student wasn't taking responsibility for my decision to come and have a lesson.

Cathy: We are going to raise questions this morning about the many ways we communicate in each moment of our teaching lives, examining our basic assumptions about teaching, and looking at both general principles and a few of the many specific means-whereby for communicating.

How will we keep the doors open between the teacher's world and the student's world?

We are in communication from the first moment we talk to a student on the phone. . .

Jeremy: Ring, ring.

Cathy: Hello. Cathy speaking.

Jeremy (old woman voice): Hallo dear. Do you teach Mr Alexander's techniques?

Cathy: Yes.

Jeremy: Well, can you tell me what his remedies are? I've got an awful back…

. . . to the first time our student comes to the studio . . .

Cathy (knock, knock, knock – very timidly)

Jeremy (opening door, booming Aussie voice): G'day! . . . (no answer) . . . Hallo? Come in! come in!

Cathy (*timidly coming in, as Jeremy watches)*

. . . to meeting a group for the first time . . .

Cathy (to the Congress audience): Welcome, it's a pleasure for me to be here to introduce the Alexander Technique to you. It's a deliciously simple tool that can have amazing effects in your life.....

The teaching process

To a certain extent, your ideas about what is important about communication in teaching will be based on your idea about what teaching is. Personally, I like to remember that the root word for education, *educare* means "to draw out." My job as a teacher is to draw out the wisdom of the student. Thich Nanh Hanh, in his book, *Peace is Every Step,*[2] said, "A teacher has to give birth to the teacher within the student."

Jeremy: I'd like to build on Cathy's description by defining how I want to function as a teacher. I work to a very simple formula – whatever my pupil thinks I said and whatever my pupil tries to practice – *that* is what I communicated to them. Between my intention and their perception, is the space of communication, and I am solely responsible for how my words arrive at the other side of that space. A consequence of this formula is the thinking that says, "There are no difficult pupils, just inflexible teachers". So I see it as my responsibility, as a teacher, that my pupils perceive the information as I intend it to be perceived.

Cathy: The concepts that Jeremy and I will talk about today are general enough to apply to your work no matter what your definition of teaching is – no matter what your definition of the Alexander Technique is. If you had to define teaching in one sentence, what would that sentence be? You might take a moment here to think about, even write down for yourself, your definition of teaching.

In some way, each lesson, each class begins with walking through a doorway.

The lesson starts with a knock on the door

On both sides of this door are two different worlds. As a student, this moment is an important one. When I walk through this doorway, I am walking into the unknown – whether I am a new student or a long-time student. I have signed up for this lesson or class, arranged to pay for the lesson, got in my car and driven to the lesson, and have now walked to the front door and am knocking on the door because there is something that I need, something that I think that this particular person, this teacher, can help me find.

Jeremy: For me as a teacher, the first person I want to communicate successfully with is myself. To remember to watch myself and take care of my coordination is the only way I can also take care of my student. I am also about to go into the unknown, and I know from my past experience that I am more equipped to go into the unknown if I have accessed the coordination of my whole self. I have chosen to be a teacher of this work because it fulfils a higher need in me, and it is good if I can regenerate the purity of my motivation as I start out to teach another lesson.

Cathy: On each side of this door are two different worlds. As a teacher, it is a moment for me to acknowledge my world, my "conditions of use present", and to know that my world is about to expand to include someone else's world, if it is a private lesson (or many "someone else's" worlds if I am teaching a group lesson). In a lesson, it is my job to walk with someone else in their world, while being present to myself. I think it is very important to remember that both teacher and student are walking from the known to the unknown.

Jeremy: Joining my pupils in their world, while continuing to give attention to my own coordination, is the greatest challenge I face in this communication process. I used to think communication began from my side of the lesson – I had to "show them" and "tell them" and "teach". But one day my teacher Marjorie Barstow said, "You have to begin with your pupil's thinking." Then I realized that first, I have to discover about *them*, I have to start from *their side*, not mine! As we move together into the unknown, it is important that I shape my lessons differently to fit each individual pupil.

Constructive thinking

Cathy: The first and most important key to communication which Alexander teachers possess is our ability to use constructive thinking so as to have good use of ourselves. In *The Universal Constant in Living*, F. M. said that his work offers us "a new pattern providing [us] with the means of changing and controlling our reactions in the face of the difficulties which are inevitable in [our] attempts to pass from the known (wrong) to the unknown (right) experiences essential for the making of fundamental change."[3] With this new pattern of coordination we are able to see and hear our student clearly. When I was preparing this talk, I enjoyed remembering how Marj taught me, very indirectly, about communication from the moment that she began helping me learn to teach. Here's specifically how I remember her teaching me.

If I wished to teach, I would say to Marj in one of our group classes, "Marj, I would like to work with teaching."

Once I had someone willing to be a student for me, I would start to rise from my chair and Marj would say, "Cathy, what do you notice about yourself?"

If I could describe what I noticed, which might include my thinking, my feeling, or my moving, and if I could "use my constructive thinking" to improve anything that needed improving, I would be encouraged to continue in the lesson I was giving.

The next question Marj would ask from her chair across the room would be, "What do you notice about your student?"

Again, if I could answer, we would go on with the teaching. If, however, I was unclear, negative, mumbling, or unable to prevent interference in myself, my lesson would be over for the moment, and Marj would suggest, "Why don't you think about that?"

It was quite a while before I made it all the way across the room to my student.

Demanding work, for which I am infinitely grateful. By attending to my coordination, I became acquainted with what I would later realize was both honesty and kindness to myself.

The order of Marj's questions is vital. It was not until I could constructively work with or answer the "What do I notice about myself?" question that we even moved on to noticing anything about the student.

I was expected to articulate what I saw, I was expected to talk to my student while moving well and speaking clearly. Since one of the ways in which our students learn is by imitating us, this process that Marj taught me ensured that I presented an improved coordination to my students.

This attention was the beginning of creating a constructive relationship with the student. The essential elements of good communication – looking, listening, thinking, speaking, and moving well – were taught to me *before* I even began to include using my hands as part of teaching.

The questions which Marj asked me required me to be honest and to think constructively in teaching. I learned about honesty with myself; and I learned to think constructively in teaching. Once I learned these things for myself, then I could be honest and constructive in relation to my student.

Jeremy: For my first ten years of teaching, I didn't have the benefit of Marj's wisdom, so I had to learn in a different way about how important it was to first think constructively about myself while teaching a lesson.

Twenty years ago, after I finished my training, I often associated teaching with a state of anxiety. With experience, I noticed that whenever my pupil said something nice about my teaching, this anxiety evaporated, and then I felt I could teach well. However, I soon realized that I was setting up a pattern of needing these strokes to feel successful as a teacher – and this placed an unfair burden on my students. What was more constructive for our communication was when my confidence as a teacher wasn't dependent upon their feedback. When I was self-assured from my own side, my students felt a greater freedom to be critical of me, to express their doubts and confusion.

How did I go about this? I came up with a simple mantra, "Trust the principles – they work." So when a problem arose,

– rather than be directed by my feelings of anxiety which by now I had recognized as an unreliable guide for teaching – I told myself to trust the principles. If things weren't working, I said to myself, there was a reason for it. So instead of panicking, if I eased in my neck and let my head lead my whole body so as to look constructively at what was going on, I would find a clue.

What was amazing to me about this plan was that, time and time again, it worked. By finding my clue, I gained a pleasurable experience through trusting the principles, and soon teaching became learning, and the learning became fun.

Cathy: The ability to use my constructive thinking is one of the basic skills that I bring to this doorway to an unexplored world. Each of us – teacher and student – brings into this world our own stories. It is from the interweaving of our lives, our stories, that the teaching and the learning emerge.

Ways of understanding communication
I. Analysing the conditions of use present

There are many, many excellent systems for gathering information. What's primarily required is a genuine interest in your student. It's essential for us as teachers to cultivate our curiosity, to ask the simple questions, to be willing to "not know" the answers.

In the next section of this talk, we're going to look at a practical, common sense approach to gathering information.

First, with curiosity as your guide, here is a scenario:

(Jeremy knocks at the door as Cathy fusses with her looks.)

Cathy: *(Opening door)* How can I help you? [He doesn't like me, I can tell.]

Jeremy: I want to play the piano without any wrist pain. [What does she think I want?!]

Cathy: Uh, I teach the Alexander Technique. [This is never going to work.]

Jeremy: Well, can you help me or not? [What's the bloody point?]

Cathy: Here, let me show you. [I hope this works. I hope this works. I hope this works.]

(After some work.)
Jeremy: Oh, that feels good. [I just want to get out of here.]

Cathy: Oh, you're doing great. [It might work!]

Jeremy: Oh, I like your teaching. [Maybe I can salvage something out of this.]

Cathy: One of the ways in which this teaching situation could have worked better is if the teacher had had a bit more clarity about the circumstances of the lesson – about her/himself as a teacher and about the student.

Figuring this out involves asking questions.

As a guide to learning the art of questioning, I like to use a set of questions that was developed by an acting teacher named Uta Hagen[4]. When I teach communication, I like to start with them because they are simple, comprehensive, and full of common sense. It is from this basis of common sense that other communication techniques emerge. Jeremy and I are now going to illustrate how you might use this set of questions to untangle the communications of the scene that you have just observed.

Cathy answers questions about the teacher – Jeremy answers questions about the student.

Who am I?
Cathy: I've been teaching the Alexander Technique for two years and I need to land a job.

Jeremy: I am a music student whose wrists are hurting so badly I can't play the piano anymore.

Where am I?
Cathy: I am downtown in my teaching studio.
Jeremy: I am in a strange part of town that I have never been to before.

What time is it?
Cathy: It's morning on my day off from waitressing.
Jeremy: It's 60 minutes before I have to be at school for an assessment that I haven't prepared for.

Who and what surround you?
Cathy: I am with my new music student in my studio carefully decorated with many objects I have collected.
Jeremy: I am looking at this weird poster of an egg that says "poise" under it – huh?

What are the circumstances?
Cathy: I worked late at the restaurant last night and got up early to teach this lesson. The music school has sent this student to me on a "trial" basis to see if the Alexander Technique works.
Jeremy: I slept in, missed breakfast, and have to be at school soon.

What do you want?
Cathy: I want to help my student get the information he needs so that he doesn't hurt and so that, hopefully, the music school will give me some permanent work.
Jeremy: I want her to tell my teachers that I will eventually be OK and should be given some time off to get better.

Is there anything in your way?
Cathy: I'm incredibly nervous and all I can think is, "I have to make this work. I have to make this work."

Jeremy: My wrists hurt, and I am sure I am wasting my time with all this "crystal crap". I really don't believe that Alexander work will do me any good.

What are you doing to get what you want?
Cathy: Each time I start worrying about doing this lesson right, I renew my constructive thinking – asking for ease in myself so that I can see and hear my student and help him learn what he needs to learn.
Jeremy: I have given up my valuable time to try to find a new approach to be able to stay at the school and continue playing the piano.

Replay the "Fix me Please" Scenario – different subtext first for teacher, gradually for student.

(Jeremy knocks at the door as Cathy moves delicately towards it.)

Cathy: *(Opening door)* How can I help you?

Jeremy: I want to play piano without any wrist pain.

Cathy: Come and sit down for a minute and talk. (*They both sit down.*) Tell me what's going on.

Jeremy: My wrists hurt too much to play piano and. . . *(Cathy still listening)* well – frankly, I am frightened that I will be thrown out of the music school!

Cathy: Wow, that is frightening. Let me explain a bit about how the Alexander work has helped other pianists so you can get a sense of how it might help you. (Jeremy *looks relieved.*)

Cathy: That scene was a bit different, wasn't it? The teacher still had the same issues, but she had a constructive plan to deal with those issues.

With a little preparation – using what Mary Cox referred

to (in her presentation, "Emotion") as a "realistic appraisal of the situation and the environment" – these people are in better communication.

The other day, Claude AnShin Thomas said that when we teach "we can't help stirring things up"; that our job is to "provide an environment in which reaction can take place safely."

It seems to me that, by both using the Alexander Technique and becoming conscious of as much as possible about myself and my environment, I am doing my job in "providing an environment in which reaction can take place safely," since my teaching space and I are major elements in my student's environment.

For a bit of fun, let's see what happens if each of you takes a moment to answer these questions about yourself as you sit here in the music auditorium in Freiburg (if you prefer, imagine yourself with one of your students).

Wer bin ich? *Who am I?*
Wo bin ich? *Where am I?*
Wie spät ist es? *What time is it?*
Wer und was umgibt mich? *Who and what surrounds you?*
Was glaubst du, was geschehen wird? *What are the events—before, during and after this moment?*
Wie stehst du zu dieser Situation? *What is your relationship to your role here, to where you are, to the time, the people, the surroundings, the events of to-day?*
Was willst du? *What do you want? your want for right now, your want for the day, your want for the Congress, your want for this year, your want for this life?*
Empfindest du etwas als störend? *Is there anything in your way?*
Was tust du, um zu erreichen, was du willst? *What are you doing to get what you want?*
And the one I add to Uta Hagen's list, "Wie gebrauchst du dich, um zu erreichen, was du willst?" "How are you using yourself to carry out your actions?"

Cathy: In other words, in Alexander's words, we are "analysing the conditions of use present" in the widest sense. Our use of our self is one part of the conditions of use present. The circumstances of the activity we are engaged in is another part.

Now, we've all answered these questions for ourselves; and our students have their own sets of answers to these questions – undoubtedly quite different from our own. A genuine curiosity, along with the ability to see and to hear clearly, will aid us in gathering bits of information from our students' world.

From what you see and hear, what could you guess about these students?

Use the doorways...

Cathy (knocks on door)

Jeremy
I was teaching a group workshop and a half hour into the workshop, the stiffest, angriest arrival to a workshop that I'd ever seen entered the room and said:

Cathy: My daughter came and dragged me out of the house and dumped me here because she said I needed it.

What questions might you ask this student? or

Jeremy (knocks on door).

Cathy: A physician arrives. As I start explaining the Alexander Technique to him, he interrupts . . .

Jeremy: Don't bother with the explanations. I don't go with all this pseudo ying yang vegetarian crap. Still, my musician friends say this works, so just do it to me!

Again, what would you guess about the student? What questions would you ask? or

Cathy (knocks on the door).

Jeremy: I open the door and let and say "hi" as the student rushes past me to my piano saying . . .

Cathy: Hi, I'm Sue, and when I play the piano my wrists hurt and I want you to see what I'm doing?

What would you guess about this student?

As you notice, my questions to you have been, "What would you *guess* about the students involved?" It's important to know that you are guessing and to ask rather than assume that your guesses are correct. The guesses help you to formulate questions that may help a student who is "stuck" in their lesson. Even a wrong guess might elicit the information that you need. Assumptions can be disrespectful; guesses and questions give your student the opportunity to learn.

I like to remind my students that questions are a gift that you bring to a teacher. Questions can also be a gift that the teacher gives to the student. What a question can do is to open doorways into fixed patterns and beliefs. Questions are, by their nature, an invitation to movement. Questions are also a way to initiate an experimental attitude in our work, as Lucia Walker and Kevan Martin talked about in their presentation, "Concepts".

Sometimes there is no direct answer to the question in the moment, but a door has been opened. Creating the opening for change is a vital part of the lesson. The poet Rainer Maria Rilke wrote:

> Live the questions now.
> Perhaps you will then
> gradually,
> without noticing it,
> Live along some distant day
> into the answers.

II. Three important processes of communication

Jeremy: In preparing our talk, Cathy and I decided it was important to talk specifically both about the lesson itself *and* the time before the lesson. Because so much happens to create the context of a lesson, it is a trap to think that the lesson itself is the only part of the communication process. The means of a lesson includes the approach of your pupil before any real learning starts.

It was Annie Hall, the late Art Director of *Direction*, who first taught me this lesson. I had arrived with the proofs one afternoon to face her famously ruthless red pen, when a scrappy looking little flyer that I had prepared about *Direction* slipped from my folder and fell to the floor. She looked at it, picked it up by its corner as though it stank and demanded:

Annie:
What is this?!

Jeremy:
Well, it's a flyer about *Direction.*

Annie:
Jerry . . .

Jeremy: The Art Director of *Vogue Magazine* explained . . .

Annie:
This is the first experience anyone has of *Direction*. Look at it. What is it communicating to you?'

Jeremy:
That this is a scrappy journal on the AT, put out by someone in a hurry who isn't taking much care for precision.

Cathy drops the flyer on the floor.

That was what I was communicating—not just the words as I imagined—but the holistic experience people had of my flyer. On that note I believe it is right for our societies to fuss about logos, professional appearances, and succinct, accessible descriptions of our work. This time is a crucial moment in the ongoing process of communicating our work.

There are several processes that shape the communication environment of your private lesson or group workshop. They don't need to be haphazard processes – we can actually plan the conditions of use present so that our communication is the most effective.

Now, I want to look at three processes involved in preparing a lesson: research, rapport, and planning content. As an example, I will talk about planning a public talk or a group lesson.

To start with the obvious, any communication process comprises three interdependent elements – the teacher, the pupil, and the ideas that are being taught. In an Alexander lesson the ideas are, of course, Alexander's practical discoveries. Remove any one of these three components and the communication process can't happen. Have you ever tried to give a talk to an empty room? Or stood before an audience and can't remember what to say? Or been to a lecture when the speaker didn't show?

The next step in organizing our thinking is to realize that we have two stages to consider: first, preparing our lesson; second, teaching our lesson.

At this point, all I have done is lay out the basic structure behind any communication process.

The first of these is research. This is where the questions we led you through earlier fit into the scheme of things. If you've taught this person or group previously, then part of your research is getting their feedback.

As we are looking at planning a group, let's briefly examine each question from that perspective:

"Who am I going to teach?"
What is the professional background and agenda of these

people? Are they choosing to come, or is it compulsory? Are they professionals – athletes or musicians or a mix? If it was a group of physical therapists, for instance, it might mean brushing up your anatomical vocabulary, or have a reference book handy, in case you get stumped.

"Where am I going to teach?"
Always, always find out as much as you can about your work space – the best option being to visit it personally prior to the presentation. It's no good planning an active class for dancers, only to arrive and discover a hard, concrete floor; or a semi-supine talk-through in winter in a room where the heating is inadequate; or make the mistake I nearly did in Japan of planning a whole lot of processes with chairs, only to discover that they didn't have any! Often, you can never anticipate the problem until you've seen the space.

"When am I going to teach?"
Are your students likely to come to the class fresh and ready to think, or tired and ready to be bored? Is this just a one-off class or the first of a series? How long do you have – will everyone be on time and there till the end? In Japan, for example, it can be very important to finish on time, as people often have trains to catch but are too polite to tell you. Your extra five minutes of teaching might mean they arrive home an hour later.

All these questions lead you to achieving the next important aim of running a group: building rapport with the people in your group. Building rapport is dependent upon you knowing something about your students:

The importance of building rapport is that you want to get your students on your side, you want to enrol them to work with you, not against you. In this connection, Alexander said: "Don't come to me unless, when I tell you you are wrong, you make up your mind to smile and be pleased."[5] That's a lot to ask from a group of strangers, but we can facilitate things far better if we can communicate with them in a way that encourages them to listen.

I learnt this the best way you can – through direct experience. In the early 1980s I was invited to run a workshop at an Easter celebration with a group of Sanyasins – or "Orange People" as they were known then. It was all very loose and free, so every teacher had to describe his or her workshop so the 40 odd participants could decide where they wanted to go.

I was fresh and frightened in those days, so I offered a fairly safe description, saying something like:

> The Alexander work is about constructive conscious control, it is about discovering our habits of use that are harmful and, through the processes of inhibition and direction, learning to re-educate the use of ourselves so we can restore the vitality of movement we once had as children.

At the time, I thought it was rather good, but then came the big moment… How many people wanted to come to the Alexander workshop? Three hands went up. It was cancelled.

The next day I had another chance with a new group of people. This time I thought about who these people were, I thought about their belief structures and their own personal agendas and what they wanted from this day of "celebration". In short, I thought about how I could communicate with them more effectively. So when my time came around again, I explained:

> Alexander work is a sensation, a new feeling – it can't be described, it can only be experienced. In my group I will use touch to help *you* transform the inner experience of who you are being. This touch has the power to transform your whole being, your whole life.

How many people wanted to come to the Alexander workshop? 35 hands shot up. It was a great success.

What happened? I got into a rapport with these people. I spoke to their needs, their wants – I got their curiosity peaked. I also answered some questions that I haven't mentioned yet, questions that fulfil the next moment in the communication process: *planning the content.* To build a complete rapport with these Sanyasins I also had to ask myself: "Why are they here?", "What do they want?", and "How do I do it?"

"Why are we here?" and "What do we want?"

Getting people to think about these questions is an almost universal beginning to any successful workshop – and for a good reason. It creates a focus for both teacher and pupil and starts shaping the "how" of the lesson.

However, as teachers we still make our own plan – we don't follow the pupil's plan. A first-time student might say that they are here because their back hurts and what they want is an exercise that will fix it. We listen to that perspective and then find a way to lead them on to a new one. The point is, we need to know how they are listening to us, because that filters everything we teach them. We've all had to teach people whose response to what they hear is: "This sounds like a load of psychobabble." Great communicators can transform that agenda – provided they realize it is there.

How do I do it?

This is the moment when we start to make some important choices, based on the conditions present. We start planning the content of our group, based on what we learn. Is this also true of the private lesson? Do we consider its content every time? This may sound like an odd question to some of the experienced hands in the audience, who may be thinking, "Well, the content of the lesson is the Alexander Technique – what else is there?"

Of course that's right, but I think the newly qualified teachers in the audience, and those about to qualify, are thinking about this question a lot. After many years of teaching, this process becomes so intuitive we often forget we are making choices – it all seems to flow so easily. But if you think back to your very first private lessons – wasn't this a question that occupied you?

Come to think of it, even touch was originally the result of a choice by Alexander in planning the content of his lessons. He didn't start out touching, but he soon found it an effective means-whereby, so he started to include it more. Nor did Alexander ever stop this learning process, as he indicates in his description of giving a lesson to "the stutterer" in *The Use of the Self*: "It is impossible in the space at my command to put down all the details of the variations of the teacher's art that were employed to bring my pupil to this point, *for a teacher's technique naturally varies in detail according to the particular needs and difficulties of each pupil*" [my italics].[6]

That's all I am really talking about, becoming aware of "the needs and difficulties of each pupil." Perhaps this is a question we could all ask – what are the variations of your teacher's art? What prompts you to change your teaching technique? How do you structure a first lesson or an introductory group?

III. Using language

Cathy: All of these steps require flexibility to hear, to see, to speak clearly as we walk with our student through the many doorways of the lesson. It's a little like an Alexander lesson – the parts of communication don't work unless the overall coordination of communication is in place.

Another specific tool in communication is word choice. What words do you choose to use? What words do your students choose to use?

Language, both from our students and from ourselves, is important in this process. You can hear how F. M. Alexander listened to students and chose his words in some descriptions we have of his work. Goddard Binkley reports several conversations with F. M. in his diaries.[7] His September 11 1951 entry reports that Alexander "repeated the orders, constituting the means-whereby. . . But right here at this point, I interfered with myself."

> *Goddard*: I did not "rise" from the chair.
> *F. M.*: There, you are trying to get up.
> *Goddard*: But it seemed absolutely impossible to me that I should be able to stand up from the position I was in.
> *F. M.*: Well, there you are! You see, by what you have just told me you were not inhibiting the desire to get up. In fact, you were thinking about "getting up from the chair."
> Goddard laughs.
> *F. M.*: You see, it's all a matter of belief and intent.

Cathy: Much of what I learned about using language came from watching Marjorie Barstow teach. She was masterful as a listener and a chooser of language. People who knew Neurolinguistic Programming, a system that identified the ways in which good teachers and communicators communicate, often commented that Marjorie Barstow used language exquisitely. As I began to teach, some of those people would ask, "Have you studied NLP?" and when I said no, they would say, "Don't bother, you already use it." I decided to learn some of the terminology when I started doing more teacher training because the terms help me to identify the contribution which clear listening, looking, and intent make to good communication.

Jeremy: I have also studied NLP as a tool for researching the communication process. I don't see NLP as something separate from the communication process it describes. Every great communicator uses these techniques without exception – to be a successful communicator it is not necessary to study NLP. NLP is simple a set of labels used to describe the different processes that constitute excellent communication. Like Cathy, you may be naturally doing some of the things discussed in the next section of our talk.

Cathy: Language can give you clues about how your student thinks and learns. You get the language clues from the questions you ask; the invitations you make to the student to participate, to take responsibility for their own learning.

Earlier, I mentioned that the way Marjorie Barstow helped me to learn to teach involved seeing, hearing, and moving. Interestingly, both NLP experts and education researchers say this is a good idea. They talk about it in relationship to learning styles.

Education experts have identified three major learning styles: learning mostly either from seeing, from hearing, or from moving. They suggest that educators include elements of all these ways of learning in order to effectively reach all of their students. Even if someone has a preferred way to learn, everyone learns better if they receive the information in all three styles. What I learned from Marj, is to include observing (sight), listening (hearing questions and answers), and moving (in the movement of the lesson).

As an example of how a specific communication tool might help an Alexander Technique teacher, let's see how knowing about learning styles might be helpful in an Alexander lesson.

The student who favours visual learning might say: "I see it like this. When I'm playing tennis I'm not doing well at returning the serve. And the more I try, the more it looks to me as if I can't do it."

To match the student's preference, the teacher might say, "Let's look at the moment before the serve."

Or, for hearing preferences: "Listen, when I go to take my exams, all I hear in my head is how I don't know anything, and everything I write sounds stupid to me. And then, suddenly I'm so tight, I don't know what to tell myself."

The teacher might say, "I hear what you are saying to yourself."

Or, they may learn primarily through movement:

"I just feel so restricted when I'm moving onstage. It's as if my body feels everyone's eyes on me and I just want to jump out of my skin."

Rather than match the preference, a teacher could decide to go outside the student's preference to help him change his perspective: "Do you hear what you are saying to yourself? Let's look at things differently."

What we are doing as we listen to and suggest changes in people's messages to themselves is that we are teaching them how to talk constructively to themselves. Teaching them the difference between constructive thinking and non-constructive thinking. Marjorie Barstow sometimes called this "redirecting your thinking." NLP would call this "reframing". Mary Cox did this the other day when she changed the word "danger" to the word "possibility".

The example I used, the labels "matching" and "mismatching" from NLP, is just one of many ways to redirect a student towards "constructive thinking."

To do this effectively, you listen well, and make no assumptions. We hear words often, and think that we know what someone means when we hear them. That's not always true.

I was teaching a class at a university, and a student's neck was getting tighter and tighter. I said:

"What would happen if you asked yourself for ease in your neck so that your head can move, so that all of you can follow, so that you can sit in this chair?"

He was getting tighter and tighter, so I asked, "What are you saying to yourself?"

He said, "I'm trying to get my head to float up."

To myself I said, "Did I say anything about floating heads?" To my student I said, "You know what? Heads can't float. They can rest and move easily on top of your spine. Let's look at this again."

I hear that in German you have two different words for neck – one that means only the back of the neck, "Nacken", one that means the whole neck, "Hals". Which word you choose would radically change the meaning of the directions.

Jeremy: This relates to another important development in this era of the global community – today there is so much more crosscultural teaching going on, making it doubly important that we listen for our assumptions about how our words are being heard.

I recently had a direct experience of this. As many of you know, I have moved to Japan and started a training school in Tokyo. Before coming to Europe, I discussed the translation of Alexander's concepts with my Japanese wife, Jaldhara Koyama-san, who is a both a professional translator and a teacher of the Technique. As a translator, she was trained by Professor Yuzuru Katagiri, who has been with us this week. One striking communication problem they faced concerned translating the whole concept of non-doing, of letting or allowing something to take place.

Take the simple expression "Allow my neck to be free." Now an uninformed interpreter could translate this with the expression, "Kubiwo raku nishite kudesai."

Hearing this phrase, a Japanese speaker might either perceive it as meaning simply "free my neck" with no idea of "allow" or "let" being in there at all. But more likely – and much worse – they could conceive of it as an order such as "*make* my neck free". The difficulty is that, in Japanese, there is no word that successfully translates this concept of "allow" or "let". They just don't have it.

There is no magic solution to this. My wife, for example, says she personally overcomes this problem by using the word "urushite" which, directly translated, means "forgive". Personally I love this concept – I must "forgive my neck to be free". Of course when a Japanese speaker hears this expression, they find it as peculiar as you do. However, it is a skilful use of language, as it demands that the listener seek out the meaning of this phrase. With almost every beginner, this marks the beginning of their journey into understanding the nature of non-doing. And, if you reflect a little, it isn't really such a strange idea. Forgiveness is a kind of release – to forgive, you "let go" of the idea of getting back at someone. In fact, in Japanese the word once had the meaning "release"; while in English we still say, "Stop holding on to your grudge – let go of it." Forgiveness and letting go are definitely related.

The Alexander community owes a great debt to Professor Katagiri, who has taken meticulous care that the translation of Alexander's concepts into Japanese keeps intact the paramount importance of non-doing, and the sequence of the directions. For those of you who understand the Japanese language – and I can't number myself among them – I have heard that this is quite a feat and a subject for an entire presentation all by itself.

Cathy: The meticulous care we give to listening to the clues our students give us is a great kindness to them. Ultimately, this attention helps them formulate their own particular language for change.

While we have been focusing on language, there is another non-verbal "talking" – expression, gesture, and movement also communicate meanings. As Alexander Technique teachers we can watch this nonverbal talking with great subtlety. We can watch how someone's use of themselves and their words go together. Our overall ability to observe coordination gives us a lot of additional information about how our students give meaning to words.

For instance, I was teaching a group of Alexander students. Whenever they went into activity, they would initially get an improved use of themselves, and then at the moment they reached for something, or began to talk, or to type, they would lean backward to do it. Puzzled, I asked them to tell me what they were thinking, what they were telling themselves. What they said was:

"I'm saying, 'free my neck, so that my head can move forward and up so that my back can lengthen and widen so that I can stay back from the book I'm reaching for, or stay back from the person I'm talking to, or stay back from my computer'."

Stay back! They were making non-endgaining a physical doing of pulling away from what they were doing – putting themselves at a mechanical disadvantage. Again, it was *both* looking and listening that gave me the clues I needed to help them out.

Similarly, I worked with a singer who came to me primarily because she couldn't bow at the end of her performances without some danger of falling over. I watched her sing and her use was beautiful. I watched her bow, and her coordination fell apart. So I asked her, what do you tell yourself when you start to sing, thinking that it might give me a clue as to how to work with her bow. I can't remember exactly what she said, but it was something like, "I pull my head back and tuck my chin in and lift my palate and make the air go through a straw . . ." and she said eight or more other things that would turn nearly anyone into a pretzel trying to do. But when she said it, her head moved up, and her body followed and she looked and sounded gorgeous. If I had only listened to her words, I might have messed up a plan that was actually working quite well for her. Since I could see it was working, I found another way to teach her about bowing.

(As a side note, it was important that I could tell her that the words she used would turn most people into a pretzel. When I told her, she said, "Oh, is that why my students do such strange things when I tell them to do these things?")

Jeremy: I once saw Marj give a superb piece of teaching which integrated every element we have been discussing – and more. By the way, those who know NLP will recognize here at least a dozen techniques all rolled into one – and done within 30 seconds!

We were sitting in a circle at the end of a workshop in Australia in 1987, when suddenly a woman blurted out:

"Oh it's awful! Terrible! The way people use themselves, the tension they carry around!"

Needless to say the woman herself was demonstrating the very tension she was riling against. I thought: how is Marj going to handle this? What she did surprised me.

She immediately pulled herself down too – copying the woman's use – and in a similarly harsh tone of voice answered:

"Yes! It's terrible!!"

Immediately the woman eased a little – I assume because she appreciated Marj's agreement with her. A few people laughed. Then Marj shifted her voice towards a softer tone, delicately starting to move herself up again while saying:

"And don't you feel sorry for them, walking around with all that tension?"

"Yes, I feel sorry," the woman agreed, also in a softer tone.

Then Marj moved right up while using her hands, as she often did, to indicate the "forward and up" movement and added, with a twinkle in her eye:

"And don't you feel lucky – that you know something that they don't know."

"Yes," the woman answered, now also moving up and obviously thinking about what she had learnt at the workshop: "Yes, I feel lucky."

Language, when coordinated delicately with our use, is easily as powerful a tool as is our touch.

IV. The importance of desiring outcomes

Since we have been talking about the lesson itself, I want to return to my discussion of the structure of communication, now discussing three processes involved in teaching the lesson itself: desiring outcomes, starting a lesson, and getting feedback. To begin, I want to ask the question: what drives the communication? What keeps our pupil's curiosity peaked, their listening tuned, their motivation high?

Boiled down it comes to this: they desire something. No matter how weak it is, everyone has some kind of desire before the start of a lesson. This desire affects many things. A person with severe back pain, desperate for help, is going to learn very differently when compared to an adolescent boy pushed into lessons by an over-protective mum; his only "desire" is to get his mum off his back by fouling up your lesson!

We can encourage a pupil's desire for lessons by helping them look forwards to a desirable outcome.

Generating a strong desire for an outcome is not to be confused with endgaining – which characterizes an inadequate means of reaching an outcome. Alexander never wrote that goals in themselves were harmful. In fact, in *Man's Supreme Inheritance,* he made it very clear that we need them:

> It is the wish, the conscious desire to do a thing or think a thing, which results in adequate performance.[8]

But a goal alone does not equate with strong desire. If our pupil's desire is weak, what do we do? Resigning ourselves to their weakness of purpose discounts our ability to inspire, to lead, to somehow unravel from within the student a purpose that will excite them to continue their lessons. The greatest teachers in our community do this because of their own clear vision of the work. This shows that it isn't just something from the pupil's side. It is important that we, as teachers, have a desire for something too. Why is it that one teacher has so many pupils returning for lessons, while another keeps striking out?

Whenever a person clearly sees the potential outcome of our work, they are motivated to have lessons. Teachers who have this vision become great motivators of pupils. The vision is a force that drives the lessons to continue. What I am saying is that when the expectation of what can be achieved is strong enough, it becomes the very force that drives its own accomplishment.

As an example, listen to these words of Alexander, taken from "Evolution of a Technique":

> I began to see that my findings up till now implied the possibility of the opening up of an entirely new field of enquiry, and I was obsessed with the desire to explore it.[9]

Does that sound like a man without goals, without desires, without an outcome in mind? "Obsessed with desire" he describes himself. So we have to ask – can being "obsessed" with a goal be good thing? Is having a strong desire for an outcome important in our work? And looking at Alexander's achievements, we would have to answer, "Yes, it is".

Whenever I teach children, for example, I take advantage

of this idea. Children are naturally competitive, they enjoy testing their skills against each other and having fun while they do it. If you can convince them that Alexander lessons are going to help them run faster, jump higher, yell louder, and kick further, they will throw themselves into learning with glee. When I do it, they all eagerly line up for their reminders, before running off and having a lot of fun experimenting with their new coordination.

Watching them and hearing their laughter is fulfilling and another important moment in the communication process: *getting feedback*. This is a another key process of our communication; in an Alexander lesson it includes using touch to know what's going on – I think we all understand the importance of that. People learn at different speeds so we want our communication to be calibrated to their speeds. If not, our pupils can start to feel overwhelmed or inadequate. We want to create an atmosphere of success, not failure, and this means being sensitive to how the ideas are being implemented and understood.

V. The role of feedback

Cathy: What enables us to use communication tools and structuring tools well remains our ability to listen and to see, as well as a curiosity and flexibility of thinking that allows us to walk with someone in their world. In that moment we encounter the richness of each individual's unique abilities to use themselves well. Marj said,

> I don't believe in giving lessons in silence because I want to know what my pupils are thinking. I am not making a mechanical person out of them; I want my students to know what I'm doing; know how they experience it, talk it over with them.[10]

What I find, when I talk things over with my students, is that they can uniquely become their own teachers.

In one of my recent workshops, a student kept having trouble making a change in what she was doing in her coordination. I asked her if she wanted to make a change. The student is a pharmacist, and suddenly she was telling me a story:

> I have a patient, and a doctor and I have been working with him for several years to get him to change his diet, to take a drug, and take up an exercise program. Now, he's dying, he's ready to change, and he's asking us to help him, and it's really too late. It's really sad and frustrating. But, if I can ask people to make changes, I could certainly decide to experiment too.

In her struggle to move into an unknown experience, she was comparing herself with the patient in her pharmacy. She very brilliantly led herself through a change in thinking that I could not have dreamed would be available to her.

Storytelling

This story of the pharmacist brings me to a favourite communication tool in teaching – storytelling. I know that F. M. Alexander told stories. Marjorie Barstow certainly told stories. I'm sure you remember stories that your teacher has told you.

Our students tell us stories from their lives, the stories out of which their own transformations can take place. The pharmacist's story is a stunning example of this. They can also be very short stories, just glimpses of how a student constructs their world.

The next story is one I often tell in beginning classes. A young man who had been taking classes for a while, and who, after many weeks, still had a really tight neck, and was really beginning to hate Alexander class, comes into the room one day, he arrived a bit early,

(Jeremy walks in and sits down.)

Cathy: Hi, Ron.

Jeremy: Hi.

Cathy: Do you want to experiment a bit?

Jeremy: OK.

Cathy: What do you notice about yourself today ?

Jeremy: My neck is really, really stiff.

Cathy: Yeah, I can see that. Look, let's not try for a big change. This is about delicate change, delicate movement. Just see what happens when you decide to do a little less work here. Just a bit of ease here. . .

(He turns and he looks up at Cathy.)

Jeremy: My mom always said I'd lose my head if I didn't keep it on.

He looked all of about 4 or 5 when he said it. And I could just imagine this little boy who started holding his head on. And now as a 24-year-old actor he was still holding it on.

Cathy: Ron, she didn't quite mean it that way.

He said that what happened was, that he stopped tightening his neck, got scared for a moment, then remembered what his mother had said. He had a very silly week after that. He would be walking somewhere, notice that he was tightening, and then laugh and remind himself that his head would stay on.

How many things does a simple story tell a new student? It may tell us that we have our habits for very good reasons; they may be faulty reasons, but they do make a kind of sense; that it's OK to feel resistance to the process, that it might indeed take some time; that even though a change may be initially scary, it can end up being something that we can laugh about. It may bring up lots of different things.

Stories are indirect because I'm not talking about the student or students I am teaching in the moment – I am talking about someone else. Some of the stories are about me, some are from students I have taught. Do note that I preserve my students' privacy when I tell the stories – that's vital. I don't draw the conclusions for the students who are listening; they get to hear the story and take whatever information from it they find useful.

As a side note, experts on adult education say that this quality of indirectness is very important in adult learning. Indirectness "offers the people the protection they need to discover their own learnings"; again, this brings out the teacher in the student. Some technical notes on storytelling: teaching stories usually have beginnings, middles, and ends; they have a problem in them that is solved. With luck, they might also be humorous – humour also helps people learn.

Jeremy: No talk on communication could end without discussing one of the most effective tools that we Alexander teachers have – our unique quality of touch. I have my own understanding of touch within the teaching context, but I certainly don't expect everyone to agree with me. 500 Alexander teachers all agreeing on something is highly unlikely, and potentially unhealthy.

The first question I ask myself is what do I want to communicate through my touch? Over the years that answer has changed so that now I have a number of options to choose from. When I first started teaching, what I wanted – as I mentioned previously – was to generate a "wow! gee-whiz " response from my pupils, so I could feel good about my teaching.

As I began to practise more constructive thinking during my lessons, I felt that the real purpose of my touch was ontological – to offer a person an experience of themselves as they are, not as they are trying to be. In a way, this lifts their perspective out of the cluttered forest, and up to the mountain high, so that for a brief period they can really see the direction that their lessons are heading in. I felt this could both inspire and motivate them to continue their lessons. And it did. It worked.

I had been teaching for ten years in this way, when I finally overcame my prejudices and encountered the teaching of Marjorie Barstow. She presented me with a radically different viewpoint, and another option that I hadn't even considered. Marj didn't want to change me much at all – she wanted to give me a tiny experience, not a big one.

Many, many times at her workshops, I would see Marj help a student to change their coordination, then immediately, she'd take her hands off and ask them what they thought had happened. "What does that do for you?" she'd often ask us.

If the student didn't clearly answer, then it was often the end of the lesson. If Marj said to you, "Have a little think about that," you knew it was time to go and sit down. Actually, I found it fun, because I knew if I understood the change, her eyes would light up, and she would say, "That's right!", and then I would get a whole new piece of teaching from her. If you wanted a long turn from Marj, your understanding of how your coordination was changing had to keep up with her touch.

This is why Marj was famous for touching a little and asking a lot – an approach that seems to be characteristic of the Barstow lineage of teachers. It is yet another approach to communicating Alexander's remarkable discoveries and, for myself, a new option to add to the already valuable tools I have gained from my original training in England. I take the view that no single approach is the right one, for the simple reason that no two people are the same. Let's thank heaven that our earth is full of diversity, our Alexander community included.

Cathy: I'm always surprised when I'm referred to as "touching a little, asking a lot." I teach with my whole self, so I use whatever means seems the most effective in the moment.

When I do use my hands in teaching, as I think I frequently do, it is not something totally different from my words; it is an extension of them, an extension of my constructive thinking, another invitation to my student's whole self.

The beauty of beginning to learn to teach the way that I did is that I had clear, honest, kind guidelines for communication before I began to use my hands as part of that communication process.

"Taking care of myself" was expanded to include "Watch your hand as you reach to this person." "Thinking of my student" expanded to include "Let your student shape your hands." In this way, I can clearly meet each student as they are at the moment of the lesson.

Everything that has been said about verbal communication applies here. The same precision and clarity of thinking. The same discipline of thinking constructively.

Touch is communication, an invitation to movement, a call to the teacher within the student. Honesty and kindness infused in the conversation.

Conclusion

Jeremy: I think that being true to oneself also means being true to our higher purpose in life. I decided to become an Alexander teacher one night in 1974, when I had the startlingly simple realization that fear distorted my coordination, while love and compassion freed it up. From that moment on, for me the work became an expression of my higher purpose. Alexander remarked that "belief is a muscular activity", and I think that's right. Our use manifests our beliefs, so that a significant direction coordinating any communication arises out of our motivation or purpose in doing it.

Before every lesson, I want to ask myself: "Why am I teaching this person today?" You can always get a quick, pat answer to this question, yet a sincere period of meditation can bear many unexpected insights, each one furrowing deeper into the heart of your life's purpose.

What do you want to achieve by communicating Alexander's discoveries? Really? Is it just to earn a living? Do you also want your pupil's praise? Is there a higher purpose, connected to your spiritual beliefs? How would you express this for yourself? This could be another valuable line of enquiry to consider.

We and our pupils benefit when our higher purpose is constantly directing our activities. As Alexander once remarked to a pupil:

> The essence of the religious outlook is that religion should not be kept in a compartment by itself, but that it should be the ever-present guiding principle underlying the "daily round", the "common task."[11]

Irrespective of whether you are a believer or nonbeliever, whether Christian, Muslim, Jew, or Buddhist, all spirituality boils down to the same thing. It is, in the words of the Dalai Lama, ". . . [the] goal of developing a good human heart so that we may become better human beings."[12]

Starting your lesson with a good human heart, while seeking to better yourself and the lot of your pupil, I believe can overcome almost any obstacle to communication. It can dissolve almost any prejudice, almost any cynicism, almost any fear on the side of your pupil. Within this context, I believe communication can almost "do itself" – take place without interference.

Cathy: In learning to teach with Marj, in her persistent asking, "What do you notice about yourself?", I learned about being honest with myself. Because when I am not honest, I am not using myself well, and that shows up as an interference in my coordination. I also learned about kindness to myself: because any time that I am not kind to myself, that also shows up as "pulling myself down". Marj never spoke directly about it – she just told me to think about it so I had to figure out how I could talk to myself.

After some time, I understood that kindness to myself was part of my constructive thinking; I understood that if I was to be a teacher of this work, honesty and kindness to myself were required. Each lesson that I teach, each class I meet teaches me more and more about this.

When I am honest and kind to myself, I am able to hear and see my students clearly. My curiosity is genuine, my compassion for them grows out of a coordination that fuels my willingness to see and to hear them; to choose to be honest with them; to choose kindness. It is from this perspective that I am able to choose from my communication options, to choose the most appropriate means to teach.

F. M. Alexander said in *The Universal Constant in Living*:

> Being true to oneself in the sense advocated here presupposes being true to others, and if this had once been established not merely as an ideal but as a habitual reaction for several generations, the resultant sense of responsibility might, I believe, lead to a consideration for others and their well-being, such as never yet, except in isolated instances, resulted from educational, religious, or other means for the cultivation of desirable human qualities."[13]

We've been playing with doorways to lessons, because doorways are an archetype for this moment of going from the known to the unknown.

Jean Shinoda Bolen, in a book titled *Crossing to Avalon*,[14] talked about the special qualities of a doorway:

> In fairy tales, legends, and science fiction, the main character often arrives at a "gateway" that is both a special time and at a special place. Here and now, she or he must choose whether to step through and go beyond the known world: only once in a hundred years does the impenetrable briar hedge that surrounds the sleeping maiden part to allow the prince to pass through; a protagonist in a science-fiction fantasy can enter the stargate or portal to another dimension only if he or she gets there at a precise time; . . .

In this portal, we are in an "in-between zone", a state in which we are neither who we used to be, nor who we are becoming. It's like standing in a doorway.

Each time we teach, we are standing in such a doorway. Every day it is a sacred place for me. We are moving into unknown territories together. Honesty and kindness born out of clarity of coordination are my tools.

When I hear that knock on my door, I take my tools to the threshold, and begin a new adventure.

References

1. Due to time constraints this presentation was not delivered in full at the Congress. For this book the authors have made some cuts from the full text.
2. Hanh, Thich Nanh *Peace is Every Step*, p. 55.
3. Alexander, Frederick Matthias *The Universal Constant in Living*, p. 206.
4. Hagen, Uta; *Respect for Acting* (New York: Macmillan Company, 1973) p. 82.
5. "Notes of Instruction" in Alexander, Frederick Matthias *Alexander Technique* edited by Ed Maisel (Thames & Hudson, London, 1974) p. 10.
6. Alexander, Frederick Matthias, *The Use of the Self (*Centerline Press, Long Beach, USA, 1984) p. 73.
7. Binkley, Goddard *The Expanding Self* (STAT Books, London, 1993) p. 104.
8. Alexander, Frederick Matthias *Man's Supreme Inheritance* (Chaterson Ltd, London, 1946) p. 63.
9. Alexander, Frederick Matthias *The Use of the Self* (Gollancz, London, 1985) p. 37.
10. Barstow, Marjorie, *Direction* Vol. 1, No. 2, p. 12.
11. "Notes of Instruction" in Alexander, Frederick Matthias *Alexander Technique* edited by Ed Maisel (Thames & Hudson: London, 1974) p. 8.
12. His Holiness the Dalai Lama *Words of Wisdom* (Margaret Gee Publishing, Sydney, 1992) p. 22.
13. Alexander, Frederick Matthias *The Universal Constant in Living*, p. 209.
14. Bolen M.D., Jean Shinoda *Crossing to Avalon* (San Francisco, Harper Collins, 1994) pp. 7–8.

Jeremy Chance trained in London in the 1970s with Paul and Betty Collins (now Langford) and later trained with Marjorie Barstow. He has been editing the Alexander Technique journal *Direction* for the past fifteen years. He has written articles about the Alexander Technique for a wide range of journals and magazines. He is currently running a teacher training programme in Japan, where he lives with wife Jaldhara, also an AT teacher, and their daughter Angelica.

Hieidaira 3-Chome 38-20
Ostsu-Shi, Shiga-Ken 520-0016
Kyoto
Japan
Tel/fax: 077-529.2881
e-mail: jeremy@alextech.net

Catherine Madden began training with Marjorie Barstow in 1975 and has been teaching Alexander's work since 1980. She is currently Artist-in-Residence for the University of Washington Professional Actor Training Program, Director of The Alexander Training and Performance Studio in Seattle, and teaches in training programs and post-graduate trainings internationally. She is a Sponsoring Teacher for Alexander Technique International.

11042 27th Avenue NE
Seattle, WA 98125
USA
+ 1 206 543 7170
e-mail: cathmadden@aol.com

Concepts

Lucia Walker and Kevan Martin

Hello!

It seems to me that the congress is about getting together and renewing our commitment to what we are teaching and learning. It's about nourishing our passion for the Alexander Technique, or what you see your work to be. It's about getting clearer about what really inspires or moves us. I am certainly finding opportunities to do that.

We see this presentation as an opportunity to raise questions; it is not our intention to provide answers, solid interpretations or definitions. I'd like to encourage you to allow yourself to have new questions, or see familiar questions in a new way. We will present you with big concepts and small experiments, by means of which we can investigate those concepts.

The first concept I want to introduce is *consciousness*. Kevan will describe how he sees consciousness and how he is investigating it in his work. We both have a similar commitment to the idea that consciousness is a quality of *us*, of our being. It is not something separate that enters us or works us from outside. It's a quality of who and how we are.

We will also address the concept of *unity*; believing that our consciousness, our perception and our ways of understanding and being are a unified whole.

That leads on to the third concept, which seems to be a central theme at this congress, and is very important to me personally, *presence* or the *present moment*. For me it is closely connected to unity. It's about the individual being connected to the present moment and being fully alive.

I see *presence* as having implications that are practical, interpersonal, related to performance of any kind, and spiritual. We can all say when someone "has presence", or when we feel ourselves to be more or less "present" at any moment; but what that quality is and how we can practice it is more difficult to identify.

The concept of *learning* is linked to these previous ideas and to my work as a teacher and my reasons for being here.

Kevan raises some issues as a scientist that excite me. One is that in order to learn something you have to *differentiate* in some way between the various possibilities. This involves doing something wrong. You have to make the mistake before you can learn something.

It seems to me that F. M. Alexander was a wonderful model of learning and I've looked to learn from his example. One of the things that seem central to learning is to refuse to impose our previous map of reality too strongly on what we perceive. To a certain extent we have to rely on this but to learn anything new we have to make space, to hold back from our previous model or understanding. As Alexander said "How can we learn what we don't know if we keep on doing what we do know?"

Our *perception* is a very rich field of investigation and in his talk Kevan will explain more about levels of perception which are unconscious and will be unlikely to come to consciousness. We can become more and more aware of what we perceive but there is always a high proportion of unconscious information involved. Even that unconscious information is affected, organized and processed by our previous assumptions which are often sense based. Kevan will also talk about the necessity for *action* in the process of perception. We act in relation to the world in order to perceive what is happening.

I would like to finish with a quote from Krishnamurti and a poem by Emily Dickinson.

> Ideas are not truth and truth is something that must be experienced directly from moment to moment. It is not an experience which you want. That's then merely sensation
>
> *The First and Last Freedom* by J. Krishnamurti

The Brain – is wider than the Sky -
For – put them side by side –
The one the other will contain
With ease – and You – beside –

The Brain is deeper than the sea –
For – hold them – Blue to Blue –
The one the other will absorb –
As Sponges – Buckets – do –

The Brain is just the weight of God –
For – Heft them – Pound for Pound –
And they will differ – if they do -
As Syllable from Sound –

Emily Dickinson

On the brain

Emily Dickinson said it all. The brain is truly astounding. It is built on a such a scale that it's not unreasonable to compare it with the universe. The cerebral cortex of the brain contains 100 000 nerve cells in every cubic millimetre. In each cubic millimetre there are 4 kilometres of nerve fibres that connect the nerve cells together and about 100 million connections. In the whole brain there are 10 billion nerve cells each making about 1000 connections with each other. When we consider that just 17 nerve cells can potentially be connected in more different ways than the 1080 atoms in the universe, then we realize that the 10 billion nerve cells each of have provide our 3 litre volume of brain with an extraordinary potential. Yet, perhaps surprisingly, our brains are very alike, thanks to our genes and a common environment. Thus, we can readily communicate with each other using a very sophisticated language and, by and large, we agree on what we perceive. But the question that faces all of us is how we understand something of such immense complexity. For the scientist, this challenge is immense, particularly if we want to understand how the water of the physical brain is transformed into the wine of consciousness.

How do we do science?

The process of science, whether investigating how the brain works, or the outermost reaches of our universe, is to explore questions about nature, to make models of the world and then test them by experiment and observation. This is how we ourselves can gain knowledge, but we can easily fool ourselves (and do!) if we do not design the experiments well. It is too easy to get the results that fit your own preconceptions if the experiments are not well-designed Indeed, a feature of science theories is that they are frequently counter-intuitive, they do not follow common sense, they are in a real sense "unnatural". The most successful scientific theory of all time is the quantum theory of the atom, yet even Einstein did not accept it, because it did not accord with his intuitions about how the universe was organized. If the scientist has too fixed an idea about how the world works then nature will inevitably show up the scientist's error if the experiments are carefully done. Scientists design experiments so they can compare the differences between an unperturbed condition (usually called the "control") and another, perturbed, condition. The theoretical model predicts what the difference between the two conditions should be, and if is not, that is, if there is a difference, it means either the experiment was not done correctly, or the model is in some way incorrect.

The models that science creates are designed to be simplifications of the "real" things and are thus always in some degree incomplete. This is what makes it continually challenging: how do we make the most compact and accurate description of nature? The process of experiment in science is to make checks of how consistent a model is of reality. We throw the model out if it really is too inadequate as a description of our experimental observations. For example, none of us here would now accept Descartes' model of how the brain works, yet in its time it was the most advanced scientific theory of brain function. Descartes' model of how the brain works was based on his introspections about how he supposed he must work and his knowledge of the latest technology of his day. He introduced the notion that the physical body is simply a machine that is interfaced to a non-physical soul via the pineal gland. These two aspects combine in his famous illustration of how light from an arrow is captured in the eye and transmitted to the pineal gland where the soul directs the body to point at the arrow by inflating the muscles by means of tubular nerves (figure 1).

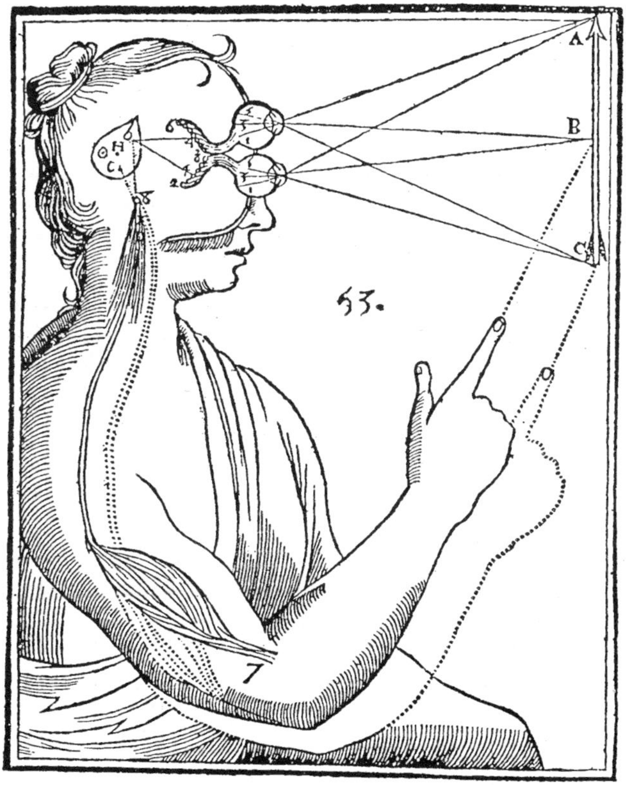

Fig. 1. Illustration from Descartes's work.

Error-driven learning

That we continually reject previous models and try to devise better theories and experiments to test them means that, from one viewpoint, science is a long catalogue of errors. Paradoxically, science's greatest contribution to humankind is not the artifacts it produces, whether labour-saving machines, or cures for diseases, or new processes for improving our environment. It is in diminishing error and so removing doubt. However, the process of science provides for a continual refinement and transformation in our knowledge of nature. It presents us with continual challenges to our existing ways of thinking about nature. It is through this process of apparent failure that we ourselves learn. Our models of learning in artificial neural networks show us that learning in these networks only occurs if there is an error between the actual and the desired behaviour. It is the error signal that drives the learning by, for example, altering the strength of the connections between nerve cells. In animal learning, the error between expectation and actuality also drives the animal to attend to the stimulus more and this accelerates learning. Being wrong is more help if you do want to learn. This is insight has been used to good effect in training Olympic level decathletes. Traditionally, coaching methods have tried to make the athlete repeat exactly a particular optimal motor pattern, say in throwing the javelin. However, to improve such a habitual pattern has proved difficult, and some coaches have discovered that rapid improvements can occur when they ask the athlete to deliberately perform non optimal actions – say, throw the javelin into the ground in front of them, or too high in the air. This accentuates the difference between constructive and unconstructive ways of throwing a javelin long distances and this information can be used for more effective learning.

Doing it deliberately wrong may be much more helpful if you want to learn than trying continually to get it right. The reason is simply that by breaking the normal patterns of experience, you can achieve a better discrimination of perception and a better differentiation between similar patterns. This is evident in children with language impairments where their problem is an inability to distinguish between different sounds delivered at speed. The solution is to prolong the sounds and separate them in time from one another. If the child attends to the new sounds then they can learn to differentiate the different sounds and this leads to a speeding up in their comprehension. This active process of differentiation does not "expand consciousness" it just expands the range of different things of which we can be conscious. How often does it happen that once we are made aware of something of which we were previously unaware, e.g. a particular bird's song or a particular advertisement, we then hear it or see it everywhere?

Attention

Our capacity of awareness is not unlimited. In fact, we can simultaneously attend visually to no more than about seven separate things. If we add visual distractors, we degrade the ability to perform tasks in visual perception. If we add auditory distractors, we need not degrade performance in visual perception. This is fortunate, because if we could not divide our attention to some degree at least, we could not listen to a lecture and watch the lecturer, or drive a car and continue a conversation while "keeping one ear" on the car radio.

Active learning

To acquire knowledge about the world, we need to be active. Yet so much of teaching demands passivity! "Sit still, be quiet, concentrate, and just listen to what I'm telling you." But just compare, for instance, the difference in your knowledge of a new road route if you drove or if you were just the passenger. The passenger, being passive, finds it much more difficult to re-navigate the route, yet both passenger and driver saw the same road, the same landscape, from the same vantage point. But the driver is active in deciding where to steer the car, the passenger is not. The driver has to take many decisions if he or she is to achieve the desired goal. Of course, much of driving is unconscious, but this does not make it passive. A route can be learned in a single drive. Such "single trial learning" is a feature of our abilities. We do remember many things for a lifetime after having only been exposed to them once. This is an extraordinary ability that seems not be exploited in the classroom, where repetition is more often the preferred method of teaching.

Even when we are stationary and looking at the scene in front of us, we can be engaged in an enormous amount of active exploration. Do the experiment now – just look at the room or what's outside and observe how you "look". What you'll notice is that your eyes do not stay still, they move more or less automatically as you scan the scene. You don't have to decide consciously where to look. You'll notice that you look at different things in the scene, but you do not look at all parts of the scene with equal amounts of time. Why is this? Parts of the scene are more salient, that is, they seem more significant or interesting, and so they occupy more of your "looking time". You pay them more attention. Many details in the scene are simply ignored. If you have a choice of looking at a rock or an animal, you tend to look more often at the animal and much less at the rock (even if you are a geologist). This indicates that we are interested in extracting a particular selected set of information from the scene, and moving things are particularly interesting for us. This is not surprising. We attend more to things that are more important for us, and what is important for us is determined by our own history of experience. If a family walk together through a city, the father may notice the location of the good restaurants, the mother may notice the cinemas or the parks, the children may be much less discriminating, but probably notice many other things that are not interesting for their parents. Each of us in some sense occupies his or her own unique world, selected from the vast range of possible worlds presented to us by our senses. The miracle is that we can still make sense of it and communicate our understanding to each other.

Active perception

No parent needs persuading that every child at all stages of development expresses a huge amount of behaviour. We usually interpret this as the long process of discovering how to direct movement in a coordinated way, but that is only a part of it. Movement is also essential for forming a coherent perceptual representation of the world, where "world" should be interpreted as including all of us, in addition to what's "out there". Both as children and as adults we continually experiment physically with the world. We hold it, pat it, walk on it, taste it, chew it, throw it, touch it, talk to it, smell it, and so forth. All this action is the means by which our senses, particularly our distant senses like hearing and seeing, come to gain knowledge of the world and, most importantly, interpret the world. As children this activity is how we come to know what pieces of our world are part of ourselves and which are not. This knowledge is now so embedded in us that we simply take it for granted. Yet if we try to build machines that emulate even one portion of our behaviour we encounter major difficulties. Marvin Minsky, one of the pioneers of artificial intelligence at the Massachusetts Institute of Technology (MIT), once made the following observation:

> Our first foray into Artificial Intelligence was a program that did a creditable job of solving problems in college calculus. Armed with that success we tackled high school algebra; we found, to our surprise, that it was much harder. Attempts at grade school arithmetic, involving the concept of number etc. provide problems of current research interest. An exploration of the child's world of blocks proved insurmountable, except under the most rigidly constrained circumstances. It finally dawned on us that the overwhelming ma-

jority of what we call intelligence is developed by the end of the first year of life.

Minsky 1977, cited by Carver Mead 1989

Thus all the things we take for granted – our abilities to perceive, think, remember, act – are effortlessly available because we are built the way we are. We do not need a programmer to figure out for us how to see out mother's face, nor can our mother teach us. Most of our first year of life is spent acquiring knowledge about the world and developing motor skills without us being taught how to do it. Most of language acquisition occurs quite independently of instruction – our parents do not teach us grammar, yet by the second year of life we appear to know most of the rules. The development of these extraordinary properties, including the development of consciousness, is inseparable from the development of the structure and function of ourselves.

Lucia: That was a huge amount of information for us all to absorb. I can see those neural connections dancing. I am really struck by what Kevan said about *error*. About the presumptions and assumptions that our system makes, and that we make consciously on top of those. Our task in learning *and* as scientists is how to suspend some of those presumptions in order to find out something else.

We need a *beginner's mind*, an *experimental attitude* as Alexander had when he made his discoveries. There is an outcome, but if we are too attached to understanding and logging the outcomes in terms of our current model then we don't find anything out.

So the "game" with these experiments is to be as *simple* as possible. The issue of what it "means" and how "this" connects to "that" is not the first step. The first step is to observe what happens.

Game 1

Swivel in your seat to find a partner and face each other.

i. One person closes their eyes.
The one with eyes open is the *observer.* Pass an object to your partner who is ready to receive it without knowing what it is. They have *to wish to take something from you.* Don't talk about it.

ii. Same exercise with your eyes open.
The problem with our "quickness" to understand and analyse is that it prevents us from noticing. Observation takes time. Pass the object back and forth without discussion, without analysis.

iii. Last stage. One partner *takes* the object from the other. But this is *not* a psychology game. Stay simple.

iv. One person closes eyes and leaves hand open. The partner lays object on hand.
To discover what it is the first person has to *move,* to touch it more actively.

The issue raised here is how much we do that we are not conscious of and don't need to be conscious of. How responsive our coordination is.

Game 2

This issue of how much information is unconscious fascinates me. Is it possible to make it more conscious? There are layers and levels of what we can become aware of. This next experiment involves *waiting* to access information you may not know you have.

> Again in partners. One closes eyes and touches their partner's knee (or other preselected place).
>
> Very often we go straight for the place, make a slight error and feel around.

> *Wait* at the moment of decision and *allow* a picture of where your partner is to be there. (You may not *see* this so much as *know* it). Wait, then touch, and I think you'll find much greater accuracy.

Take time to register information, to let yourselves absorb it. That's the flipside of taking *time* to register information you don't yet have. You also need a space for that.

Adaptation

Kevan: One of the most important properties of biological organisms is their capacity for adaptation. It is this property that allows us to survive in a world that is forever changing. In the course of a day we experience a wide variety of light levels, from dim light, electric light, sunlight, evening light to moon or starlight. If we measure the change of light intensity that we experience it is over a range of at least 10 orders of magnitude and if we measure the wavelengths of light reaching our eye we find again an enormous variation in these different conditions. Yet things do not change colour, they do not become blurred, they do not disappear, they do not bleach in brightness. This all seems to us normal, but if we start to take pictures of the same scenes we find out that the colours of the pictures change when we move from artificial light to sunlight, we have to lengthen the exposure times considerably from day to night, which means that we cannot take sharp photographs of moving things in dim light, and so on. The reason that we effortlessly cope with this varying world where the camera cannot is that our brain, like the rest of us, has many adaptive mechanisms for coping with these changes. These mechanisms ensure that what we register is not the absolute level but the relative level of light or sound, taste or smell, movement or touch. The camera, by contrast, measures the absolute level of light, and this difference is the reason why we have to use a light meter instead of our eyes to measure the correct level of light before we take the picture.

Our eyes are not light meters. We can show these adaptive mechanisms more formally in experiments. For example, in Figure 2 are a series of vertical lines, called gratings.

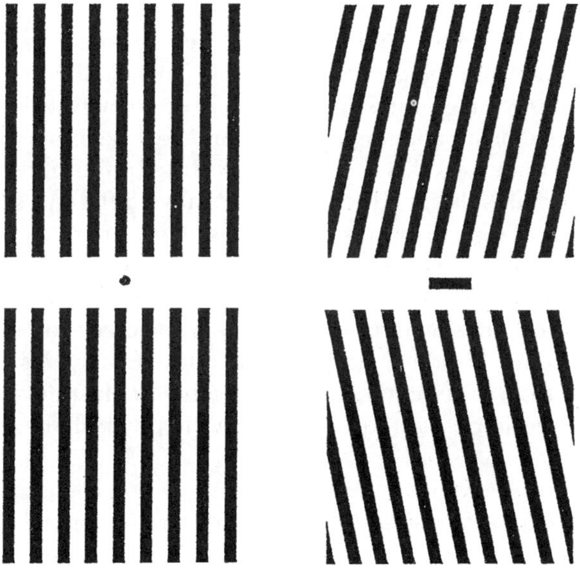

Fig. 2. Gratings.

There are two test gratings, which are identical, and two adapting gratings, which are tilted. First look at the little black dot between the test gratings (left pair) and note that both gratings are vertical. The task is then to scan the short horizontal line between the adapting gratings (right pair) for about a minute. (Don't fixate on one piece of the line, move your eyes back and forth along the line). *Do not look away*! Then after a minute look immediately at the black spot between the test gratings. Do they still look vertical? Do they still look identical? No they don't. What you have experienced is the tilt-after affect. The two vertical test gratings look tilted after adaptation. To understand this we need only to know that in the visual system there are neurons that are sensitive to different orientations, and that these neurons are organized in orderly "orientation maps" in which neurons that "like" vertical, sit next to neurons that "like" nearly-vertical. The tilt illusion occurs because the one-minute viewing of the adaptation grating tires the neurons that "like" gratings nearly vertical. The effect of this is to make the response of neurons neighbouring relatively stronger. This means when you look at the vertical gratings again, the balance of activity is biased away from the adapting gratings and the machinery of the brain interprets this as a tilt. The central point here is that our brain is designed to look for relative differences. It has no way of measuring absolute values of anything. Adaptation is its great strength for it allows us to extract sensible information and establish perceptual constancy, despite a wide range of variation in physical world. The perception we have is generated by the wiring we have in the brain and is inseparable from its function. This is dramatically illustrated by our ability to impose interpretations on the physical world.

Imposing our interpretations on the world

A second important thing to be reminded of is the paramount importance of experience in determining our perception. We see things the way they are because we have interacted with them in a particular way. Of course, there are certain constants, like earth's gravity, the motion of the earth relative to the sun, the size of the earth relative to us, the density of the atmosphere, and so on, all of us have experiences in common and thus it is no mystery that, by-and-large, we agree on how the world seems to us. But the fact is that the millions of stimuli that bombard our sense organs every second are strongly filtered and interpreted by experience. When we view the two outlines below (Figure 3), for example, we see one as a flat hexagon and the other as a cube. Yet the hexagon can also be interpreted as a tilted cube and, with a little practice, we can impose that interpretation upon it. The cube itself has two possible interpretations. Just look at it for a few sec-

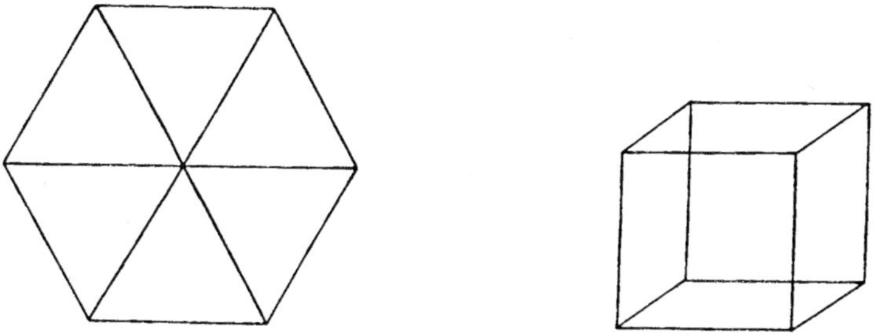

Fig. 3. Hexagons and cubes.

onds and it will flip between the two – one in which the front face points downwards and to the left, the other where the front face points up and to the right. This happens more or less of its own accord, unconsciously. It is difficult consciously to change the rate at which its flips. The reason it flips is because the neurons that give rise to one interpretation adapt and the group that gives rise to the competing interpretation takes over until they too adapt. So your perception of the orientation of the cube flips back and forth and the rate at which this happens is a measure of the time of adaptation.

Thanks for participating in these experiments.

Lucia: We're coming to an end soon. Thank you for your attention and participation.

I want to remind myself and you of the concepts we raised. I hope that we have increased our ability to hold an experimental attitude and to open ourselves to receiving new information. I feel there is something important about learning how to detect when the models we already have interfered with our desire to learn more. It's quite a test, but central to our work here!

Scientists get attached to their models and we as teachers can also be over-reliant on the models we currently hold. Somehow – as well as being clear about what our beliefs and values are – it's important to make situations and experiments where you can allow that model to be adapted, re-adapted or changed.

That connects for me to the focus or point about us all meeting together in a large group; that we communicate with others with slightly different models. If we can take time and *wait* to access more information and more knowledge, our own patterns of thinking will be influenced. That's an exciting process; to discover how we can make that process of change possible, and to become aware of which parts we do *not* have the ability to affect are both exciting.

I've enjoyed how Kevan has shed light on the issue of *unity* by pointing out how the processes of perception of consciousness and of physiology are not separated in us. Even in our action in the world these cannot be divided into separate components.

He also confirmed the importance of an ability to *make mistakes.* That if we can distinguish and *differentiate* between doing one thing and doing another, we have more choice and greater possibilities for learning, which is something I'm sure we are all passionate about.

Of course *presence* is related to all of this. The connectedness of our thinking, feeling, moving our selves with others and the world around us. The practice and exploration of this is very important to me. As is our concern with the ability to be *with* the action in the present moment. *Now.*

Kevan will finish with a story. Thank you again for your attention.

Kevan: Ramon y Cajal (1852–1934) was one of greatest neuroanatomists the world has known and a contemporary of the great neurophysiologist, Charles Sherrington. He was a prolific investigator who laid the foundations of our modern knowledge of the structure of the brain. At one point he became addicted to chess. This addiction distressed him greatly as it distracted him from his neuroanatomical investigations. In his autobiography (*Recollections of My Life*) he describes how he cured his addiction by a process that should be familiar to Alexander Technique teachers and might serve as a useful text for discussion with their pupils. This reminds us that science is not an abstract process, but is an integral

Kevan Martin, Professor of Systems Neurophysiology and Lucia Walker, teacher of the Alexander Technique, presenting "Concepts."

part of our culture and our way of thinking about nature. As individuals, the difficulties and delights of doing science are not qualitatively different from anything else we pursue; the process is the same:

> But how was I to cure myself thoroughly? Feeling myself incapable of an inexorable, "I do not play anymore," . . . the only supreme remedy which occurred to me was the *similia similibus* of the homeopathists: to study the works upon chess thoroughly and reproduce the most celebrated plays; and besides to discipline my rather sensitive nerves, augmenting the imaginative and reflex tension to the utmost. It was indispensable, also, to abandon my usual style of play, with consistently romantic and audacious attacks, and stick to the rules of the most cautious prudence.
>
> In this way, expending my whole inhibitory capacity in the undertaking, I finally attained my desired end. This con-

> sisted, as the reader will have guessed, in flattering and lulling to sleep my insatiable self-love by defeating my skilful and cunning competitors for a whole week. Having demonstrated my superiority . . . the devil of pride smiled and was satisfied. . . . Thanks to my psychological stratagem, I emancipated my modest intellect, which had been sequestrated by such stupid and sterile competitions, and was now able to devote it, fully and without distraction, to the noble worship of science.

Professor Kevan Martin studied Logic and Metaphysics, Physiology, and Psychology for a Bachelor's degree at the University of Cape Town. He continued with a B.Sc. Honours degree in Physiology and a Masters degree in Civil Engineering (cum laude). He did his D. Phil. Degree in Developmental Neurobiology at Wolfson College, Oxford. He was a Junior and Senior Research Fellow at University College Oxford from 1979 to 1995. In 1996 he moved to Zurich where he established the Institute of Neuroinformatics (of which he is Director); it is a joint Institute of the University of Zurich and the Swiss Federal Institute of Technology. His research is on the cerebral cortex where one of his long-term projects is to explore the physical basis of thought. He has studied the Alexander Technique for several years with many teachers.

c/o University/ETH Zurich
Winterhurerstr. 190
8057 Zürich
Switzerland

Lucia Walker is based in Oxford but travels and teaches widely. She qualified as an Alexander Technique teacher in 1987 with Dick and Elisabeth Walker and teaches individuals, groups, and on teacher training programmes. She is also a movement teacher and performer with particular experience and interest in contact improvisation, improvisation, and in developing a deeper understanding of the qualities of "presence".

15 Hurst Street
Oxford OX4 1EZ
England
+44 1865 726307
e-mail: walkup@which.net

The Use of the Self in Ancient Egyptian and Classical Greek Cultures

Hans Georg Brecklinghaus

> More than any other people of antiquity or of modern times the Egyptians owned a sensory perception of balance: order by balance.
>
> *Gregoire Kolpaktchy* [1]

The concept of the human being which includes the spiritual, mental, and physical use of the self, is mirrored in the fine arts of every culture. This is true not only in terms of content and gesture, but also in terms of movement style, and body structure. I want to explain and substantiate this statement with reference to the cultures of Ancient Egypt and Classical Greece. I published my findings in a book last year[2], and I would like to present here a rough overview of my findings and some interpretations of that material.

In my analysis I have used the structural approach of Dr Ida Rolf, the founder of the Rolfing method of Structural Integration of the human body. I am sure that you will be able to translate this model into terms applicable to the Alexander Technique.

The structural point of view defines structure as the relationship between the parts of the body and as the relationship between the body as a whole and the gravitational field of the earth. If the body parts of a standing person are aligned vertically, the inner central axis of the body coincides with the vertical direction of gravity. It is a precondition that the counterforce, i.e. the resistance of the ground, can be fully used for an upward lift in the body. In this case of an optimal body structure, gravity and antigravitational force create an equilibrium of forces, and almost no muscular effort is required to stand upright.

Optimal or not, a person's structure manifests itself in movement, as well as movement manifesting itself in structure. Body structure is the solidified result of repetitive movements and postural patterns, and vice versa: body structure is the individual frame which defines those postures and movements which are possible for a given person.

With this in mind let's take a look at examples of Egyptian art which I will contrast with works of art of classical Greece.

Depictions of people pacing – like the High Priest *Ranofer* (statue, appr. 2500 BC) – were frequent subjects of Egyptian sculptures, paintings, and reliefs.

Structurally taken, the main segments of *Ranofer* – with the exception of the thorax, which is slightly tilted back – are in a horizontal position, vertically arranged around the midline.

Pacing persons were often shown in a peculiar "artificial" posture in between standing and walking. The heel of the posterior leg remains on the ground. This leg and the upper body remain in a nearly vertical standing position. The anterior leg is moving forward. It is longer than in anatomical reality in order to reach the ground. This is a situation of transition, a moment which combines the posture of standing with the movement of walking. It may be understood as the combination of polarities: static posture and action, immanent movement and actual movement.

The famous statuette of *Tut-Ench-Amun* (1340 BC) harpooning a hippopotamus is an example of more dynamic movement. A sense of ease emanates from the sculpture, created by the extension mode of movement.

The whole body is reaching forward, showing the intended direction of movement, but a second direction is also present: the body uses gravity and transmits the kinetic energy from the ground. There is a fine diagonal connection between the extremities passing through an open and long transit between lumbars and sacrum. Shoulders and back keep their full length and width. The only deviation from the optimal structure – and this is not typical for Egyptian art – is the anterior shift of the head and neck.

In archaic times Greek artists took Egyptian statuettes as models for their own works. But typical Greek deviations from an economical structure are to be seen already at that time: the forward tilted pelvis and sacrum, the extreme and highly tensed anteriority of the lower lumbars and a kyphotic thoratic spine. One example is the *Young Man from Samos* (530 BC).

Later, in the classical period, Greek artists moved away from the simple forms and developed more complex forms with particular aesthetic elements. This included segmental rotations, counterrotations, tilts, and intrasegmental torsions. However, we have to distinguish postural elements like the side-tilt of the girdles caused by the phenomenon of one leg bearing the main weight of the body (standing leg) and the other leg taking no weight (free leg) – we have to distinguish such *postural* elements from actual *structural* deviations. So we have a mixture of structural aberrations and chronically poor posture. An example is the *Greek Girl* (470 BC)

Differences of posture and structure in Egyptian and Greek art are also apparent in the genre of sitting persons.

Many examples of Egyptian art show people working or playing sports and games. The sculpture of a *brewer* (2450 BC) presents a figure working in a "folding" manner. Knees, pelvis and trunk are balancing each other. Front and back have an equal length, they are open and wide. Ankles, knees and hips remain flexible. There is a fine transition of strength from the ground up to the middle and from there into the arms. The perceptual orientation is directed into the surrounding space as well as rooted in the ground.

There are other examples of sculptures of people working which express this kind of good movement pattern. The typical gracefulness and ease of Egyptian persons working or playing are due to the extension mode of movement.

Egyptian artists worked with an elaborated set of rules, the so called canon. One aspect of this canon is of special interest for us. In paintings and reliefs a person was always represented with a frontal shoulder girdle and with the pelvic girdle in profile – that means the depth of the pelvis and the breadth of the shoulder girdle were shown. This representation is called *aspective*.

The aspective is a structural order in space, and is defined by the three axes of extension: the vertical (extension up and down), the horizontal (movement to the sides) and the saggital axis (movement forward). Each axis has palintonic properties, and the relationship between the three axes is ruled by the right angle.

Comparing more than 200 sculptures and more than 350 paintings and reliefs, I came to the conclusion that Egyptian art shows only a few deviations from the structural ideal.

In contrast, Greek sculptures, reliefs, and paintings very often show severe deficiencies in terms of structure and movement. Most of the time the pelvis is in an anterior tilt with a sharp bend at the transition between pelvis and lumbar spine. Frequently the thorax is collapsed and the chest constrained. The outer layers of muscles are usually overdeveloped. On the other hand the Greek artists introduced *perspectival* representation, the phenomenon of weight-bearing leg and free leg, and the more refined drawing and sculpting of anatomical details into fine art. In addition, they were the first people to show individuals expressing particular emotions related to their personal situations.

How did valued and well-used principles of an integrated body find their way into Egyptian art? And what caused Greek artists to develop their own style?

We know that outstanding sages and physicians like the famous *Imhotep* (living 2600 BC) had great skill in massage, treating dislocations, and restoring the tonus of the pelvic diaphragm following childbirth. Nevertheless, those medical papyrii which have been preserved do not prove the existence of a *theoretical* knowledge about structure.

But we do know that the leading artists in Ancient Egypt observed bodyshape and characteristic movement patterns very precisely. Furthermore, there is evidence that the people of Egypt actually used economical movement patterns.

Lutz Weber, a student of sports from Cologne, has written a diploma dissertation on the Egyptian technique of rowing. He experiments prove that Ancient Egyptian paintings show exactly how the Egyptians rowed. [3]

Here is a summary of his description of a sequence of rowing in Ancient Egypt: The rower is standing on both feet and pulls the oar by using his own weight. Meanwhile he is slowly coming into a sitting position. At the end of that movement one leg is moved back to render possible a supported sitting down/standing up movement by using the resistance of the ground. Bending from the hips and supported by his legs he brings the oar back into the starting position.

There must have been an *intuitive* knowledge of what economic structure and movement is about. But this discovery did not satisfy my curiosity completely. My supposition was that the exploration of Egyptian consciousness and spirituality, the study of the Egyptian attitude to the world and the human being, would provide me with more profound answers. And that was indeed the case.

The source and function of art in Ancient Egypt were essentially religious. Art was mainly a magic tool. Sculptures of the Pharaohs and divinities in temples preserved the spiritual power for people. The Egyptian word for sculptor was "one who gives life".

The education of artists took place in the *House of Life*, which was also the place of education for medical doctors and stood under the guidance of the priesthood. Therefore the *House of Life* was a manifestation of the still existing unity of religion, science and art.

Sculptures of the god of artists and of creation in general, *Ptah*, are frequently shown standing on a pedestal which depicts the hieroglyph of the goddess of cosmic and earthly order, called *Maat*.

That is: the base of art was *Maat*, the personification of cosmic and earthly order. To accomplish this order in spiritual issues, in politics, and in daily life was the most important moral rule for the Egyptians; and the outstanding part of the cosmic order in the Egyptian consciousness was the principle of balance. The value and significance of balance may be found in all areas and levels of Egyptian life. Therefore the image of a human being in art also had to be in congruence with the cosmic principle of balance. For the Egyptians it was not important to show individual characteristics of a person, but to meet the essence of the human being. And this essence included the balanced shape of the human body. In Ancient Egypt language the word for essence was the same as that for shape.

For the Egyptians, vertical and horizontal relationships were an expression of cosmic order, for which they used the symbol of the sun orbit. The sun god in the morning (in the east) was called *Chepri,* at high noon (in the south) he was named *Re,* in the evening (in the west) his name changed into *Atum,* in the night (in the north) his name was *Osiris.*

The sages used this model as a paradigm for analogical descriptions of physical and metaphysical relationships. Geometry and especially the right-angle were used as a kind of symbolic language for their knowledge, built not by rational logical thinking but by inspiration, imagination, and analogical thinking, which were the basis of human consciousness at those times.

One example: the relationship between matter and spirit was represented by a vertical polarity (palintonicity). The material world was understood as a manifestation of the spirit, originating during the process of an "in-folding" or *involution.* And the *evolutionary* process was seen as the unfolding of a spiritual self.

This relationship between matter and spirit was expressed additionally in a horizontal polarity between form and meaning. For the Egyptians, form and shape were full of spiritual meaning or wisdom. And vice versa: meaning was function, and expressed itself by the shape of matter, by structure.

In the Egyptian world of symbols, the vertical was of great significance. The Ancient Egyptians experienced the cosmic force of the sun in the process of being upright. And although they didn't speak explicitly about gravity, they were aware of the gravitational and antigravitational forces in polarity. It's striking that they introduced the base line in reliefs and pictures and the pedestal in sculptures as an illustration of the fact that human beings have to settle a matter with gravity.

There is another point which is also impressive. In Egyptian thinking one aspect of the human being, the *Ka* of a person – in the European tradition of esoteric thinking it's called the ethereal body – is responsible not only for the shape, the form of the person, but also has the function of keeping the person upright.

There was a wide range of metaphysical considerations which the sages in Egypt associated with verticality, horizontality, and depth. To mention only a few: the vertical stood also for the polarity of the inner being of the self in the world, being spiritually centred, honest, and so forth; the horizontal stood for "the doing of the self in the world"; and depth stood for a special aspect of *doing*, for entering the material world. The simultaneous presence of standing and striding expresses the balance of the self between being and doing.

This simultaneity is a moment of doing in the presence of being. In addition, this peculiar representational mode reflected the Ancient Egyptian belief that they came from the timeless space of the spiritual level, at the same time entering the level of the physical world in time.

The transition from the culture of Ancient Egypt to the culture of Classical Greece was a fundamental change in thinking and in mental orientation. The Greeks no longer felt themselves embedded in the cosmic order, as the Egyptians still did; instead, they confronted the material world and their own subjectivity. To understand the world and themselves they developed logical, rational thinking, which created in art a method of seeing in "perspective", based on a split between the subject and the object. This became possible by the development of the consciousness of the "I".

It was the time of individual heroes like Prometheus, Heracles, Odysseus, etc. The spiritual theme was "know yourself" (the motto at the entrance of the Apollonion mysteries at Delphi). The fate of an individual person became an important topic in art. Emotional expression was shown, and the body mirrored personal biography. Degenerations of the body structure and random movement patterns are visible components of the individual subject.

The Greek tried to escape from the cosmic order in favour of a subjective, self-willed existence (like *Prometheus* rebelling against the gods). In Greek art of the Classical and Hellenistic periods, the representation of the human body changed: the limbs of the body broke out of the axial order and randomness was introduced. Patterns of compensation were developed to keep the body in a sufficient balance.

The phenomenon of the weight-bearing leg and the free leg is a good example of the introduction of compensatory balance, which replaced balance around a vertical line. The leg taking no weight (free leg) tries to free the body from gravity – from a law of cosmic order – by shifting the weight to the other leg. The Greeks tried to find their balance by fighting against gravity, which is a part of cosmic order on earth. But of course they could not win this fight: the weight-bearing leg and the free leg are a compromise.

The transition from Egyptian to Greek art is also a transition from intrinsically dominated movement to an extrinsically dominated one. The representation of overdeveloped, extrinsic musculature is typical for strongly war-minded cultures like that of Greek antiquity, in contrast to comparatively more peaceful cultures like Egypt.

The Greeks took big steps forward in the development of human consciousness and of fine art. But whenever you go forward you leave something behind, you abandon or lose something. The Greeks lost the feeling and the artistic expression of the higher order and of the economical movement of the human body. They partly lost that portion of the self which is greater than the personal ego.

This becomes more visible nowadays, because today we as human beings don't want to lose the achievements of the Greeks but we are trying to regain some of the qualities the Egypts had. Those qualities are: nonlinear, analogical, and intuitive thinking, a refined body awareness, less attachment to our ego – to sum it up: a transformative kind of use of our self.

Works of art like statues influence us at a conscious and a subconscious level. They influence kinaesthetic feelings, the emotional approach to life and our spiritual approach. In that sense the representational mode of human bodies in the fine art of Ancient Egypt can be used as an extensive and versatile symbol for our evolutionary way of growing upright in both the physical and metaphysical sense. Therefore these presentations of body-structures can be understood as an educational ideal and a useful subject for meditation and for analogical thinking in our time.

References

1. Gregoire Kolpaktchy, French Egyptologist. Quote from: G. Kolpaktchy (ed.), *The Egyptian Book of the Dead* (Bern 1970) p. 47.
2. Hans Georg Brecklinghaus, *Die Menschen sind erwacht, du hast sie aufgerichtet. Körperstruktur und Menschenbild in der Kunst des alten Ägypten und heute* (Freiburg/Br. 1997). English translation in preparation.
3. Lutz Weber, *Versuch einer Rekonstruktion der aegyptischen Rudertechnik in der 18. Dynastie* (Cologne, 1978).

Hans Georg Brecklinghaus is Dipl. Päd. and certified Advanced Rolfer and Rolfing Movement Teacher. He has practised Rolfing since 1983 and is the author of *Rolfing: Was es kann, wie es wirkt und wem es hilft* and *Die Menschen sind erwacht, du hast sie aufgerichtet, Körperstruktur und Menschenbild in der Kunst des alten Ägypten und heute* (1997).

Stadtstrasse 9a
79104 Freiburg
Germany

Making Good Use of Complementarity

A possible lesson from science

Ernst Peter Fischer

If I understand it correctly the Alexander Technique is understood by its practitioners as a means of understanding man. This goal constitutes the first good use of complementarity, since usually a scientific or medical method is used to dissect or analyse something or someone, and one hardly encounters a technique designed or understood as a way to create an image of something or someone.

The idea of complementarity

It seems to me that the Alexander Technique is not only making *good* use of complementarity, but that it is making *excellent* use of this idea that was introduced into science in the early decades of the 20th century, with 1927 as the best candidate for being the decisive year. The principle of complementarity was first spelled out by the great Danish physicist Niels Bohr, who then tried to come to terms with some very strange physical observations that occur when we explore the atomic world (these findings will be described shortly). Bohr's idea states that scientists will always find contradictory descriptions (explanations) of nature (reality) that are equally justified; their complementary aspects show up in experimental set-ups that are mutually exclusive. Complementary theories are thus both right, but none is true by itself.

The whole

If I understand it correctly the Alexander Technique is based on the convincing insight that any living organism is a whole that cannot be split into parts. The idea of complementarity expresses in a similar way the fundamental insight that, deep down in the heart of matter, one encounters an atomic reality that is a whole that does not consist of parts. This whole does not possess any parts because there are none.

This may sound surprising to most readers, but I will explain this statement as I go along. While one certainly has no difficulty in understanding an organism as a unit that needs to be looked at as a whole without separable parts, one nevertheless may wonder about the notion that the atom, too, is a whole that has no such parts. Doesn't an atom consists of electrons, protons, and neutrons all arranged in a coordinated fashion, with protons and neutrons forming a nucleus that is surrounded by a cloud of electrons? How can I say that atomic reality is a whole that has no parts? And what has this to do with the psychophysical unit that you as practitioners of the Alexander Technique are interested in?

Entanglement

The strange feature of the microscopic world that I just mentioned is called entanglement ("Verschränktheit" in German), and it was discovered to be the most important aspect of atomic reality around 1935. It was discovered by the most famous physicist of our century, Albert Einstein, whose name also comes up in connection with the eclipse of the sun that will be the great event of tomorrow (11 August 1999). An eclipse that could be observed by scientific means in 1919 was used to test Einstein's theory of relativity that he had put forward in 1915. Einstein became famous all over the world when observation proved his theory to be right, and many people think that this constitutes his greatest achievement.

But I think his greatest contributions to physics were made in 1905 and 1935, ten years earlier and twenty years later. In 1905 Einstein opened the road to complementarity by discovering that there is a dual nature of light – light behaves as a particle as well as a wave – and in 1935 he described entanglement as the essence of matter or the essence of physical reality. This happened after the French physicist Louis de Broglie discovered in 1924 that what holds true for light also holds true for matter.

It should be pointed out, however, that though Einstein discovered the first instance of complementarity, he disliked the idea very much. For the rest of his life Einstein hoped to overcome complementarity and replace it by the new unity that he dreamt of. Einstein wanted a "One", not a "Two" as a unit. But complementarity tells us that the only unit we can hope for or that we can experience is made up by Two that are One. I personally think that the Alexander Technique is based on a Two that acts as a One. The Two can be found in the psychophysical unity of the pupil, or the Two can be found in the unity of teacher and pupil in a lesson.

Actually, on the picture on the invitation to this congress one can see directly the Two that is One by looking at a hand on a back. We see a unity consisting of two elements that achieve their true meaning only as a whole, i.e. as the one thing that we are seeing. Seeing in general is a single event in which a figure is perceived in front of a background. Our awareness is concentrated on the figure but we can shift it to the background (and vice versa).

The nature of light

Let me return to Einstein and his early detection of complementarity when he realized that the nature of light could not be interpreted in a straightforward fashion. For centuries scientists had understood light as a collection of waves propagating through time and space. Then Einstein came along, and proved that things were a little bit more complicated. For example, light assumes the quality of particles if it interact with matter, and light travels as a wave when spread out. Thus light is a wave as well as a particle. This dual nature of light – the duality of light – was named "complementarity"; it expresses the fact that both qualities are real and genuine properties though they could not be observed simultaneously in a single experiment. Complementarity holds that wave and particle are mutually exclusive aspects of light that are both necessary in order to fully understand light.

Please note that light moves along like a wave as long as nobody observes or interferes with it. If you do so and interact with light by picking up some of its energy, you change it into a particle. In other words, light behaves a little like we do. As long as we are left alone, we act in one way, and as soon as we are observed, we act in another way. Here again we see the hand of the teacher on the back of the pupil. Without his or her "interferences" we behave according to our habit – according to our manifestation of a constant, as you would call it. But with the hand and the teacher's "interference" we can influence that habit and change it for the better. One's own awareness becomes the teacher's hand in the long run; this shows how our perception of the body may be equivalent to the experimental observations Einstein and other physicists have made.

Einstein discovered the dual nature of light in 1905 – he was then an unknown clerk and only 26 years old – and it took nearly two decades before physicists realized that not only light but also matter itself exhibits this dichotomy. This was proved in 1927 – the year the term complementarity was introduced into the natural sciences – and even electrons, protons, and the atoms they are part of, are both waves and particles, with the particle aspect being the more dominant one – mainly when electrons show up in huge numbers, e.g. in an electron beam. Within a single atom the movement of single electrons is more readily understood by thinking in terms of clouds made up by a wave-like entity. Electrons surround a nucleus like a cloud and they move around like a particle on an orbit only when they are observed in an experiment. Here again the treated electron behaves very differently from the untreated one.

Bohr's complementarity

With the dual nature of both light and matter as a basis, the Danish physicist and philosopher Niels Bohr introduced the idea of complementarity into physics by saying that a complete understanding of physical reality requires complementary descriptions. (The word "complete" is at the root of the term "complementarity".) Complementary descriptions are true but neither taken alone is sufficient or true. Complementary terms refer to experimental situations that are mutually exclusive and thus contradictory. Nevertheless, they belong together, and only together do they provide a complete description of a certain "reality."

A famous example of a pair of complementary descriptions of a single physical reality is found in the conflict between Newton and Goethe in their descriptions of the nature of colour. While Newton starts from the wavelength of a ray that is isolated from the sunlight, Goethe starts directly from what is given in nature and available to the observer. While Goethe is interested in experiencing colour as a sensation in a qualitative way, Newton wants to determine wavelengths in a quantitative fashion, and he wants to measure it as a physical appearance.

Many of you may have heard of the wave–particle duality without realizing its consequences for our understanding of reality. If an electron is a wave as well as a particle, it is a point in space and spread all over space at the same time. To be more precise: complementarity says that if you fix an entity at one point in space, you distribute its qualities all over space. If you measure an electron at point A, for example, you change what that same electron does at point B. That may sound strange already, but the truth is even stranger. Assume two electrons colliding, and assume you measure the position of one of the two elementary particles. Call this point P. In this case you not only change or influence this electron at another point, Q, you also interfere with the second electron and influence it – wherever, or whatever, it is.

Particles of atomic dimensions are non-local entities that are closely correlated in such a way that a change in one of them induces a change in another, and the most important point is that this correlation of individual and separate entities occurs simultaneously, that is, it takes no time at all to show up and act. This instantaneous correlation of particles is called entanglement. Its existence has been proved by experiments beyond any reasonable doubt, and it truly demonstrates that reality is a unity. Atomic reality is a whole that has no parts that can be separated from it, as I emphasized in the beginning

This is one of the strange, but correct, ideas of the modern physical discipline called quantum mechanics. It is based on a whole (the quantum) and it generates a whole (the entanglement). For the purpose of this paper, however, another aspect is even more important. It is the fact that the idea of complementarity provides us with an insight which reunites the two aspects of reality that we usually refer to as "mind" and "matter". We also talk about the split between "body" and "mind" – "Körper–Geist" or "Materie–Geist" in German.

Classical physics thrives on the assumption that matter is void of mind, that there is a world without me (see Box 1) or without an I – and quantum physics tells me that this is an illusion. When I dig deep enough into matter I neither arrive at another piece of matter, nor do I arrive at an empty piece of space one might call "nothingness". When I come to the heart of matter, I arrive at myself – I cannot escape the observer who is "me". Wherever I go, wherever I travel, in the end I will arrive at myself.

Western Physics: A world without an I Eastern Metaphysics: An I without a world

Box 1: Complementarity between East and West

The Cartesian Cut

The important point is that the observed particle is different from the particle left alone. In other words, observations create facts – something that is already inherent in the term "fact" which is derived from the Latin *facere,* meaning "to do". Facts are made, and they are made by us, something that holds equally in German, where the corresponding term "Tatsache" demonstrates the "Tun" in the "Sache".

Observations generate facts, they generate properties that are not present without them. In other words, the old cut between a subject's "I" and an object's "world" is no longer acceptable. This cut is for historical reasons called the Cartesian Cut and is named after the French philosopher René Descartes. We have to close this cut, and complementarity shows us the way. Making good use of complementarity means mending the Cartesian Cut, but it means more at the same time. For example, it means that we can separate neither the mind from the body nor mind from matter. We have to treat both in a symmetrical fashion, and here we arrive at something that western culture and western thought have tended to neglect as the result of Christianity. In the Christian tradition matter is treated with disrespect and isn't considered to be on a par with mind. In the same spirit we treat the body with disrespect and don't expect it to be of equal complexity in comparison to the mind. (Of course, there is a whole industry that supplies body lotions, body care, etc., but this is only the other side of the wrong coin, since in this commercial culture there is only body and no mind at all.)

Making good use of complementarity: Part One

Making good use of complementarity means to handle the body with care in the sense that it is not only an object but also a subject. It is my subject and by perceiving my body I experience the same situation as an observing scientist who studies natural phenomena. My perception of my body is an observation and as such it will influence what this body does, how it operates and functions – for better or for worse.

It is, of course, trivial to say that I move and behave differently if I act under conscious control. But the idea of complementarity allows me to give a more detailed description in this respect which I will explain after a final detour.

I not only mentioned that we cannot separate mind from body, I also mentioned that we cannot separate mind from matter – "matter" understood in the widest possible sense as the stuff that makes up the material world that we can bump into or throw around. Just as we may have mistreated our individual bodies, we may have mistreated matter in general, and this failure has become more and more obvious in recent decades. We have mistreated matter by constructing an atomic bomb or by ruining parts of the environment. We have done this by means of science, by applying rational methods and by doing logical analysis of conscious thoughts. When asked to prevent these wrongdoings and find another direction for the future, philosophers and ethicists answer by pointing to human reason ("Vernunft" in German) for help, and they have repeated that suggestion to no avail for decades.

Complementarity gives a different answer, namely by stressing complementary aspects of the human capabilities used so far. Making good use of complementarity (see Box 2) means to rely on love (of nature) instead of logic. It means to try feeling, as well as thinking. It means to use not only your intellect but also your instinct, and it means to take subconscious thoughts as seriously as the conscious ideas in your mind.

Logos	– Eros
Thinking	– Feeling
Conscious	– Subconscious
Intellect	– Instinct

Box 2: Complementary qualities

Of course, you must never forget the other side. Don't give up thinking when you experience feelings, just get both complementary functions to operate in balance.

Making good use of complementarity: Part Two

Now we are ready to apply complementarity to treating your own body as a patient who needs care because of pain. As far as I can judge (as a person without any experience as a therapist and with only marginal knowledge of the Alexander Technique), making good use of complementarity in this context means to look for complementary aspects of what you were doing all the time before you perceived yourself as doing something. Here is a list of possible ideas and suggestions: Don't act subconsciously, act in a conscious way (something that can be learned); don't rely on your habits, but try to become aware; don't just follow your instinct, but follow your ideas and reason; don't only care for your body from the outside, but care for it from the inside.

You will note that this advice for the individual is complementary to the advice for the whole of nature. The reason for this can be explained by the fact that an individual is complementary with respect to the whole (quite analogous to the particle–wave duality).

What we have to learn in order to be capable of doing the above is best expressed by the term "perception". Perception is the key to changing how science treats matter, and perception is the key that can help to change the way a human being treats his or her body. Making good use of complementarity means learning to perceive the world and the body, thereby introducing the subject's mind into an objective fact. We need this addendum to find the road to truth. This road is very narrow and difficult. In order to be successful we have to find a passage through the danger of sterile rationalism on one side and the perils of blue-moon mysticism on the other side. We should be aware that mankind can tumble down either way and prepare ourselves to make good use of complementarity.

Ernst Peter Fischer is a physicist and biologist, and Professor for History of Science at the University of Konstancz. Among his books are *Die zwei Gesichter der Wahrheit* (1987), *Die aufschimmernede Nachtseite der Wissenschaft* (1995), *Aristoteles, Einstein & Co.* (1995), and *Das Schöne und das Biest – Wissenschaft und Aesthetik* (1998); English translation *Beauty and the Beast* (1999).

Mozartstrasse 10
78464 Konstanz
Germany

Marjory Barlow Masterclass

Learning by being aware of being wrong

What I want to start of with is to talk a little bit about being wrong. I find that most people in training courses are absolutely terrified of being wrong. This is very bad, because if you are afraid of something you make a lot of tension. People – particularly people who run training courses – don't really understand that our only means of learning is by becoming aware of what we are doing wrong so that we need not do it. There is this idea that you've got to try and be right; there is no such animal – truly. We are on a pathway which is going from wrong to something a little bit better. There is no such thing in life as perfection. It is such a pity that we waste so much energy being concerned about being wrong, instead of using the awareness we have of what we are doing wrong to learn. We are all wrong. It is an inevitable process. We wouldn't learn without it. Alexander used to say "The only thing you will ever know in this world is when you are wrong." He knew from experience that nothing could happen until he discovered what he was doing wrong. What is important is that we know what is wrong, because that is how we are going to learn what not to do.

Because we are all afraid of being wrong, it is very important to encourage your pupils: when they do something well, compliment them. There is far too much criticism. You come away from a lesson feeling like a worm. And that is such a pity, because this work is meant to be fun. It isn't meant to be torture.

It is the teacher's job to see to it and if it goes wrong, it is the teacher's fault. A favourite saying of Patrick Macdonald – if it went wrong in a lesson – was: "Not your fault, my fault." This is a very good attitude for the teacher to have.

Always praise your pupils if there is the slightest excuse to do so. Don't praise if there is no reason. But if they do something good, let them know. How are they going to know the difference otherwise?

Hands on the back of the chair

I think sometimes people are baffled as to why we do these things like hands on the back of the chair. Everything F. M. taught us had a purpose – in itself, but also as a basic good use of ourselves that can be adapted to many things. People say we don't need to do those old "procedures" – we never called them that – but they don't understand why. All the things that Alexander taught us in the way of these basic things are adaptations. I noticed that a lot of training courses don't teach hands on the back of a chair.

First: my neck to be free, my head to go forward and up.

Bend your knees, then come forward. F. M. used to say, "Take two bites at the cherry." F. M. taught the monkey in two stages. Go down there, then come forward. Don't try and do it all in one, because it is very difficult to put your knees away, keep your back working, and come forward all in one fell swoop. Always go down in two, but you can come up in one.

It is very important to remember that your shoulders belong with your back. We use the shoulders as if they are part of the arms and the neck. It ain't so. They are part of the back. So if you can say to yourself during the day "My shoulders belonging with my back," you'll make life a lot easier.

The teacher will take your arm, you say "no," and then you take hold of the chair very gently, but firmly with straight fingers.

Now allow the wrist to be in, think of pulling to the elbow as you think of widening the upper part of the arm as you widen the back. These are F. M.'s exact words when he was doing this with us. Straight fingers, the wrist in. (Some people teach with the wrists up in the air. Alexander didn't.) Pull to the elbow. Think of widening the upper part of the arm as you widen the back. At this point F. M. used to say, "Final refinement: just think of very gently lifting and stretching the top of the chair." Don't do it, but think it.

Pulling to the elbows is very important, because when you are holding on to the chair the tendency is to push forward from the elbows, but he liked you to think of lengthening backwards. All the directions in this work are in opposition so you get that balance, but we like to go only one way – mostly down. When you are working on someone on the table, for instance, take the person as if you are over the back of the chair.

Table work

In the first training course F. M. spent a long time with us teaching us exactly how to give a lying-down turn: how to move the legs, how to move the arms, how to do the whole thing. It is complete nonsense that F. M. didn't do tablework.

He didn't have a table in his teaching room but his assistants used to take his pupils – after they had a lesson from him – on the table. If we were in difficulties when working with people, we would go and knock on his door, and he would come and help us. But he spent a lot of time training us how to do the lying down work. We only had one table at Ashley Place so we had to take everybody on the floor. It was wonderful for our legs because we had to go into a deep squat to get the head. When you wanted to take the arms or legs you went down on one knee. It was very good for our backs as well.

He thought lying-down work was very important, because he said that if you have got a pupil lying down they haven't got to worry about their equilibrium or losing their balance which is a usual thing as you change the poise of the head and as you change the work the back is doing. The pupil can get very wobbly. But when they are lying down, all they have to do is think. He said it was a wonderful opportunity for people when lying down to pay attention to their orders. It is a very good opportunity to think. And none of us like thinking, we like "to do."

F. M. always started a lying-down lesson with the legs out [down]. People say, "But doesn't that make the lower back come up?" Well, in some people it does, but it doesn't matter, because as you work the back will go down. You can't get it right at the beginning.

Eyes

The connection between the poise of the head and the eye position is very, very close. If you ask someone to think of their head going forward, they nearly all drop their eyes down, and if you ask them to think of lengthening, they do a sort of maiden's prayer. Watch that with your pupils.

It is also important to look at something, but not to stare and fix. F. M. used to turn us around facing a painting. We didn't know what his purpose was. He then turned us back and said, "Now, describe the painting." Of course, none of us had even looked at the painting. We had been looking inside our heads which is a fruitless exercise.

F. M. would not allow you to shut your eyes, because he said that all that happened was that you would look inside your head to see which way it was going.

When working with someone it's important to look at them, to see what's going on. Some young teachers, when working on me, look everywhere else but at me. I don't know why that is. It is as if they feel they can't think unless they are looking into outer space.

You've got be aware of your environment at the same time as what is going on inside you. It is a double process.

Inhibition

If you can just get them to stop and inhibit, the thing does itself. There is nothing wrong with us. F. M. used to look at us and say, "You are all quite perfect – except for what you are doing." Nature will do it for you. With this work we work in accordance with the law of Nature. Most things which the human race are doing are dead against the laws of Nature, so we have a lot of help – if we just can get out of the way.

But what is important is that we know what it is that we are doing wrong, because that is how we are going to learn what not to do. Not what to do, but what *not* to do.

By the way, everybody should read Fiona Robb's *Not to Do* about her lessons with Margaret Goldie. I have read it six times and it is a wonderful document of actual lessons day after day, based entirely on what F. M. taught her. No frills, no fuss, just pure Alexander.

Directions

Direction is a thought. Only a thought. Because what is the matter with you is what you are doing already. The directions are primarily preventive. That's what F. M. used to say. The purpose of the orders is to prevent.

Think what happens before you have any lessons: messages are going from some part of the brain to your body to make your habits happen. If you interfere with the part of the brain that controls this arm, what happens? You can't move the arm! There is nothing wrong with the arm. What has gone wrong is the communication system, the nervous system.

F. M. could never have discovered this work if we weren't dealing with the brain and the nervous system. It was only because he discovered that if he could inhibit, if he could say "no" when he got a stimulus, and give a different set of orders, the new orders would prevent the old thing from happening.

The way F. M. used to explain it is: if you live in a forest and you always go from point A to point B, you'll wear away a path. One day you think: maybe there is an easier way, so you start going another way. Then you have two pathways. Then you decide the new one is better, and gradually the grass will grow over the old way. He used that as an illustration of what actually happens in the nervous system. The more you can use the new pathways, the sooner you can rid of the old one. The other illustration he gave was: You are laying down railway lines along which a train eventually is going to go.

The most real thing you've got apart from inhibition is the ability to send, to project those messages from your brain through your nervous system to the different parts of your body.

F. M. was very clear about the directions when he was teaching you. Sometimes he would make you repeat them out loud, asking you, "Now, what orders are you giving?" And he would expect you to say the whole rigmarole. Sometimes Alexander would talk about other things – it varied, but he spent an awful lot of time making you rehearse the directions. It depended on the circumstances, how much work you've had and so on. But certainly in the beginning, he would even make you say the orders out loud in the lesson.

A lot of teachers say that it is no good teaching the directions early on because pupils only go wrong. Pupils are going to go wrong whatever you do. That is what teaching is: allowing the pupil to go wrong so that you can help them back on to the right path. You mustn't be afraid of them going wrong. We all have to go wrong, it is how we learn.

When teaching, remember what Shakespeare said in *Hamlet*: "Suit the action to the words, the words to the action." That's what you have to do when you are teaching. I know it is not the general practice these days. I find a lot of teachers work with their hands, but they are not making their pupils use their brains at the same time. To me, that isn't teaching, because what are the pupils going to do when you are not there? Memory alone is no good. You've got to train them in the lesson of how they are going to think when you are not there. I find that some teachers don't do that. They rely on the experience given by the hands, but that isn't enough. It is like learning the piano. You have a lesson. You go home and there is not even a piano in the house. You go back the following week for another lesson: nothing has happened. How

Marjory Barlow teaching in her masterclass.

could it? This work is like learning a musical instrument. Only the instrument is yourself. It is much more difficult, because the piano doesn't have bad habits. You do.

It's interesting that a lot of teachers when they have got someone lying down say "forward and out" when lying down – I don't do that. Because the orders are internal. It is the relating of part to part that is important – and not to do with the ceiling and the walls. It is not a spatial direction. You can be standing on your head and still order it to go forward and up in relation to the rest of yourself.

Working against the wall

Working against the wall is a thing which Alexander taught us in the first training course. It is very useful. You stand with you heels about three or four inches from the wall.

F. M. used to say to have the feet about the width of the hips apart. The feet are not completely parallel: the toes are turned out a tiny bit. Most people, when asked to turn their toes out, turn their heels in, which brings the legs closer together.

You go back to the wall, giving your orders all the time, and then bend your knees, which bring you down the wall. Inevitably, as you do that, the lower part of the back goes back against the wall. You haven't got to force the back back. Everything in this work is indirect. You stay there a little while with your knees bent. The tricky bit is when you start to straighten the knees. The tendency then is to pull the back in again. You don't have to try and keep it back, but have that idea that you are going to lengthen and allow the back to remain back as you straighten your knees.

It is a great thing to use movement if you want to make a change in yourself. F. M. used to say that if you suddenly realize you're wrong, say sitting in a chair and slumping, don't try and alter it but give yourself a stimulus to move, just a little bit. He used to demonstrate this: he would sit in a chair and slump right down and then he would gradually, gradually move a little bit. By the time he had done it about three times he would be right up again. Don't try and get it statically. If you think you're wrong – which is most of the time – give yourself a stimulus to move. Then you'll get the experience in the movement. Otherwise we are just feeling out.

Whispered "ah"

One of F. M.'s favourite stories was that of two comics on the stage. One of them falls down. The other says, "What's the matter with you?" "It's all right," says the first man, "I forgot to breathe."

The most important thing after giving your orders is to think of something funny to make you smile. F. M. insisted on this. If you think of something funny from the inside you get a natural smile which releases all the muscles of your face and your jaw and everything else. It isn't a question of making a grimace. He used to say that if you can't think of something funny at will you certainly can't give orders. I never quite understood that but that is what he said. I like to give you the things he said so that you make your own understanding of it.

Allow the jaw to open. When we go open the lower jaw we try and lift the upper jaw off the lower one, and the whole head goes back.

Let the tip of the tongue touch the top of the lower teeth. F. M. used to say, "A nice lot of alliterations." The idea is for the tongue to be flat.

Then whisper "ah." F. M. used to stand in front of us and do it with us. He used to say it is like gas escaping from a pipe. No throttle sound or anything like that. You don't have to do anything with your throat or your vocal cords, just expel the breath.

Then close your mouth and don't take a breath, it'll be there. If you don't interfere with yourself, if you are freeing your neck, directing your head forward and up, and your back lengthening and widening, you won't be able to help breathing in. It is a secondary thing. We all think of breathing as something primary, but is dependent entirely on your use. We had great training in that when we were preparing to do the Shakespeare plays. That's why I don't agree with Lulie Westfeldt who said it was a waste of time. All through my teaching life I have had actors, singers, people who needed that kind of help with their breathing. Indirectly. You can't teach breathing directly. The moment you try to, you interfere.

He used to say there isn't a single cell in your body that isn't altered by you doing a whispered "ah" because the food of the cells of the body is oxygen. Every time you are doing a whispered "ah", you are getting more oxygen into your system. If you are not feeling very well, or you've got a bit of a hangover or you are on a boat which is rocking a bit, if you do whispered "ahs", you'll be okay. It is a wonderful cure if you are seasick. Lulie and I went from the coast of Maine to a small island about 20 miles out on a very rough day. All the other passengers were nuns. They were all very sick. Lulie and I sat in the front and did whispered "ahs" all the way across. We were fine.

When Alexander was training us to do the Shakespeare plays at the Old Vic and Sadler's Wells Theatre, the whole thing was based on the whispered "ah". We had a big double room in Cromwell Road, where we used to rehearse. Sometimes he would stand at the far end of the rooms and make us do the whole of *Hamlet* in a whisper. Woe betide if he couldn't hear us!

When I came to record F. M.'s books I didn't know that the training that Alexander gave me in how to use my voice would still be there after 60 years. Because his books aren't easy to read aloud. Those sentences go on forever. It was no problem – no getting out of breath. Once you've got it, you've got it.

Incidentally, F. M. also made us use vowel sounds. There is a whole sequence: "ay, ah, aw, at, ee, et, ai, it," etc. And he used to make us vocalize, having done quite a lot of whispered "ahs". I haven't written them down though. It is a long sequence. Patrick [Macdonald] may have written them down because he was very keen on them.

Preserving the Technique

How are we going to preserve the Alexander Technique in its basic essentials, in the way that F. M. formulated it for us, without getting distracted by 101 other things? It is very important to keep this work pure. And it is very, very difficult. But if we don't work that, the whole thing is going to explode in all sorts of different directions. I don't mean that new things can't be discovered about the work, but if we lose sight of the basic principles and the basic teaching that he gave us, the work won't last. I have great faith that the work will last because I think it is too important, this knowledge is so important for humanity. In a sense we are only at the very beginning of its history. It is only a 100 years after all since Alexander discovered the work. One of the things which will ensure that we are able to stick to what he taught us is reading his books.

Transcribed, abridged and edited from Marjory Barlow's three masterclasses, given on 10, 12, and 13 August 1999.

Marjory Barlow is the daughter of Amy Mechin, F. M. Alexander's sister. Marjory trained with F. M. Alexander 1933–36. She married Dr Wilfred Barlow in 1940 and has two children.

4b Wadham Gardens
London NW3 3DP
England
+44 20 7722 1884

Notes from a Workshop

Elisabeth Walker

We use the Technique to make our lives better, easier, in a way more simple, and not more difficult. It is not meant to stop us doing things, but to help us do them better, whatever we want to do. I had at a workshop a conductor who said, "I've stopped conducting because when I conduct I use myself so badly." That's the wrong way to go about it. We want to use ourselves better, to do what we want to do better and better, remembering to take time to think – to inhibit and direct.

I'd like in the first instance to have someone who I'll take in and out of a chair. I think chair work is important, because we use ourselves quite badly for sitting and standing. This is one of F. M.'s things. My first lesson with him was in and out of a chair quite a lot.

F. M. would always look to see that people hadn't got their feet together. The feet should be just under the hips, and I remind you there is a chair there – not to think I'm going to put you on the floor at this point. The thinking is the important part. The thinking is, that you're not going to think too much of that chair, you're going to think of not interfering here at the back of the neck, and here under the chin. That's it! So your head is balancing freely on the top of the spine, you're allowing the ribs to contract and expand. Great! She's breathing. You go on with the breathing, and you go on going up, and let the knees go. It is wonderful to have people that know about this work to demonstrate with.

Now, I'm very keen on using the arms and the shoulders. This pupil has beautiful free arms – so many people pull themselves down by their shoulders; they make their arms heavy, and that helps to pull them down. You're not one of those, it seems – at the moment. It is very important to get the direction of the neck free and the shoulders going one away from the other. As I take the arm, don't tighten the back of the neck. Those shoulders are going nicely one away from the other, the rib cage is moving beautifully, and I often use a touch which F. M. did, to encourage the rib-cage to move, or not necessarily to encourage it, but to stop it fixing.

So you're going to stand, but you're going to think of not interfering here, that's it, back back, heels down to come up to stand. It's brilliant when you've got an easy customer! [laughter] Great! Now from there, you're going up nicely and you can take a step.

Hands on the back of the chair

You're all used to hands on the back of the chair. F. M. liked us to do it every day, because it incorporated all the directions: free neck, the back back, the good monkey, good free arms, everything that you needed for putting hands on pupils.

We're going to go into monkey in two stages. You go on up and just let the knees go; and now hinge from the hips – wonderful, I like working with teachers. Don't tighten under the chin; lengthening the fingers, directing from the shoulder to the elbow, from the wrist to the elbow, straight fingers, and opposing thumbs. The chair is low, but I can't make it grow. Don't tighten under the chin. Just let your knees go a little more, that's it. So you've got that lengthening of the back, that's nice, and go on breathing, allowing those ribs to move. That's it, lovely, and the long fingers, free wrists, straight fingers, opposing thumbs, and keeping this width here. We've lost a little bit of the width here, so we'll take the hands off and start again. Nothing wrong with that. It just gives another opportunity for a bit more thinking. The more opportunity we have for thinking and going through the thinking process again, the better. Never mind being wrong.

Question: When I put hands on the back of the chair, I tend to stand closer to the chair. How close should I be?

I don't find it particularly important. I think it is quite a low chair for putting hands on, but never mind. We often have to approach low things. Quite often, if people have to reach low things, I get them to do it on their knees.

Now, we'll go through that again. You go on: that shoulder going out that way, this shoulder this way, and nice ribs, that's it. And you're going to release the knees quite a lot, and now hinge at the hips, great, yes, that's a beautiful back, is that OK for you? Go on up there, you've got this width now, shoulders, straight fingers, directing. Some people say "pull to the elbow", I say "direct"; I think "pull" sounds a little strong, but you can use whatever thoughts or words you like.

Question: You said how nice it was to work with a teacher. I wonder if you could say something about why it is nice?

It is because they respond to every thought, and it is there almost as soon as I am. Whereas with an inexperienced person, it takes quite some time. You have to wait before they get their thinking going, their responses going. But with some of these experienced teachers, the responses are so quick and that's such a joy, isn't it?

Musicians seem to shorten a lot in the upper arm and pull down here – pianists especially. I point it out and get them to observe the use of their arms. I think they've been told as a child to drop the shoulders, and they've grown up often with that habit pattern. That's how it seems to me, it is so common, particularly in pianists, that tightening.

Going up on toes

I think we'll do something like going on the toes. I'm running through different activities so you see some of the games we get up to. So, you're going to go on going up there, and allowing the ribs to expand and contract. You go on, up there, don't tighten under the chin, just let that head go on going on up there. And now I'm going to put my hands on your back, and I want you just to come back to my hands from your toes. That's it, on your toes. Now, heels down to the ground. All was well until, at the end, you threw the hips forward on the way down. But going up you did brilliantly. On the way down don't throw this forward. Let's go though that once again. You're allowing this neck to be free, your shoulders are going one away from the other, right under here, so, again, don't pull yourself down under the upper arm. It's a great place for contracting under there. You go on going on up there, and let your back come back to my hands, and now stay coming back, back, back, and let the heels down. Good. You should all be able to be noticing where they're improving.

Question: Where did you have your hands?

All sorts of different places. I was doing it right on the shoulder blades. So again you're going up there nicely, sometimes I'll do that with hands on the sides of the rib cage, but I don't want to be lifting in any sense, and sometimes that can encourage them to feel one's going to lift, so I'm putting them here on the shoulder blades. Let your back come back, your neck be free, go on going up, and back back, that's it, heels down. OK.

When I have someone holding on to their hips and throwing themselves forward, then I find the only way is to take them at hip level. So you go on thinking a lot of not interfering with the head and neck, letting your back come back, and don't think of sitting, think of freeing the ankles, very important, free ankles. You can all think of freeing your ankles as you free your necks to sit on your sitting bones. Go on up there, and now go on with that thinking, and just let the knees go. Similarly there are some who want to push with the legs to come out of the chair. And again I often come back to hip level again. You think of the neck being free, let your back come back to my shoulder. Back to come up. And that's really a great way if people are keen on stiffening their hips. Just let that head float up there. Have the shoulders going one away from the other, lengthen, that's it, right out there. And don't be afraid of lengthening in all directions, and allowing the ribs to contract and expand.

Question: My pupils often ask me, "Did I stiffen?" and they want me to tell them. And I want to encourage them to realize it for themselves.

Maybe they did stiffen. It doesn't matter what they've done in the past, it is the moment that matters.

Some people hate being wrong. They can't stand it. However much you tell them it doesn't matter being wrong, they get worried. So I don't often tell them if they're not doing very well. Because this work is often difficult for people; they think it's difficult, so don't make it more difficult for them. You want to encourage them on their way. That's why I often say "good" or "great", etc.

Question: Do you ask them to give a little post mortem?

Yes, I sometimes ask them, "Now, how was that for you?" and they'll say, "Oh, I'm not sure", or they'll say, "Oh, that was wonderful", or, "light". Its quite good to get them to notice what's going on. When they say they stiffen; yes, we can think or inhibit a bit more, you can always be that much better. It is no good to get them upset.

Now, you're going to do some squatting. Have your feet a shade further apart, and you're going to allow this neck to be free, you're going to go right up and out of the hips, and let the knees go, that's it, lovely [laughter]. It makes a difference if you come right out of the hips and don't go down into them.

Question: At what point in your lessons do you teach that?

I teach it a lot to pregnant women – not in the first three months, but later on in pregnancy. I get them to practice squatting, holding on to doorknobs. But a lot of people are afraid of squatting. We don't squat in the West, do we? Lucia, my daughter, brought me back a wonderful picture of an elderly washerwoman in India, squatting with her washing, looking so poised and balanced.

Question: You very often look at the person's head and face or eye when you are working. I wonder is it somewhere particular that you are looking?

Yes, I find it very important to watch their head and neck. I think it is very important to use the eyes as well as the hands, to observe everywhere. You want to look as well as to listen with the hands to what's going on.

There we have that lovely balance of the head on the top of the spine, nice and free, not tight here, nor under the chin. You're going right up there. So, if you are going to squat, would you like your feet a little further apart? Good. Go on going up there, and I'm going to help you here. So, freeing the ankles, you come out of the ankles, out of the hips, and let the knees go. Great. You've squatted before? I thought so. Back back, heels down to come up. Yes. I think we should all follow the example of our Eastern friends and squat and kneel and use our joints.

Some people who are squatting tend to come onto the inside of their instep because they're not free enough in their ankles. But ideally the ankles should be, you know, just in the same way as when we're walking or standing. With people who don't squat readily, I put a book under their heels, and if there's anyone who doesn't like squatting, we try that. It makes such a difference to start with. We'll just do one more squat with Sylvia. And she's going to let her head lead, up there, and a nice back here, and free ankles and let the knees go forward and the hips back. That's the way. Just let the head come forward just a little more. Now do you notice any difference? There's a big difference, a big stretch in the back. Head forward, back back. Before there was a wee bit of holding on there, and it made a big difference to your back.

Question: Can you say something more about your processes when you're working?

I think it's such an instinctive thing, your communication with your students, you get to know them in so many senses. You get to know them by touch and by look and by voice, by so much.

Question: Do you just visualize where the bones are or does it just come to you?

I don't find that particularly important. For instance, people often have strange shapes, but they can use themselves within those shapes. People have a bad kyphosis or lordosis and they can still use themselves better within that shape.

Question: Do you take pregnant women up that way when they go into the squat – I mean, when they're very, very big?

You have to see every person, and how they are. Sometimes it is better for them to get onto hands and knees, but each one is so different. Some are very athletic and agile right at the end and some aren't. I just see each one as they are.

Question: Did F. M. teach you a whispered "ah" that had an oral arrangement or was it something you picked up in the training?

He taught it during the training, yes. As far as I can remember, and it is quite long ago, he taught us to think of something funny, to smile, but again, we had to go on allowing the neck to be free. That was the important thing, allowing the neck to be free, thinking of something funny, smile, to allow the jaw to drop, tongue to the top of the lower teeth, and say "aaaaahhhhh" [laughter].

So once again, we're allowing the neck to be free, that's it, think of something funny, smile, and allow the jaw to drop and say "aaaaahhhhh". Now again, this is something I use with women in labour, it's the best possible thing, in the first stages of labour, as soon as they have contractions, they say whispered "ahs" and usually three whispered "ahs" take the time of a contraction. And it makes all the difference in the world, because they're not tightening up, they're allowing the breathing to continue, they're not "ohhh" (demonstrates restricted in-breath) like this, it is really so important, so tell your friends.

Question: I was wondering if this was F. M.'s original way, we have to put our lower teeth forward in front of our upper teeth and we go from there?

As far as I remember, no mechanical thing, other than just watching that when they drop the jaw – that's it.

Question: How should the smile be?

The smile has to stay round the eyes, you can't keep a grin – that's it, yes. People do tend as they drop the jaw to stick the jaw out.

Question: Were you trained to say "ah" or "hah"?

No you mustn't put the aich (h) in. Which language do you speak? German? I think it would be the same. Its "ah". [Demonstrates] You mustn't do "hah" [demonstrates] that gives you a glottal stop. That's it, just opening. But it is quite difficult to get newish people to leave out that "hah", they want to put in the glottal stop. The ah is just a sound and it's a sound to get the throat really open.

Question: Do you teach with shoes on or off?

Whatever they like. They're usually more comfortable with them off, and of course when they go onto the table, I like them off because I like to put hands on the feet. I think it is unimportant. If they come in high heels, I talk to them about that [laughter]. Some want to wear high heels. But it does make a difference to their balance, and so we sometimes practice a bit of both, if they're in high heels, walking barefoot or with the heels, so that they notice the difference.

Pupils often come to me saying they want better posture. I don't like that word. It describes a position and the Alexander Technique helps freedom in movement and coordination by stopping interference with inherent good use.

Elisabeth Walker trained in 1935 as a radiographer and worked with Graham Hodgson in London with whom she x-rayed royalty and many celebrities. Later she worked at King's College Hospital. In 1938 she married Dick Walker and together they completed their training with F. M. Alexander in 1947. She and her husband, Dick Walker, lived in South Africa 1949–60. They started a training course in Oxford in 1985 which Elisabeth Walker continued after her husband's death (in 1992) until 1999.

63 Chalfont Road
Oxford OX2 6TJ
England
+44 1865 558477

Conversations with Erika Whittaker

interviewed by Bruce Fertman

Impressed by Erika Whittaker's deep personal and philosophical understanding of the work, at both the first and third International Congresses, I chose to begin a dialogue, via letters and tapes, with Erika. Martha and I invited Erika to Philadelphia in the autumn of 1995 to teach at the Alexander Foundation. The experience was unforgettable. Later, Erika and I co-taught classes for A.T. teachers in Sydney, Australia.

It gives me pleasure to share with you some of Erika's perceptions of Alexander's work.

Conversation I: Spreading like strawberry jam

I am talking to you from Melbourne, and we will try and see what we can do with our tape. It would be fun to see if we can use the tape as a way of exchanging ideas and of communicating.

I want to welcome all your friends who are sitting with you and who are listening to this more as a way of communicating, of sharing an idea, or process. The old concept of a teacher is one who knows, imparting knowledge to one who does not know, a rather one-sided business with strong overtones of right and wrong. And of course the pupil always wants to do well, thinks in terms of pleasing, pleasing your parents, pleasing your teacher, pleasing yourself not least, and that all comes into it when we have a strong teacher–pupil relationship.

I am becoming more and more aware of changes in communicating in my lifetime. We walked a lot more. We sat together over meals longer.

When I was eight, my Aunt Ethel gave me my first Alexander lessons. I had lying-down turns on the floor with the simplest of directions, suited to a child. One of them was to think of your back spreading like strawberry jam on the floor. And when she gave me lessons in a chair, she made up funny songs.

My Alexander lessons were an amusing mixture of fun and responsibility for my use. Aunt Ethel really kept me on my toes, but it was always fun. We both made up jokes and called each other funny names. She hated her name, Ethel. She said I could call her anything I liked, but please don't call me Ethel, Aunt Ethel, so I called her "Pip", because she looked like Pip of the "Pip Pip Squeak and Wilfred" comics of that time. So Pip she remained for the rest of her life, to me and my brothers, and to many students of our first training course.

So as you can see, my attitude to Alexander work is conditioned by a very happy start. That early simplicity has remained with me all my life.

Conversation II: Stay in touch with each other

To graduates, I give three suggestions.

A Zen master lived up in the mountains in China somewhere – very hard to get at, far away from anywhere. He was known to have three secrets in his teaching. A certain monk managed to get there one day, with much trouble, and the monk asked the master if he would give him his three secrets.

The master said: "Yes, all right, you've taken a lot of trouble to get here. I will tell you. Now the first secret is: *pay attention.* The second secret is: *pay attention.* The third secret is: *pay attention.*"

Those who have worked with Marj Barstow will know that that was the strong point of her teaching. She made you pay attention, not for a long time, but when you were doing some activity, you were to pay attention to what you were doing *relative to the activity.* Paying attention is not an endgaining. It's simply paying attention, and that's a very important point to understand.

F. M. could always tell with his hands whether you were paying attention, but he didn't stop you. When he was working with you his hands kept moving about in such a way that you did pay attention. But not in an endgaining way. You didn't try to do something. You allowed it to happen because you were getting the right sort of help. You allowed it to happen, and then you had an experience of a kind of use which was totally unexpected, wonderfully strong, and very supportive.

After I graduated in London, with Alexander, I first of all went away. I had so much Alexander in my life for so many years that I decided I needed some fresh air. So I went. My father was living in Philadelphia. I went to see him there. Then I stayed with Lulie Westfeldt in Richmond, Virginia, where she was teaching at a kindergarten school. And after that I had several months holiday in the United States, where I met a lot of people. It was wonderful.

Then I went back to London, and was immediately drawn back into Ashley Place. I taught, as a pair, with Irene Stewart. We gave our lessons together. One person had the head and one took the back, and then whatever movements you make, the person with the head is in the lead and the back fits in with that. We worked that out very efficiently all the time we were working at Ashley Place.

I think that one of the important things for students, those that you particularly get on well with, is that you stay in touch with each other.

Conversation III: Doing the things you're interested in

Don't be in a hurry to expect students. If you need the money, earn the money in some other way. But don't endgain over earning money on Alexander lessons, because the Alexander work will suffer – yours, as well as your pupils'. I think the ideal way of attracting students is to work in totally different surroundings: work, say, in a bank, or in a library. Whatever place you work in, you attend to your own work and to "the work".

But you might have somebody who works with you, who keeps on saying, "Ooh, my shoulder's giving me a lot of problem." All the time you're working, of course, you must have a look round and see. Watch other people's use, see how they go about things; see how they're endgaining; and you begin to sort of read people after a while. Not in a critical way – not that that's bad and that's good – but simply for interest. There is no good and bad in this kind of observation. But you can see what is happening. And somebody might say to you: "Ohh, my shoulder is giving me a lot of trouble," and of course, you've been seeing these people, this person. You know that person's use. Well, then you can hop in there and you can say, "Right, I think I might be able to help you." And there's a pupil.

Get experience working at somebody's school, an Alexander School, where there are a lot of pupils coming and going. The main thing I would say is, don't have any expectations at all. Go on doing the things that you are interested in.

There are infinite ways of seeking and receiving help. The person we had in our time, in Alexander's time, was Irene Tasker. She was what you might call a born teacher. She was wonderful. If you had any problem with the work or with yourself, or working with others, or with teaching, or when you were working with children, you'd ask her and she would say, "All right, you don't understand that. Come over here and I'll show you." And she did.

And my Aunt Ethel Webb, she always had the simplest answers. We'd be having a great problem with something and she'd come along and simply say, "Oh, look, you can't do that with that pupil. Look, they're coming down. So you take them up."

Never work away at somebody. You have to use your teaching ingenuity.

It must never get so that it gets into a situation with no solution. If you can turn it into a joke, so much the better.

Don't take your teaching seriously, and don't think about teaching.

Conversation IV: "Between us"

At the Alexander Congress in Sydney when I said "I am not a teacher," it so startled everybody. I meant just that. I am not the figure of a teacher, the person who knows, as against the pupil who doesn't know. I don't want to see it that way. If I am working through the Alexander work, I want to share it with you. I want to show you how maybe you could improve whatever it is you are complaining about. But I must not endgain, and you must not endgain and, between us, we'll work out something.

When you are teaching a pupil, you want that pupil to be happy, and of course the pupil is paying you. So, we work out some routine that becomes sort of a charm, something that you will turn on with everyone. But you can't do that with Alexander's work; it is entirely unique; every moment is different. Turn it into fun, into something amusing to do. Your pupils will be very grateful, and they'll learn. And you will learn.

The conversations with F. M. in his lessons were about anything that happened to be going on in the world. I remember Mussolini at that time was making a lot of noise in Italy. I think there was a plan for the Italians to invade Abyssinia, in Africa, and F. M. was raving about "Musso." He couldn't stand "Musso." "Musso was up to this, and Musso was up to something else." And, if you wanted to have a bit of variation in your lessons you would ask him, you know, "What's the latest about Mussolini?" and off he would go.

It was very good fun, and some of the best lessons we had from him were when he was talking about something very interesting that was going on. But that all goes to show that it is never, never, a very dull business of routines, or what they now call procedures. I think it is rather a pity these procedures have got locked into boxes, because that is not what it's about.

When it came to our being given our certificates, by F. M. in London, we had actually had four years of training. The original plan was three years, but then F. M. wanted to give us a bit more time so that we didn't rush out and start teaching.

He wanted to slow that up. He wanted us to understand more and more about what his work was really like, because he knew with his own career how sensitive this teaching work is.

Conversation V: "I never use the words 'Alexander Technique'!"

Irene Tasker was a very, very experienced teacher, and quite a few of us did work with her later on. She was always very willing to help us, and to do work with us, any time we wanted to. But we had to make our own way.

I was working at Ashley Place, to get lots of experience, which I did. Then the war came and that broke the whole thing up.

By that time, I was married. I was living in the country. I had my own daughter, and as she was growing up we had animals. We had geese, goats, and later, we had horses. I became a very good driver of a horse trailer. My daughter went show jumping, and I had to drive her all over the place. I stayed in touch with my Alexander friends, but I didn't want to be an Alexander teacher out in the country where I was. I was too busy.

I came back into teaching later, after I went to Australia. Somebody came one day and said, "Why aren't you teaching Alexander?" And I thought, "I've got time now, haven't I?" I did have time. My own interest in Alexander had become very much more acute. I had done a lot of reading, I had gone to university and studied another language. I went to university when I was sixty. I enjoyed that enormously. All the time, Alexander was in the background.

I never conceived of it as a subject in isolation, not like a university subject. It is something for living. And it widens all the time. Alexander had the way of finding out what you yourself are about in a total pattern. Not just how you are psychologically or practically, but how you function altogether as one.

I came across in the old writings of the old masters, things that fit in exactly with Alexander's work. It must be a living pattern of our lives. And it is infinite in its variety. Alexander work is never just chair work and the kind of things that you do in a lesson. Those things that Alexander was doing with people, he was simply helping them to become aware of their use in everyday life.

I never use the words "Alexander Technique." I think it indicates something that you can learn and then do, and even be judged on. It is not that. It has infinite variety, and it is always growing.

Conversation VI: Great fun

You ask about our first training course, how our days were divided. We had two hours with F. M., from 10:00 till 12:00, and in the afternoons we met to find some way to continue our mornings' work on our own. But how? F. M. gave us no instructions. No guidance.

As students we must study. We must show interest and initiative, and you must, you know, be very much on the ball all the time. That is proverbial for students, who want to show their teachers that they are really enthusiastic about what they are doing. But there was the other carrot that was dangled before us as well: at the end of the three years, we would be teachers and we had the added incentive of being the nearest successors to F. M., who was growing old then, and one day would no longer be with us. But his work must go on. So we experimented through observation. F. M. was forever telling us to observe what was going on around us, not just how people used themselves and how they moved. But also everything else that was happening around us. We observed each other with writing. That occupied us for quite a while. It was very, very informal and great fun. F. M. never asked or wanted to know what we were up to. We got used to that, as we had learned by experience that he never told anybody what to do.

F. M.'s lessons were so remarkable for his pupils because of the way he used his hands. And these hands, as I see it now, were so remarkable in that they reflected what F. M. observed with his eyes and his own use experience.

If somebody came into the room, he would take one look at them, and he would know exactly where that person's use needed help. Of course, he wouldn't tell them, because the moment you tell somebody that, they say, "Oh, that's something I'm doing wrong, so I must put it right." And they'll concentrate on that. So, that is why he criticized very, very little in lessons.

And so, because he didn't give you that criticism, you relaxed, and you were treated by the way his hands seemed to be reshaping you, which felt so good, and you seemed to be expanding, feeling strong, simply because you had let go of all your tensions which were now replaced with an all over, entirely new coordination.

Conversation VII: The decision is *you*

When you say "no," you have given yourself space and time in order to make your decision. You do it, or you decide not to do it, or you do something altogether different. The choice, the decision is yours, the decision is you... "No" is not a postponement. It means truly stopping in a final sense. Then you have all the time in the world to choose what you will do, while you remind yourself of your orders, or your directions, or your constructive thinking, or whatever you call them, so then you are master of your own decisions.

Then our activities become nothing special. Time is of little consequence, and results are no longer of much concern. What a relief, and how pleasant!

Conversation VIII: A very real person

> If only we would love the ancients more, and copy them less.
> Kakuzo Okakura, *The Book of Tea*

"Hello Erika? This is Bruce. How are you?" Erika answers promptly. "I've had quite a good day. I was sitting for quite a while in a train station, watching people. Suddenly I began to see people, the whole of them. It was quite remarkable. I could see exactly where, if I were to lightly place one finger in a particular spot, with a particular decision, in a particular direction, then that particular person would and could only free directly up, from head to toe. Truly seeing person after person. I'm eighty-five years old, and today I am finally beginning to see."

Late autumn. Erika had just finished teaching for the Alexander Foundation in Philadelphia for seven days, six hours a day. We drove to the park to be outside by the river. Our senses were open. Emerald-green-headed ducks were swimming below huge golden-leafed maple and oak trees. I could see that Erika felt happy, satisfied. Just then a strong, soft wind blew through Erika's thick hair. All at once, in slow motion, the translucent leaves seemed to let go of their branches, in great numbers. A haiku by Issa flashed through my mind:

> Simply trust:
> Do not the petals flutter down,
> Just like that?

I was just about to share my poetic thought with Erika. Then I realized that I had just tried to hold on to that moment, and in doing so had lost it. Erika had not. So I stopped, letting my lips lightly close, and said nothing. Instantly, I re-entered the real poem, standing next to a very real person, and a very real teacher *who teaches without teaching*.

Erika, thank you.

The Academy of Music (Musikhochschule) in Freiburg, the site of the Congress.

Recreation time.

Forum: Special Interest Classes

Exchange of practical work.

The Cranio-Sacral System

Its hidden influence and its support in an Alexander lesson

Hillegonda Boode

When we want to make use of the knowledge of the cranio-sacral system, there are two ways of going about it; to use it as

1. a therapy for people who have had severe damage especially in the core of the body (head, neck, spine, or pelvis), and also in tissues connected with traumas.
2. a tool to understand more about the state of the client; as a background tool in a profession, for instance, in combination with the Alexander Technique.

In this workshop the emphasis will be on the second point.

I would like to refer to the talk I gave in Engelberg in 1991 (*The Congress Papers*, 1991).

In the beginning of 1998 I had an accident; I fell and my left arm came out of its socket and my upper arm broke. It was an amazing but also a very painful experience.

I realized that all of my tissues, muscles, and nerves had come under extreme stress. It took more than one year to recover. But during that year I gained more and more insight into what was going on in my whole body.

Initially, my arm seemed a separate entity as if (apart from the pain) it didn't belong to me. I recognized the feelings Oliver Sacks described in his book, *A Leg to Stand On*. Working in an "Alexander way" with my right hand on several painful places on my injured left arm had helped. But from my work in cranio-sacral therapy I had learned that the arms have to be able to rotate inward and outward at the shoulder socket in a kind of rhythmic pulse, about six to eight times a minute, in sympathy with the whole cranio-sacral system. I could feel that my arm was stuck in the position of the "inward" rotation. My injured arm had to relearn how to turn out from this inward position in order to reconnect with the rhythm of the whole. This was the work that needed to be done.

To accomplish this, I found that I needed to stay longer with my right hand resting on one place on my left arm, and slowly give more and more pressure until the pain reached a certain border. Then there came a release such that my right hand seemed to be pushed away by the injured arm. It was as if the pain had found its way out.

After months of work, session upon session, the feeling of wholeness in my body came back. My arm was again under the influence of my cranio-sacral system. I tell you this story because my experience led me to the conclusion that:

1. the connective tissue is the main organ of the body
2. "feeling" starts in the connective tissue (do you remember the question that came up after the talk about pain by John F. Maltsbergen at the 1991 congress?).

In reference to "feeling": some weeks ago my daughter told me that for her the most important sense is "smell". That started me thinking about which one is most important to me: it is "feeling" – I don't want to miss it. Pain and also positive feelings start in the connective tissue and the message goes to the brain, as far as I have experienced.

Being Alexander teachers, we can still do more for the well-being of our pupils. Most people who want lessons have difficulties with their bodies. We know that problems often come from wrong use, but my experiences tell me that, frequently, wrong use has a deeper cause. The question is, do we want to look for this cause? I discovered in my Alexander teaching that knowledge of the cranio-sacral system makes it possible to find these deeper causes.

This workshop will not be complex and will centre on practical issues. I hope the participants, while working together, will keep my conclusions in their minds and will explore this part of the Alexander Technique for themselves. There is still a lot more to explore and to find out.

Hillegonda Boode first trained as a physical education teacher. Later she trained at A. T. A. with Don Burton. Around 1986 she learned about the Cranio-Sacral system from Robert Norett and studied at the Upledger Institute Europe, in Doorn, Holland in the following years. She works now as an Alexander teacher in Amsterdam and uses cranio-sacral therapy as a speciality when necessary.

Jennerstraat 7
1097 GB Amsterdam
tel. 00-31-206680850

A Sideways Look at the Alexander Technique

Jean Clark

I first started seriously thinking about my two sides, right and left, when I took up horse-riding lessons. As a reasonably experienced Alexander Technique teacher of over twenty years, I thought I knew something about sitting on chairs or the floor, neither surfaces being moving ones. However, when sitting on a moving horse's back, my sitting bones were being asked to balance on a surface which moved up and down, backwards and forwards, and from side to side, thus giving my sitting bones an individual experience. It was as if I was perched on two moving balls, one sitting bone on each. As I endeavoured to think of my sitting bones individually, I had much more of an experience of having a left side and a right side of my body, each with its own sitting bone. My spine became the flexible centre linking the two sides of my body, like a zip. My legs needed to free up on either side of the horse. This two-sidedness seemed to extend to include my neck, which also had a left side and a right side. As soon as I thought in this way, I could sense that my "right neck" was more dominant and "bossy" than my "left neck", tending to pull forward – this is often the habit in a right-handed person. I began also to wonder if I had had a mistaken concept of lengthening up by squashing my two sides together and pushing up through my middle, the result being that I was actually narrowing and shortening myself. A newspaper character, Andy Capp, observed once that "experience is what you imagine you have, until you have a bit more!" How true this was for me in my experience of sitting on a horse.

In this session, which is predominantly practical, we will explore together sideways movements and hopefully add to our own experience, like Andy Capp " – a bit more".

Walking sideways is our first experience of walking, after we master the art of standing upright – at the age of about one year – and, while holding on to the furniture, we raise a foot and step sideways. For adults (who have full command of their balance, and do not need to hold on to the furniture) stepping sideways becomes a rather novel experience. We can explore our understanding of F. M.'s directions to neck, head, back, and knees – particularly the knees, which still need to be directed forward and away from each other, as we progress sideways. This encourages widening of the back, and the end-gaining tendency to pull ourselves to our destination (as when we are walking forward) is mercifully diminished, in fact, we seem singularly uninterested in the destination to the extent that we can enjoy the "scenery" as we move. We need to explore stepping to the left for at least half a dozen steps and then to the right, parting one leg from the other by bending the knee and raising the heel and then bringing the other foot to land beside the first. A lengthening upward thought needs to be continually renewed, especially when changing direction from stepping left to stepping right. When repeating this for a while and then standing still, there will be more of a sense of being balanced, and centred, with all options open for forward, backward, sideways, or diagonal movement. Some folk dances promote this sideways movement, as in circle dances.

Crawling sideways on hands and knees is another novel exploration. I have sometimes found that adults, when crawling forward, over-reach and have a tendency to bring their weight too far forward and have too much weight on their arms. This tendency is diminished when crawling sideways, in the sequence of knee first then hand of one side, then knee first then hand of the other side. Progress sideways is deliciously slow, giving plenty of time to inhibit, direct and breathe. This is, as it were, a variation on homo-lateral crawling (i.e. creeping), which enhances widening and helps to reduce the tendency to interfere with the working of the back by tightening at the waist. It also encourages more widening of the upper part of the arms as one continues to widen the back, and also encourages widening in the upper part of the legs. Often our habitual mode is to clench the legs together, as if they were joined together at the top – like a wish-bone of a chicken – instead of spanned apart by the pelvic girdle. The head is still leading in the sense that it coordinates the whole organism in whatever direction has been decided, so that the head releases forward, not in this case to go forward, but to go sideways in an organized way.

These are just two practical procedures to give one a sideways look at life, which I am sure will have each of you thinking up your own.

A useful variation is to lie on one's side on the table – similar to recovery position, with enough books under your head to fill the space between shoulder and side of head, the lower leg extended, and the upper leg bent at the knee and at right angles to the trunk (being raised under the knee by a book or small cushion). Working in an Alexander way on someone in this position can be most beneficial and interesting. With one side of the trunk not weight-bearing, the rib-cage of the upper side is very free to move, and the connections of the limbs into the trunk can be explored. The pupil needs to roll over, so that both sides have the experience.

These sideways procedures bring up interesting areas for further exploration: for instance, the dominance of right over left or vice versa, which tends to bring about unwanted twists and uneven strength in one or more of the large number of paired organs, such as eyes, ears, arms, lungs, legs, etc. that we have. In identical twins, if their differentiation from a single fertilised egg occurs at a particular time in early development, the resultant twins are a mirror image of each other; one will be left-handed and the other right-handed and, in males, even the receding areas of hair on the head will be mirror images of each other. Each of us will probably have a preferred way of thinking, using either the left side of our brain, with its preference for logic and specifics or our right side, with its generalities and intuitive ideas.

In early uterine life, our body segments, or somites, divide bilaterally, enabling lateral bending movements. The development of anterior/posterior splitting allows flexion and extension. The building blocks are then together in place for spiral movement.

Professor Raymond Dart, an Alexander Technique devotee, wrote about our double-spiralled trunk and neck musculature. His advice to us was to use both sides of the body and both sides of the brain. I concur wholeheartedly with this, I hope with both sides of myself!

Jean A. J. Clark trained with Walter Carrington in London 1966 – 1969. She has been teaching continuously ever since, pupils of all ages from 3 to 93 years old and from many varied walks of life. She has been involved in teacher training, both her own students and as a visiting teacher at schools world-wide. Before training she was an entomologist working on the classification of insects in the Natural History Museum. Her birth sign is Cancer – the crab – a creature who also likes to move sideways.

104 Toynbee Road
Wimbledon, London
SW20 8SL
England

The Primary Control: Some Personal Views

Rivka Cohen

Introduction

The subject that I would like to discuss is, "aim up and stay back under all conditions, in both poise and movement". These simple words contain the essence of the Alexander Technique. By "aim up" we mean "to initiate a conscious activity regarding the use of the entire self." This guiding of direction along the body is steered by a mental order; and the guiding is both a mental and a physical act. These two respective acts manifest themselves in one unified operation.

For many years, however, I have observed that groups of Alexander teachers from different parts of the world, as well as individuals from various training programs, interpret Alexander's words quite differently. The more I am in the world of the Alexander Technique, the more I understand that these varying interpretations are not simply a question of style; they reflect differences of conceptualization. People read the same words but interpret them differently. It seems that the way we use our bodies mirrors our understanding of these words.

Normally, people don't exercise any conscious direction in the use of themselves. What seems to be natural to them is in reality a misdirected behaviour to which they are habituated. The result is that they tend to collapse or tense up – both phenomena being symptoms of the absence of an "up" direction. These forces of habit act on us unconsciously, and cause us to experience heaviness, downward pressure, fatigue, pain, and even debilitating physical conditions. We often see people who are "spineless" – i.e. without a solid back, stiff-necked, and so on. These conditions express psychophysical limitations that can be changed through the discipline of the Alexander Technique.

There are many aspects of the Alexander Technique. Often, people who are attracted to the world of the Alexander Technique are looking for an answer to some need. However, needs vary. There are those who want to improve their physical condition. Others look for a resolution to a psychological question that may be reflected in their physical world. And there are still others who search for a disciplined system through which they can work on themselves in order to improve their entire being.

Alexander's major discovery was to find the innate mechanism that is responsible for the use of the self; this he named the primary control. Thanks to Alexander, we know that the primary control involves the dynamic relation between head, torso, limbs, and feet that, when used well, produces changes at all levels of our being.

Before discussing the primary control, however, I would like to say a few words about directions, and about directions in relation to movement.

Directions and movement

When we talk about directions and movement from the perspective of the Alexander Technique, we recognize two different events. When we speak of directions, we speak of the flow of life in the body, which has sequence and timing. When it works well, it tends to expand the body into space in all directions within the limits of the body.

When we speak of movement, we speak of the motion of the body or parts of the body in space. Movement is where we take ourselves in space. It can happen in any direction we choose (e.g. forward, back, up, down, sideways). We speak of two separate events – direction and movement – yet they are inseparably joined in life. They are joined even when they move in opposite directions. For example, when we lower ourselves in space to sit, the movement is down; but the direction of the spine has to be aimed up.

Normally, mechanical repetition will not improve the quality of performance. We need to apply constructive conscious control. Learning the principle of the Alexander Technique will help. In the words of Patrick Macdonald:

> I think it might be useful to list the items that, taken together, I believe make the Alexander Technique one unlike any other. They are:
>
> Recognition of the Force of Habit
> Inhibition and Non-Doing
> Recognition of Faulty Sensory Awareness
> Sending Directions
> The Primary Control
>
> If one meets a technique that has some similarity to the Alexander Technique, run these five simple items over it and see what is missing.

Primary control

When we talk of the primary control, we recognize a complex of directions that, when put in words, says: "Allow the neck to be free to allow the head to move forward and up, for the back to lengthen and widen." Words are pronounced sequentially, but actions happen simultaneously. It is this co-ordination of opposing forces that allows the spine to maintain a constant upward direction all through the body.

The head is used well when "opposing" the torso. There is that inner movement in the body where the head moves ahead of the torso no matter which direction the head faces (forward, down, or up in space); the head rotates by moving forward and up where the spine continues its upward movement. It is also very important to point out that the use of the feet on the ground plays an enormous part in the ability of the head to create and maintain that "up" direction in motion.

We need all these conditions for the primary control to work well. If one of these parts fails to direct, then the primary control is misused. However, when the head keeps moving away from the torso, it leaves room for the torso to be released up. This process is reached through conscious mental direction; that is, we use conscious inhibition in order to change the habitual behaviour, while at the same time creating a new direction of behaviour.

The "up" of the spine is the leading part. In the proper dynamic, the head is forward and up, the spine is pointing up, and the ground is below us. However, please don't confuse "ground" with "down"! The ground activates the reflexes to go up. Ground brings the power of opposition. This is what we call "direction in action."

Only when "direction in action" exists can we move into space with the dynamic of the power of the opposition. Using the primary control in this way, we discover the unique option of moving up in space by releasing the power of inner directions without needing to tilt forward in space.

Of course, we can choose to tilt forward so long as we create "direction in action." As Patrick Macdonald would often say in his classes, "Aim up to move forward, not forward to get up."

Often we hear the sentence, "The head leads, the body follows." This sentence, however, does not describe any opposing forces that create an upward release in the use of the primary control. Here, we emphasize that it is *the upward direction* of the spine that is the leading part. When we talk about directions along the spine, we want it to be understood that we are consciously creating upward directions along the spine, even when the torso moves forward in space.

Practical application

My approach to dealing with change of habitual behaviour regarding the way we employ the primary control is as follows:

First, one must use consciousness to change from an habitual unknown behaviour involving misuse toward instructing – actively and positively – the head to move in a forward and up direction, while allowing the back simultaneously to lengthen and widen and aim up and away from the head and the limbs. (One has also to include the knees moving away from the torso and hip-socket while the feet are well grounded, allowing for their power of opposition.)

Obviously, during the process of the work to improve the use of the primary control, we also need to let go of many of the excess tensions in our use that interfere with any part of our bodies. These tensions need to be taken into consideration. Although I notice them when teaching, I choose to deal with them after I have introduced – through my words and hands – the words and *activity* of directing. (And even as we advance, we must not just release, but release in an *upward* direction.)

Conscious inhibition

As we develop our understanding of the work, we begin to recognize the constant downward pressures in our systems; and having recognized these downward pulls, we choose not to do them. Then we must choose to behave in another way using conscious inhibition. Conscious inhibition is an activity that requires a certain response to stimulation, rather than the habitual one, through the mental orders of the directions. In practice, we create a sequence of events that happens simultaneously.

Having a good back means knowledge, and knowledge can be acquired. We acquire it through discipline. You learn to attend to where your back is in relation to other parts of the body. The relationship of the parts of the body to each other creates dimension. When relations work well in action, they work in circles where the spine "up" is an axis.

I choose to teach this way, but I recognize that there are other ways of improving the use of the primary control. I have found that people often hold tensions to protect themselves against fear-filled, new situations. However, letting go of these tensions without an alternative, concrete, new direction can cause even greater fear and confusion.

"Aim up and stay back" is another way of describing Alexander's primary control. Aim up is a conscious action that works against the habitual force of habit. Aim up is activity; aim up is extension. Up is the power of life. Up is centrifugal. Up is away from down.

Rivka Cohen trained in London 1957–62 and was qualified by Patrick Macdonald. During this period she also studied with Peter Scott, Wilfred Barlow, Margaret Goldie, Bill Williams, and Walter Carrington. She returned to Israel where she taught privately for 20 years. In 1980 she opened the Haifa School for the Alexander Technique, and has qualified about 70 teachers. Cohen now runs her own training course in New York City. For the last 15 years she has given postgraduate courses in Israel, Canada, Germany, and USA.

10 Bradford Terrace, Apt. 1
Brookline
MA 02446
USA
+1 617 566 4227

The "Pivotal" Role of the Chair in the Alexander Technique:

A reconsideration and a proposal

Galen Cranz

The first aim of this presentation is to introduce participants to the social history and cultural criticism of the chair recently published in *The Chair: Rethinking Culture, Body and Design* (W. W. Norton, New York, 1998). The book will be summarized through slides showing the social history, style history, ergonomic *vs.* somatic theory and research, and the physical design implications of a somatic approach to thinking about the body.

The second aim is to focus on the role of chairs and stools in the Alexander Technique.

Third, the physiology of perching (halfway between sitting and standing) and why it is less stressful to the back than right-angled sitting is explained.

Fourth, members of the audience will have the opportunity to experience for themselves the differences between right-angled sitting and perching.

Fifth, the advantages of using a variety of postures and movements rather than relying primarily on classical right-angled sitting will be reviewed.

And finally, the session concludes with a discussion of how teachers of the Technique can encourage their pupils to design and to select their physical environment to support "good use" in a variety of postures. Specifically, we will consider places for rest position, sitting cross-legged, and crawling; stand-up workstations, including treadmills; chairs which have adjustable heights; high work-surfaces; (kitchen islands, counters, drafting tables with pneumatic lift mechanisms, reading stands) for use while perching or standing; knee space under counters and sinks for the "monkey;" lounge chairs (and adequate sleep); the ideal of movement in all environments including work and school.

Galen Cranz, Ph.D. (1971), STAT-Cert, AmSAT (1991), is Professor of Architecture at the University of California at Berkeley, specializing in the sociology of architecture. There she teaches a seminar called "Designing for the near-environment"– where the body and the environment intersect. In this popular course students design issue, chair, room interior, and experience a lesson in the Alexander Technique. She is the author of *The Politics of Park Design: A History of Urban Parks in America.* Outside of academia her interests include tai chi, swimming, farmers markets, eating, and other arts.

Department of Architecture
University of California
Berkeley, CA 94720
USA
+ 1 510 658-9330
fax: +1 510 643-5607
e-mail: gcranz@uclink.berkeley.edu

A Turn of Heart

Bruce Fertman

Full eclipse

More than five hundred of us spent a week studying, teaching, and dancing in the Black Forest. The full moon floated across the face of the sun. Worlds crossed. Time stopped.

Some of us were just beginning our studies. Erika Whittaker, a perennial student of the work for eighty years, and other great teachers, graced us by their presence, wisdom, and skill. All of us, regardless of our length of study, were drawn together, powerfully so.

In the blackness of the moon

Twenty-three years ago I naively but bravely ventured out and began introducing small groups of people to Alexander's work. These classes were less than wonderful. Nonetheless, I convinced myself that there was no other way to gain experience. Sticking to principle as best I could, I taught, trusting that, slowly, I would learn and improve. This work held meaning and mystery for me. Would others see its value?

Many did see and gradually my seeing began to change as well. My curiosity about personal use in relation to social, historical, cultural, and political life verged, at times, on the obsessive. Were we Americans spatial gluttons, spreading out all over the place, lacking any sense of containment? Were we too impulsive, overexcited? We seemed driven, more like human doings than human beings: tonus pushed more into the front of our bodies, creating strong façades; energy stolen from the legs and lower back, pushed into the chest, face, and skin.

Was I seeing a significant number of Germans who appeared to be bearing an invisible rock upon their upper backs, wanting to let themselves just fall to the ground in exhaustion, or shame, but simultaneously willing and forcing themselves to stand up, to plod on, no matter what, demanding that they work harder and better than ever, as a point of pride or as a self-inflicted punishment?

Did some people in France look mildly unsure, gently withdrawing back on one side of their bodies, as they reluctantly moved forward with the other? Was I seeing some impulse to distance themselves, to consider, to reconsider, to think, to rethink, to discuss at length, until the moment to act had long passed, come and gone, lost forever? Was I seeing torsion, asymmetry, the spiral of over-thinking, the spiral of under-doing, intertwining spirals of endless ambiguity, spinning into infinity?

Optimistically I thought, "Might these observations be the crude beginnings of a legitimate ethological study of the relationship between culture and coordination, between posture and place, between movement and meaning?"

But slowly, steadily, drifting in front of these over-excited thoughts, appeared a foreboding blackness. In the blackness of the moon I saw the contours of a face. But whose face was I seeing? I stood, staring endlessly into darkness until I recognized, unmistakenly, that face. My heart sank. It was Narcisssus.

Unknowingly, I was casting my shadow onto the world. My shadow, sometimes disguised as a German, a Frenchman, an American, or as a person living in Japan.

The matted braid

It is commonly known on this small, immensely populated island of Japan that "the nail that sticks out gets hammered down." It is, therefore, better to hammer yourself down than to have someone else do it for you, in front of others: the shame of it!

One Japanese man freed beautifully into his primary movement. His tight stomach ungripped. His pelvis ceased tucking under. His chest regained its natural tone and volume without any forcing. More air rushed into his lungs. He found himself no longer looking down, but around. His peripheral vision was expanding in all directions. "*Do deska*?" What was happening?, I asked him. He answered that he felt too important. "In my opinion," I said, "you are important. We are all equally important, no one more, no one less." He heard my words, shook his head yes, saying "*Hi. Wakademasu*" (I am here and alert and I understand what you are saying). But every part of his body and being was saying to him, and to me, that he was sticking out, and I could see and feel that his fear of getting hammered down was overwhelming. His face began to lose colour and he began to sweat. He was about to faint. I grabbed his shoulders and gave him a good shake. "Let it go for now," I told him. I invited him to sit down, to lean over and drop his head. I waited. I told him that I had helped him to have a new experience; that it was just something to think about. That's all. I began to sense, with greater humility, the tight, inseparably woven, no, matted braid between culture and nature.

A turn of heart

Formerly, in this land of earthquakes, houses were brilliantly designed to fall over, to land on the ground, flat and unbroken. Many Japanese people still live with less furniture, so much more of their lives lived close to the ground. Standing, bowing, kneeling, standing, bowing, squatting, standing, bowing, running. . . So many overly turned-in legs. I wondered why.

Was this more turned-in leg alignment, which at first appeared odd to me, wrong? Was "wrong" defined by natural criteria, by cultural criteria, or both? I saw that, in general, people's legs were considerably more flexible in Japan than in America. Why would they want their legs to be, and to look, like our legs, legs that didn't work as well? It seemed that the more I learned, the less I understood.

Times have changed. I land in Osaka airport, two hours after 5,000 people die in the Kobe earthquake. 6 AM. So many people asleep on the first floor of their homes, as their second floors drop square on top of them. We stare into the TV, into the classrooms, where bouquets of flowers stand upon the empty desks, where only yesterday young children sat.

An unusually quiet workshop given on the anniversary of the day, fifty years ago, when Americans dropped a nuclear bomb on Hiroshima, and on all of its people.

A head nurse in a large hospital showed me how she visited and talked to patients, how she bent over a person and listened and cared for that person. I watched, and then I asked her, "Who will take care of you, as you care for so many people?" She became very still, very quiet. Silently, tears began to well in her eyes. They ran down her face. She started to sob, and through her sobbing she whispered, so only I could hear, that she had not thought of herself for over thirty years.

At that moment I had a sudden and complete turn of heart. Thinking stopped. I stopped. Here, beside me, was a human being. I did not care what country we were in. I no longer saw her gray-black hair, or her Asian eyes. I saw her suffering, her loss, her sorrow, her strength, her fragility, and her courage. I saw her.

At that moment my clever pastime of perceiving cultural patterns of use came to an end, "not to a postponement, but to a true stopping in a final sense," as Erika Whittaker had often told me. Teachings from my religious traditions flooded back to me.

People are not numbers. (Post-Holocaust Jews, when they count people, do so by saying, "not one, not two, not three".) People are not types, not patterns. People are not even alike. People are universes. Each person is a world. Could I begin to see people this way, more of the time? I could, but only by way of the most mighty and delicate refusal to compare, generalize, classify, judge, label, conclude, and reject.

The unsettling truth

To Stephen Hawking, one of our great astrophysicists, we are, each one of us, like individual galaxies. In *A Brief History of Time* Hawking speculates,

> Now at first sight, all this evidence that the universe looks the same whichever direction we look in might seem to suggest there is something special about our place in the universe. In particular, it might seem that if we observe all other galaxies to be moving away from us, then we must be at the centre of the universe. There is, however, an alternate explanation: the universe might look the same in every direction as seen from any other galaxy too. We have no scientific evidence for, or against, this assumption. We believe it on the *grounds of modesty:* it would be most remarkable if the universe looked the same in every direction around us, but not around other points in the universe! The situation is rather like a balloon with a number of spots painted on it being steadily blown up. As the balloon expands, the distance between any two spots increases, *but there is no spot that can be said to be the centre of the expansion.*

I wonder. Is there a real, actual centre to our little Alexander universe? I wonder what would happen if, "on *the grounds of modesty*", each and every one of us could deduce that no one country, no one tradition, no one school, no one organization and no one person (not even F. Matthias Alexander, a star who died and whose afterglow we still see), sits at the centre of our expansion. I wonder what would happen if all of us could suddenly see and accept the truth. *There is no centre to either our big universe, nor to our little Alexander universe.* What would happen if we realized, suddenly and completely, that we are the little painted spots, little people, in relationship, floating through the night?

In all of its glory

Why then all the commotion, all the chaos, and all the collisions? Abraham Heschel, a Jewish rabbi, explains in *What is Man* that questions have answers, but that problems have solutions. Heschel writes that we human beings are not questions, but problems; problems to ourselves, and problems to others. Answers are verbal explanations. For us, an answer will not work. Solutions are real. If we are problems for ourselves and for each other, then what can move us, not toward an answer, but a solution? What exactly is a solution?

A solution is the process of thoroughly bringing together different fluid substances into a homogeneous mixture. So first we must become fluid substances. Isn't that part of what our work is about? And then we have to bring ourselves together, from far and wide, into a homogeneous mixture, into a new solution. Isn't that the reason for these International Congresses?

Still, what about our legitimate differences? Will they disappear just like that? And what about our insecurities? And what about that relentless need for us to feel right, to *be* right?

Sometimes it feels to me that the solution to our individual and collective problems, differences, and insecurities is just too hard. As I think this very thought, I can hear Marj Barstow firmly saying to me, "No, Bruce, it's not too hard for you. It's too simple for you." Is Marj right?

Could it be that there is not one great, final solution, but rather numerous, small, temporary solution**s**? Now with that very idea, I notice my neck freeing. Breathing becomes easier. Pressure dissipates. A long forgotten spell begins to lift. Softly, I am falling awake.

Upon awakening, another small solution presents itself. What if we "I"s could become "i"s? Little i's, numerous, small, temporary. Little i's, numerous, small, temporary. Little i's, numerous, small, temporary.

As I say these words, the black shadow of the moon mysteriously stops, as if experiencing a sudden and complete turn of heart. It seems to shift its intention. The great black disc appears to be moving. Ceasing to cover the light, at once, the awesome uncovering begins. Narcissus's face fades from sight. The sun *reveals itself*, in all of *its* glory.

First draft: November 29, 1998, First Day of Advent
Kommunitat, Jesburg, Germany
Completed: October 29, 1999
Erev Shabbat, Philadelphia, Pennsylvania, USA

Bruce Fertman co-directs The Alexander Alliance in America, Germany, and Japan. He draws inspiration from Elisabeth Walker, Erika Whittaker, Richard M Gummere Jr., Catherine Merrick, and Marjorie Barstow (to whom Bruce was apprenticed for ten years). Bruce brings forty years of disciplined study as a gymnast, modern dancer, martial artist (T'ai Chi Chu'an and Aikido), and Chadoist (Japanese Tea Ceremony) to his life as a teacher of Alexander's work. Married to Martha Hansen Fertman, he live in Philadelphia, Pennsylvania, and Coyote, New Mexico. They have two children.

605 W. Phil-Ellena St.
Philadelphia
PA 19119
USA
+1 215-844-0670
e-mail: contact@alexanderalliance.com

Exciting New Research

with significance for the Alexander Technique

Dr David Garlick

A group of Australian scientists in Brisbane and Sydney recently published their findings in regard to improving our understanding of the functions of the muscles of the lumbar region and abdomen (see reference at end of article) This provides them with the basis for a more rational approach to treating patients with low back pain (LBP).

Quite apart from their therapeutic approach, their findings about muscle function have considerable significance for the Alexander Technique:

1. The deep muscles of the trunk, notably *multifidus,* are postural muscles.
2. The deepest of the flat abdominal muscles, *transversus abdominis,* is also a postural muscle and it works in synergy with the *multifidus* muscle.
3. These muscles have a high proportion of non-fatiguable red fibres.
4. When back pain occurs there is wasting of the *multifidus* muscle on the side of the pain; and
5. to restore function to these affected muscles, gentle and continuous exercises need to be used, not strengthening exercises.

Muscle fibres

In humans, the generalization used to be that all muscles (except for the soleus and the specialized facial muscles) have a mixture of red and white fibres (see Fig 1).

It is now realized that the soleus muscle (deep in the calf) is not the only postural muscle with predominantly red fibres. The Brisbane–Sydney scientists discovered that deep

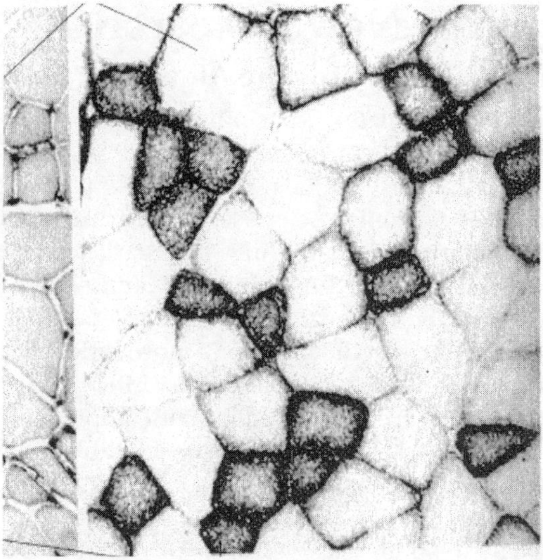

Fig. 1. A microscopic view of muscle fibres with the smaller red fibres stained more darkly.

back muscles, such as *multifidus,* and also one of the anterior or front abdominal muscles, *transversus abdominis,* are postural and contain mainly red fibres.

The actions of the *multifidus* and *transversus abdominis,* assisted by some associated muscles, result in a lengthened, upright trunk. From an Alexander point of view, the gentle, postural action of these muscles would be important in the lengthening process in an Alexander lesson

Apart from these postural muscles, most people have an even proportion of red and white fibres; this is determined genetically.

A small percentage of people have a high proportion of white fibres – making them naturally good in activities requiring strength; also, a small percentage of people have a high proportion of red fibres – making them naturally good at endurance activities.

Red muscle fibres are of two types:

1. postural red fibres (such as are found in *soleus*, the deep back muscles and *transversus abdominis*) which need continuous stimulation to retain their postural function. In the zero-gravity of space flight these fibres atrophy because they lack continuous stimulation. It is probably reasonable to say that most untrained people try to avoid sitting and standing upright and "lengthened"; they therefore lack constant stimulation to their postural muscles, which therefore will atrophy
2. rhythmic red fibres which need frequent, rhythmic activity (aerobic exercise) to retain their functions. This is particularly relevant for maintaining sensitivity to insulin (or restoring it in the case of adult diabetes). Also, body fat is burnt only in these red fibres. More fat is burnt when a person is fit from aerobic exercise.

White muscle fibres can also be generally classified into two types:

1. a mixed type (2A) fibre which has features of a red fibre and a true white fibre. This fibre can be trained to develop more features of a red fibre.
2. the main white fibre (2B) which is the usual white fibre that works without oxygen and is called anaerobic. These fibres are called into action when strength is required. They enlarge or hypertrophy with resistance exercises, such as with weights.

Activation of muscles by the brain and spinal cord

Fig. 2 provides an idea of how these different types of muscle fibres are brought into play by their nerves, which are under the control of various centres in the brain.

Before a movement can be undertaken, postural fibres and muscles need to be activated.

This is a critical point. The Australian researchers (see

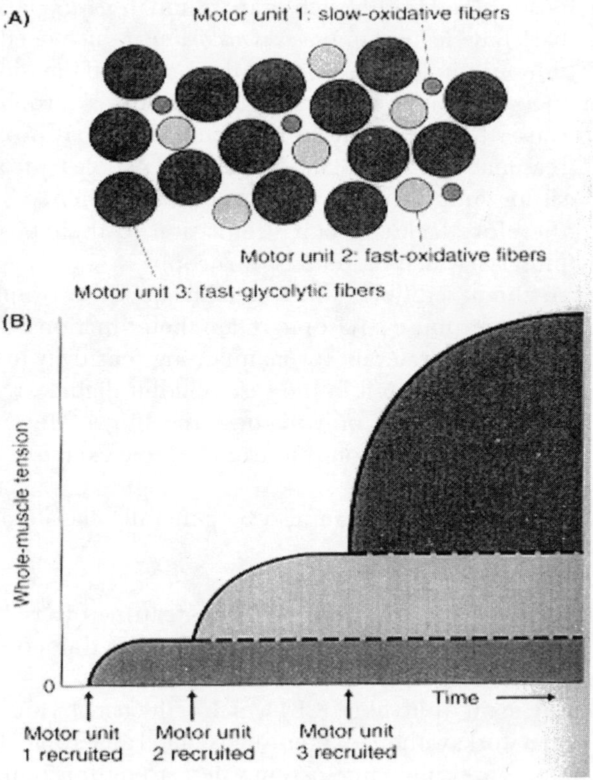

Fig. 2. A diagram of the the time of onset of muscle fibre actions as well as an indication of tension or strength developed. In the upper panel, the small dark circles represent the postural and rhythmic red fibres, the light intermediate sized circles represent the white fibres which are called mixed fibres (2A) since they have some characteristics of red and white fibres; the large dark circles represent the true white fibres (2B). The lower panel indicates that the small, red, postural and movement fibres become active first when a person moves, that the mixed fibres are then brought in when speed is required, and that the white fibres become activated when strength is required.

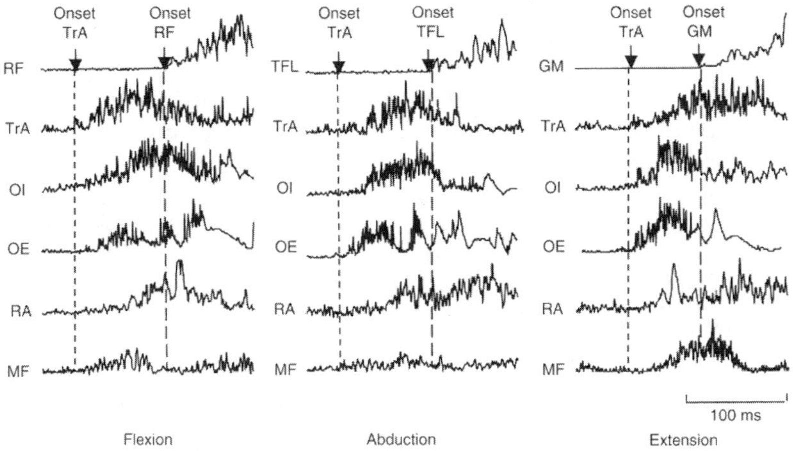

Fig. 3. Electrical activity of leg muscles when a person flexes, abducts and extends the leg. The continuous vertical line indicates the time of onset of action of the agonist for the movement – *rectus femoris* (RF) for flexion, *tensor fasciae latae* (TFL) for abduction, and the *gluteus maximus* (GM) for extension. The other muscles are: *transverse abdominis* (TrA), the internal oblique muscle of the abdomen (OI), the external oblique of the abdomen (OE), *rectus abdominis* (RA), *multifidus* (MF). (From Reference 1.)

below) have shown that weak, atrophied postural fibres do not fulfil this function appropriately.

From an Alexander point of view, it is reasonable to say that this dysfunction happens in the untrained person. The under-stimulated postural muscles do not support the person in the upright position and the person has to use other, inappropriate muscles to remain upright.

The next set of muscle fibres to be activated are the rhythmic red fibres, brought into play when movement is required.

Finally, when strength is required (the person needs to lift an object or they need to sprint or jump) the white fibres are activated.

The scientists studied normal subjects by attaching electrodes to various muscles. Fig. 3 illustrates muscle activity studied in relation to a standing subject who was asked to undertake certain movements.

In the first experiment, electrodes were placed on the *quadriceps* muscle, which lifts the leg up or flexes the thigh (*rectus femoris*); the *transversus abdominis*; the two other flat abdominal muscles (internal and external *oblique*); the *rectus abdominis;* and the *multifidus.*

In the second experiment, the electrode was moved from the *rectus femoris* to the muscle on the side of the thigh which moves the leg outwards (abduction) – the *tensor fasciae latae.*

In the third experiment, the electrode was moved to the buttock muscle (*gluteus maximus*) which causes the leg to move backwards or extends the thigh.

Fig. 3 shows how the postural muscles, particularly *transversus abdominis* and *multifidus,* showed activity before the movement occurred. The standing subject was asked to lift or flex the thigh. Before the *rectus femoris* became active to lift the thigh there was significant activity in the two postural muscles.

This was also true for the other actions the standing subject was asked to make when the thigh was abducted: the two postural muscles became active. Before the leg was extended backwards with the *gluteus* muscle, all of the flat abdominal muscles, as well as the *multifidus,* showed activity.

So postural muscle activity precedes movement.

Patients with low back pain were then studied. These patients were found to have some atrophy of the *multifidus* muscle on the same side as their pain. Fig. 4 illustrates this with a drawing of a cross-section through the lumbar region: a horizontal section which shows a smaller cross-section of the *multifidus* muscle on the painful side.

When these patients were studied with electrodes on their muscles, it was found that the activity of the postural fibres, particularly of the transverse abdominal muscle, was delayed

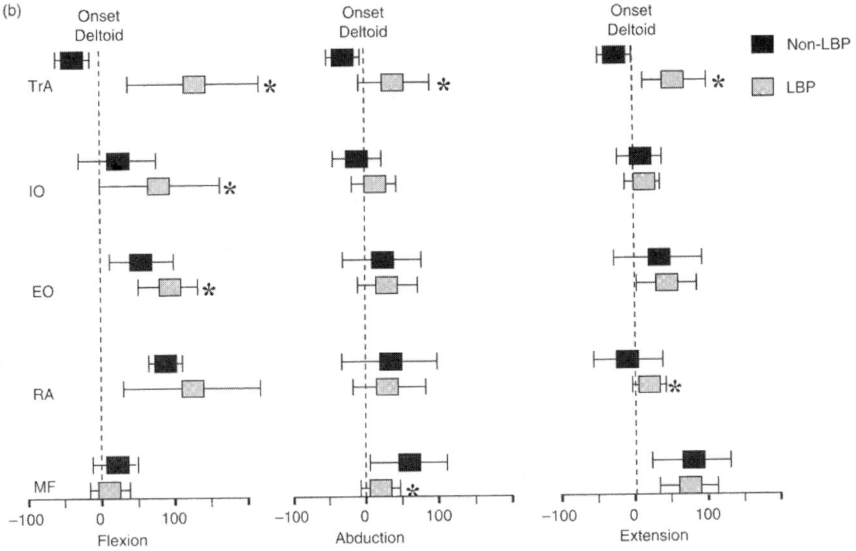

Fig. 4. A summary of muscle activities (see legend of Fig 3 for muscle names) in a number of patients with low back pain with some atrophy of *multifidus* revealed when the patient is asked to flex, abduct and extend the arm. The dotted line indicates the time of onset of the agonist activity of the deltoid muscle; from reference 1.

until after the *deltoid* muscle had begun its contractions to move the arm. Normally, postural muscles contract before the agonist or movement muscles in order for the body to be in the appropriate position.

It will be interesting for these experiments to be carried out, comparing Alexander-trained subjects with untrained subjects. One could speculate that the Alexander-trained subject would show that there is continuous activity in the postural muscles when upright and that there would be an increase in these activities preceding the movement of a limb.

Relevance

These experiments are very relevant to the Alexander Technique because:

1. They identify two important trunk postural muscles, *multifidus* and the transverse abdominal muscles.
2. They indicate that dysfunction of postural muscles results in postural muscle activity not occurring before movement is undertaken; and that the quality of the movement is affected.

This article first appeared in Direction, and is reproduced with permission.

Dr David Garlick is a medical practitioner, senior lecturer in physiology and Director of Sports Medicine programmes at the University of New South Wales. He trained as a teacher of the Alexander Technique 1985–90 with Christine Ackers.

Reference

1. C. Richardson, G. Jull, P. Hodges, J. Hides, *Therapeutic Exercise for Spinal Segmental Stabilization in Low Back Pain* (Edinburgh, Churchill Livingstone, 1999).

School of Physiology & Pharmacology
University of New South Wales
Sydney NSW 2052
Australia
+ 61 2 9697 2557

How did we get here?

Developmental movement and the Alexander Technique

Robin Gilmore

For many adults, application of the principle "head leads, body follows" may be superficial and at times counterintuitive. An experiential understanding of human developmental movement can clarify the coordination and sequencing of Alexander's primary control. By revisiting early movement patterns and reflexes, adults can "remember" how they evolved into upright, bipedal beings and find pleasure in expanding their range of movement and perception.

Since 1988, I have taught courses in developmental movement in numerous Alexander teacher training programs and residential workshops. My own exploration of this material began in the early 1980s with a number of teachers including Marsha Paludan and the late Nancy Topf, both of whom studied extensively with Barbara Clark. Clark was an early student of Mabel Todd. My other influences include the work of Bonnie Bainbridge Cohen and aspects of Bartenieff Fundamentals. Over the years I have honed the material to be a supportive component of Alexander study.

My presentation at the Congress was limited by time to a brief introduction and practice of locomotor patterns and several pre-locomotor movements. Usually I present the work over a period of several days or ongoing weekly sessions. No matter the format, I have found it works best to begin with a locomotor series from rolling through wriggling, crawling, and up to standing and walking. These movements are full-bodied and clear to understand through observation and experimentation. Here we find the underlying coordinations for contralateral movement (arms and legs moving in opposition), as well as a clear sense of the head leading the spine leading the limbs.

Once the gross developmental patterns are revisited, I take adult students further back in time to post-natal reflexes. Most of the early reflexes are superseded, i.e. have disappeared by a few months of age to be replaced by subsequent patterns. As adults we attempt to recreate subtle coordinations through clear thought messages and a sense of allowing rather than forcing an action through large muscle movements.

All of the reflexes that I present are triggered by movement of the head. From sucking with the mouth to tracking with the eyes and ears, each pattern exemplifies primary control. An infant doesn't have the strength or coordination to move individual limbs in a directed way. Rather, the initiation from the head immediately activates the spine, which in turn governs the movement of the limbs. This is not a time-delayed sequence but is in fact Alexander's "all together and one after the other" in action. I find it beneficial to slow down the sequences as I demonstrate so that students see clearly and are then able to experiment on their own. Although some may be a bit shy at first, once the mouthing and sucking are activated, most participants let go of self-consciousness and take pleasure in the sensory explosion.

Space does not allow for an in-depth description of particular movement patterns. It takes far too many words to convey what is easily understood through demonstration. There are in fact a number of fine resources which are listed at the end of this paper. I have included one book about the Dart procedures even though my own orientation to developmental movement stems from other sources. I am aware that the Dart work is taught in a number of Alexander training courses worldwide, so my inclusion of developmental movement in an Alexander curriculum is hardly singular. That said, it has given me great pleasure to offer this material at the International Congress in the presence of several graduates of the Kyoto Alexander Program (KAPPA), a teacher training course I founded in 1993 and directed until 1999. For those brave Japanese trainees who may have wondered what on earth they had gotten themselves into, a willingness to roll, squirm, stick out their tongues, and crawl has helped them to develop into Alexander Technique teachers.

Resources

Cohen, Bonnie Bainbridge, *Sensing, Feeling and Action – The Experiential Anatomy of Body-Mind Centering.* Northampton: Contact Editions, 1993. (CQ, P.O. Box 603, Northampton, MA 01061, USA; tel. 1-413-586-1181)

Goldberg, Marian, editor, *Beginning from the Beginning: The Growth of Understanding and Skill.* Self-published, 1996. (The Alexander Technique Center of Washington, DC, P.O. Box 449, McLean, VA 22101 USA)

Matt, Pamela, *A Kinesthetic Legacy – The Life and Works of Barbara Clark.* Northampton: Contact Editions, 1994. (See above.)

Stokes, Beverly. "Amazing Babies, Moving in the First Year." Video, 47 minutes, 1995. (Amazing Babies Videos, 418 St. Clair Avenue East, Toronto, Ontario, Canada M4T 1P5; fax 416-488-3063).

Robin Gilmore directed KAPPA, the first Alexander teacher training course in Japan, 1993–99, and was a faculty member of the Alexander Foundation of Philadelphia. Her Alexander study includes certification at TAF and many years soaking up the wisdom of Marjorie Barstow. She is a sponsoring member of ATI and a past board member of ISMETA. As a dancer and improvisor, she has performed and choreographed internationally.

6617 Poplar Avenue
Takoma Park, MD 20912
USA
tel/fax:+1 301 270 2399
e-mail: rglimmer@mindspring.com

Using the Five Principles

Concentrating on the lunge, toes and heels, and walking

Avi Granit

Within this workshop I would like to demonstrate the way that I work with my pupils, students, and teacher colleagues according to F. M. Alexander's five principles:

1. recognition of habit
2. inhibition and non-doing
3. recognition of the faulty sensory awareness
4. giving direction
5. primary control

My aim is that these principles will be the basis of the dialogue with the pupil throughout the lesson. I believe that when the principles are within the foreground of the conversation between teacher and pupil, the lesson is much clearer.

Initially, it is important to clarify the roles of the teacher and the pupil. The pupil must try to be responsible for his own inhibition, i.e. to tell himself to stop and not to react; he must then give direction to his primary control. However, it is not his responsibility to initiate any movement. This is the teacher's role. It is the teacher's job to move the pupil while helping him to maintain his direction. In the pupil's mind there should be a clear separation between "direction" and "movement" and of course, it is the teacher's responsibility to make this clear to him. The "directions" are the orders that we have to send from the brain to the body to encourage the body to flow; these orders help the body to expand instead of contract. "Movement" refers to the movements of the body in space.

Of course, it takes time to make this clear to the pupil, and it is an on-going process. As we all know, it is the process of learning the "means whereby" which is important, and not the end result i.e. not being "end-gainers".

So how do I implement all of this in my teaching? During a first lesson, I start with a short explanation, then I make an agreement with my pupil that whenever I ask him to do something, he should initially refuse. By doing this I try to make it clear to him that we are aiming to stop his immediate habitual reaction to the stimulus. This leaves the pupil open and receptive to the new directions that I give him using my experienced hands and my voice. While the pupil and I are working on inhibiting and on giving new, better directions, I will ask him to move. At this critical point I will help him to inhibit his immediate reaction and give the new directions to the primary control. I will continue to help him give directions throughout the movement and even after the movement ends.

Let us take the movement "toes, heels" (moving up onto the toes) as an example. There are many ways to begin working with this movement. However, in my opinion the easiest way is to initially ask the pupil to do it by himself. Most pupils will swing their pelvis forward and will hollow and narrow their lower backs in order to carry this out. Now the teacher's job is to make the pupil become aware of this habitual "wrong" reaction. I usually do this by using the mirror and also by asking the pupil to place his hands on my lower back while I mimic his "wrong" use. I try to let him feel how the back hollows and narrows. This helps the pupil to begin to understand the first principle (recognition of the force of habit) and the third principle (wrong sensory appreciation), i.e. although he wanted to go straight up he couldn't stop himself and couldn't even feel himself swinging forward. At this point I invite the pupil to try the movement again now that he is more aware of his "wrong" use. Of course, as teachers of the Alexander Technique, we know that there is very little chance of the pupil being able to improve his use in this way, but it is important for the pupil to come to this realization on his own. In this way I make it clear to my pupil that without inhibition he will just go on repeating his mistake. I tell my pupil that I will be taking the responsibility for his movement; using my hands I will help him to aim up and stay back, giving directions to his primary control at the critical moment of him moving up onto his toes. This flow is continued as I use my hands to direct him back to his heels.

I feel that by working this way and using the five principles throughout the teaching–learning process, the teaching process always remains clear to both the teacher and the pupil.

Avi Granit graduated from Patrick Macdonald's three year training course in London, England, in 1983. He spent an additional optional year teaching under the personal supervision of Mr Macdonald. In 1985 he returned to Israel and began teaching the Alexander Technique as well as teaching at the Haifa School of the Alexander Technique run by Rivka Cohen. In 1988 he began to teach the Technique to pilots within the Israeli Air Force as part of his reserve duty. He continues to teach the Technique full-time in Haifa and Tel Aviv. In addition, Avi has begun to run a monthly workshop for post-graduate Alexander Technique teachers.

9 Hayarkon Street
Haifa, 34465
Israel

Communication and Vocal Use for the Alexander Teacher

Jane Heirich

Introduction

From the first cry of the newborn to the final sigh of the dying, the human voice is our primary means of communication. As Alexander teachers and teachers-in-training, we try to clarify our thoughts and ideas, to articulate them for our students and colleagues. Do we, in this process, make the best possible use of the voices we have been given? Do we realize how important it is to think about how we communicate to our students, to fellow teachers, and to the general public in lecture-demonstrations, classes, workshops, and media interviews?

How much and what kind of voice-quality change is available or possible for an individual? How can we change our speaking habits so that we can be heard without effort, be easily understood, be emotionally communicative, and speak with a voice that is pleasurable for the listener? What role can singing play in vocal re-education, even if speaking is our primary interest? Are we making the best possible sound of which we are capable, and is it a healthy, beautiful, communicative sound?

This Congress workshop could only begin to address these questions.

As Alexander teachers we have three primary means for our communication: our speaking voices, our hands-on guidance, and our own use or direction. We also have three primary formats for communicating our work: we work with an individual student in a private lesson; we speak in a small lecture-demonstration or introductory class; or we speak in a large forum. In all of these venues, the quality of our speaking voices will contribute to the effectiveness of our communication.

Our task in this workshop was to explore the speaking/singing voice and its possibility for change. If we choose to do so, we can change both the comfort and the quality of our voice use. We should be aware that using our voices to speak and sing can be comfortable: it need not hurt, even if we speak and sing for hours every day. The optimally used voice has comfort without effort. We can also ask ourselves: is my voice pleasant to listen to? What we hear inside ourselves is not the same as what our listeners hear; and speakers/singers often make rather dramatic changes in communicative power when they change their vocal quality via some simple tools. In the workshop we employed some of these tools for vocal-quality change.

There are three reasons we might use singing as a vehicle for change. First, singing is simply an extension of speech – the vowel sounds last longer and are extended over a wider frequency range. Second, it is a good way of opening out or developing the speaking voice, because singing requires just a little bit more of whatever technical means are required for speaking. For example, singing needs more space in the throat and mouth than does speaking, and achieving this in singing can transfer back into the speaking voice. Finally, singing is a personal and social pleasure.

Before beginning the vocal activities, I elicited from the workshop participants their personal voice issues. The following is a partial list of what they presented: limited singing range, breathy voice (too much air escaping while speaking or singing), running out of breath, not being heard when speaking, not always being understood, discomfort or loss of voice after talking to groups or for a long time, and lack of confidence when speaking or singing before others.

Ingredients of basic vocal development

In the world of vocal development, as with the Alexander Technique, the concepts are simple and the tools and directions are few; however, as with the Technique, one can spend a lifetime putting the skills into practice. The vocal tools are the same, whether we are working with speaking or singing sound. Due to time constraints in the workshop, we were able to work with only three of the four most essential tools, but this paper will present all four for your exploration. Two important related matters will also be discussed.

In the workshop handout, I listed "Eight steps to vocal perfection", but in this paper I am reorganizing that material as follows:

1. Learn to release the lower jaw.
2. Learn to lift or "dome" the soft palate.
3. Learn to "open" the throat.

With these first three steps we are learning to create a three-dimensional opening of the space within the vocal tract (the pharynx/throat and the oral cavity/mouth). The benefits of this enhanced three-dimensional opening are: greater comfort, greater clarity of words, better quality, and an effortless volume of sound.

4. Learn about vowel shaping and vowel-to-consonant relationship.
5. Learn about breathing for singing, including the whispered "ah".
6. Learn to speak and sing with tactile feedback on the hard palate.
7. Learn to make vocal fold/vocal cord adjustments per pitch.
8. Learn about whole-system support for the voice.

This paper will explore games and procedures that address items 1, 2, 3, 4, and 5 (which we worked with in the workshop) and item 6, for which we did not have time. The reader will note that I have written this paper as a series of activities for each workshop participant or reader *to do*, always remembering to work with "Alexander thinking", whatever the task. I assume that Alexander teachers and training course students will have the necessary self-monitoring skills, so that all of the following activities will be done with the best possible use of the self.

Before beginning the vocal development tasks, here is the first *to do*: find a book of haiku, nursery rhymes, or very short poems. Open the book at random and read a short poem (about four lines) without any preparation. *Just do it*, not worrying about the content or meaning of the poem, but *do* observe yourself as you read. What issues come up for you when reading poetry aloud? How comfortable is your voice when you read aloud? Can you read without self-judgement, simply monitoring yourself in activity?

At the end of the following series of vocal activities, pick up the poetry book again and read another random selection and observe yourself. Is the reading any more physically comfortable? Are you more aware of what is going on with your vocal instrument? Does it sound any different to you, or to the tape recorder, or to a friend? Does the sound carry any farther, and is the sound louder while using less effort? If you work with the following tools over time, you are likely to experience some of these changes.

Essential skill no. 1: Learn to release the lower jaw

With the aid of an anatomy book (if necessary), find the temporomandibular joint, where the lower jaw fits into the skull. Use your own hands to remind yourself that this joint needs to be free and not fixed.

Make the nonsense sound "blah, blah, blah", letting the lower jaw drop down as freely and fully as possible. As Alexander students and teachers, we know that we must not force the jaw down, so persuade the muscles that control the lower jaw to release the jaw in a downward direction without disturbing your head–neck poise. If you and a friend are working together, you can put your hands on each other's faces and lower jaws to monitor this "silly speaking" activity. If you are working alone, use a mirror (which is a good Alexander tradition) to be certain that you actually are opening your mouth vertically as a result of dropping the jaw. This may feel very strange to you if your habit is to speak or sing with a closed jaw, but this first skill is of primary importance, because without a loose flexible lower jaw, all of the other vocal development tools are almost impossible to learn.

Find a simple song (a children's song, a folksong, a round/ canon, etc.) that you know, and sing it with the syllable "blah", or "la", or "ma", i.e. singing the whole song through with the same syllable on every note. Feel the loose, floppy lower jaw in your hands or watch your friend's lower jaw as it opens and closes on every note of the song. In the workshop we used two songs: the traditional German round "Lachen . . . kommt der Sommer" and another part-song with an "Alleluia" text. If you can find a song with many "ah" vowel sounds, it will be useful for encouraging the lower-jaw release, because this is the vowel that requires the most vertical opening of the mouth. "Ah" has the lowest jaw and tongue position of all vowels.

Lachen

Traditional German

Translation: Laughing comes the Summer over the field/Over the field comes the Summer, ha ha ha, laughing over the field.

Essential skill no. 2: Learn to lift or "dome" the soft palate

In order to locate your soft palate, yawn and notice how the space at the back of your mouth feels spacious and the tissues feel stretched. Look into a mirror and use a flashlight/torch to see what it looks like inside your mouth when you yawn. Make sure that the tongue is lying loosely in the bottom of the mouth so that you can really see the cavernous space available inside. This yawning, doming soft palate is the other dimension of the vertical space needed, and it complements the loosely dropping lower jaw.

Now that you have located the soft palate and seen its normal activity at the beginning of the yawn, you can spend some time learning to begin the yawn without going on to the ending crunch of the throat muscles. Find a rubber band/elastic band to play with and put your hands inside it, with one hand representing the doming soft palate and the other hand representing the lower jaw with the relaxed, resting tongue. Sense the elastic vertical stretch between your two hands as you walk around the room, yawning and saying "blah, blah, blah" with a loose floppy jaw, while all the time playing with the rubber band.

In the workshop we sang the two-part continuous song "The ocean refuses no river" as we strolled around the large room where we were working. As we walked, most people abandoned their rubber bands and used their freely lengthened arms to describe an enormous moving arc over their heads. We added the "Alleluia" and free harmonization on top of the "Ocean"

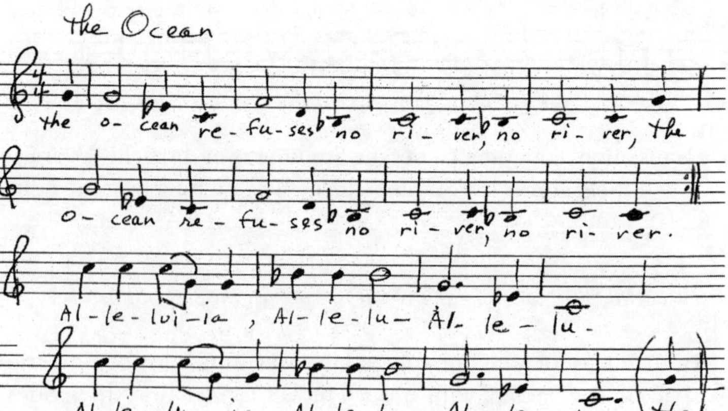

text, and the rafters began to ring with the full-bodied sound that flowed out of the 60 singing participants, as they dropped their lower jaws and domed their soft palates. We sang the continuous song with each person *allowing* the breath to return as needed, with no gasping or sucking in of air. There was always someone else singing, therefore there was no need to "take" a quick breath in order to keep going. This leisurely return of breath will be addressed later in this paper.

Try creating an image of the lifting/yawning/doming soft palate with your moving arms as you sing your chosen song with its text. Then remind yourself that it is equally important to release the lower jaw so that the mouth can open for each different vowel on each pitch. Do not be concerned at this point about *how much* opening is needed for which vowel on what pitch; but simply free up the lower jaw and yawn and let the brain take care of the rest of it.

Essential skill no. 3: Learn to "open" the throat

The third dimension of the necessary internal space for sound-making is the horizontal one. We usually call it "opening the throat", which simply means not to constrict the throat muscles. We can visualize the throat (pharynx) and the interior mouth (oral cavity) as a curved pipe that begins at the vocal cords/larynx and ends at the lips. We need to learn to imagine enlarging the cross-section of that pipe, especially in the tonsil area.

Try the following three games to help you think about this horizontal dimension of the throat while you are making sound.

1. Speak the "o" vowel while playing with a horizontal rubber band.
2. Speak the "o" vowel and sustain that sound while pretending to be breast-stroking/swimming around the room.

3. Stand up and sing the "o" vowel on any pitch while slowly swinging your whole body and arms around in a spiralling motion. The spiralling movement is easier with ankles and knees that are free to bend slightly.

In the workshop we used the Israeli round "Shalom Chaverim" and sang it in Hebrew. Some participants chose to sing the entire round using just the one word "*shalom*", which means "peace".

Shalom Chaverim
Israeli Round
Dm
*
Sha - lom, cha - ve - rim! Sha - lom, cha - ve - rim!
Fare - well, good friends, Fare - well, good friends,
Bb C7 F Dm
Sha - lom, sha - lom! Le - hit - ra - ot,
Fare - well, fare - well! Till we meet a - gain,
Bb Gm A7 Dm
le - hit - ra - ot, Sha - lom, sha - lom.
till we meet a - gain, Fare - well, fare - well.
Pronounced "Shah-lohm chah-vav-reem"; ch like German "noch".
*Succeeding voices enter.

Sing your song while working with any of the three games above – the rubber band, the swimming motion, or the spiralling – or sing your song while simply *thinking* about opening the horizontal dimension of your throat. Then try to include the first two skills from the earlier activities: the released, dropping lower jaw and the yawning soft palate. It is not likely that you will be able to maintain all three tasks simultaneously, but as with the Alexander directions, hold what you can in your mind and continue making the request, "all together in this order and at the same time".

Essential skill no. 4: Learn about vowel shaping, etc.

This skill was just barely touched upon in the workshop, yet it is very important for changing vocal quality, for being understood, and for developing genuine resonance, which allows the voice to be heard over distance with little effort. Vowel-shaping is the vehicle through which we learn the first three essential skills that result in an increased three-dimensional interior space.

With eyes closed, use your hands to draw a picture of what it feels like inside your throat and mouth when speaking an elongated or sustained "ee" vowel, contrasted with a sustained "ah" vowel. Then draw a picture of the interior space that creates the "o" vowel as contrasted with the "oo" vowel. Then open your eyes and draw the same pictures in the air for yourself or your friend. Most syllables of any word in any language contain a vowel with its own unique shape. This brief attention to the shape of each vowel inside the mouth and throat begins to create some minimal vowel awareness.

Essential skill no. 5: Learn about breathing for speaking and singing, including the whispered "ah"

We assumed that Alexander teachers and teachers-in-training were able to self-monitor their breath for ordinary daily living, and that this natural breathing would carry over into making singing sound. However, we spent a few minutes with the Alexander whispered "ah" to remind ourselves of the purpose of that very useful tool for breathing re-education. F. P. Jones is the Alexander teacher who wrote down the way that F. M. and A. R. taught and used that procedure. Jones makes it clear that *taking a breath* came at the end of the procedure and not as preparation, and that the activity's purpose was to re-educate the torso muscles for the elasticity of the natural breath we used as children. So a quick review here:

Speak an "ah" vowel with absolutely no preparation – just use the breath you have. Let the breath return. Sing an "ah" vowel with whatever breath happens to be in the system and let it last however long there is breath to use without forcing anything. Let the breath return quietly. Whisper an "ah" vowel with this same kind of non-preparation, letting it last however long it lasts. Again, allow the breath to return. Think about releasing the lower jaw as in skill no. 1 when you whisper the vowel. Then remember the beginning of a yawn and how that yawn gently releases the soft palate up into a dome, and whisper the "ah" or some other vowel. The three-dimensional opening that you have already met happens almost automatically with the Alexander procedure, because the "ah" vowel choice demands that the lower jaw drop; the inner smile ("smile with the eyes") invites the soft palate to form a dome; and the gentle whispering activity releases excess throat tension, unless you make a rough "stage whisper".

After this review of the whispered "ah" we moved into singing another song, phrase by phrase, and we allowed the breath to return at the end of each phrase before singing the next line of the song. The rebounding breath that is re-educated by the whispered "ah" exercise is the kind of rebounding breath that will automatically happen if we truly are elastic in the torso or rib-cage. The song we used was the German round, "Himmel und Erde", known in its English version as "Music

Music Shall Live

1.
Him - mel und Er - de müs - sen ver - geh'n,
All things shall per - ish from un - der the sky;
2.
a - ber die mu - si - ka, a - ber die mu - si - ka,
mu - sic a - lone shall live, mu - sic a - lone shall live,
3.
a - ber die mu - si - ka, bleib - en be - steh'n.
mu - sic a - lone shall live, ne - ver to die.

alone shall live". The group sang it several times, one phrase at a time; and we took time for the breath to return before we sang that same phrase over again. After working through the whole song in this way, we finally sang it as a round and, because the Alexander singers were quite free in the rib-cage, the breath came springing in with little effort even when we did not take extra time for the returning breath.

Choose a song that has long phrases that use up most of your breath. Instead of promptly moving on to the second phrase or line of the song, take time to *allow* the breath to return instead of *taking* it in. The natural breath will then have a chance to come springing in, and you may find that your rib-cage muscles regain the elasticity that was present in childhood.

A final game for the breath follows. Assume the Alexander lie-down position (semi-supine) with a book under your head. In this instance, you might find that less height is better than more, for you will want to feel comfortable singing in this position. Too many books under the head will crowd the larynx at the front of your throat, especially when singing. Begin with whispering any vowel as you open your eyes and look at the ceiling. Gradually move from whispering into singing, and sing any vowel on any pitch, letting the sound last however long it does. You can alternate whispering or hissing (the sustained "s" sound) with the sung tones, remembering to allow the breath to return in its own time. Do not gasp or sniff or deliberately take the breath in. Let it come in by itself, and it will do so simply *because you are not interfering with the natural process.* One important component of this game: Remember to use your eyes and look at the ceiling as you make the sounds. Looking out into the world will keep you from choking on the sound. This activity is a wonderful one to do in a group, each person choosing the vowel, the pitch, and the timing of the breath. With many different vowels sung on many different pitches and held for different lengths of time, the resulting sound can be quite beautiful.

Essential skill no. 6: Learn to speak and sing with tactile feedback on the hard palate

This skill, along with nos. 1, 2, and 3, is what I consider to be the fourth crucial tool for vocal development. The breathing re-education of no. 5 and the vowel-shaping skills of no. 4 are usually learned during the process of working with the three-dimensional opening.

This would have been the next activity had we had more time during the workshop. At the end of the session, three different participants came to me with questions, and this tool was the answer to their questions. After conscientiously learning to drop the lower jaw, and learning to remind ourselves of yawning for the domed soft palate, and thinking about opening the throat in order to create that wonderful internal space, how do we keep from getting overly focused on the internal mechanics? Looking toward the ceiling while lying down is a good starting place.

The internal vocal landscape includes the hard palate, which is the hard part of the roof of the mouth, lying behind the upper front teeth. Run your tongue from your upper front teeth back to where the soft tissue of the soft palate begins. The hard palate goes across the roof of the mouth from back molar to back molar. We can use this hard surface as a kind of "sounding board", although this is not a perfect analogy. Spoken sound can be felt as a buzz on the hard palate on its way out to the world, because sound is created by the vibration of air molecules, and vibration can be felt as buzzing. If it seems strange to you that you can feel sound, make a "z" sound while lightly touching the front of your throat. Or sustain a humming "m" sound and feel your lips tickle. Put your hand lightly on any musical instrument and feel the vibration of the wood or string or metal. Put your hand on the speaker of your stereo system and feel the vibration of the sound coming through the system.

Sound is vibration, and vibration can be sensed by touch as well as by hearing. Sing various vowel sounds on a lower or mid-range pitch (not a high pitch), and see if you can notice any buzzing of the sound wave on your hard palate. If you are sensitive to the phenomenon, you will be likely to feel the vibration whether you are speaking or singing. If your tactile sense needs to be awakened, you may find that speaking or singing the "ee" vowel is the easiest one to feel. The "ee" vowel has the highest tongue and jaw position of any vowel, hence the sound wave is crowded into the smallest space and may be felt more easily on the tissue/membrane that covers the hard palate. This hard-palate buzzing is observed and directed by the mind, and it is enhanced by use of the eyes looking to the world outside of the vocal mechanism. It is a real phenomenon that awaits our notice; and while some of us are immediately aware of it, others can only imagine the sensation of a sound wave contacting the hard palate on its way to the listener. This tool is useful only for the lower and middle-range pitches; high notes are another matter for both men's and women's voices.

Read a poem while looking at something in the distance, asking the sound wave that comes from your vocal cords to buzz the hard palate. Sing a song, remembering all the things that you learned about creating three-dimensional interior space. Use your eyes and your imagination to direct the sound up and out of that wonderful interior space. Hard-palate sensations cannot be forced but only observed, and eventually the sensation becomes clear for most speakers and singers. The sensations travel around and do not stay in just one place but, in general, the lowest pitches within your voice would be found buzzing broadly across the front of your hard palate. Try it and see what you find out.

Closure

It is unrealistic to attempt to teach vocal development through the written word, so this paper can only serve as a reminder of the sensations of comfort and the healthy fullness of sound that the workshop participants experienced. Alexander students or teachers will already have the necessary self-monitoring skills to use with these activities; and you might enjoy exploring the games, using your own or the suggested songs.

Our speaking voices can be improved in both quality and comfort, and effective communication depends on making a sound that people want to listen to. Singing is a pleasure, and whatever we learn via one mode of making sound can be transferred to the other.

This material is excerpted from a forthcoming book about the Alexander Technique and voice. Those interested in further information can contact the author.

Jane R. Heirich trained as a musician (choral conducting and piano performance) and, after completing a Master's degree at Harvard, studied vocal pedagogy for several years, followed by years of personal study of vocal anatomy, physiology, and acoustics. She completed her Alexander training with Joan and Alex Murray in 1987, and has maintained a private practice in addition to teaching a voice technique class at the Residential College of the University of Michigan.

2229 Hilldale Dr.
Ann Arbor
MI 48105
USA
+1 734-761-2135
e-mail: jheirich@umich.edu

Discovering the Moment of Choice

John Hunter

Alexander, as we now know, experimented with various vocal, respiratory, and physical education methods, and was at one time advertising himself as a teacher of the Delsarte System of Dramatic Expression. Although Alexander's work contains many resonances of Delsarte's pioneering ideas, these, and other physical and energetic techniques, were nevertheless not able to give him the means of freeing himself from the grip of "habit". It was not until that critical discovery – so well described in *The Use of the Self* – in which he found *the moment of choice*; the possibility to ". . . then and there make a fresh decision" that he was ". . . at last on the right track". In this workshop we will explore Alexander's "evolution of a technique" from sensation-based energetic, relaxation, and postural methods to the recognition of the need to re-assess mental activity, inhibition, choice, decision, volition, intention, and his successful attempt to *realize within himself* the relationship between these aspects of human functioning.

My intention in this workshop is to encourage discussion and experimentation as we go along, so please feel free to comment or contribute. As I have a particular theme, however, I would ask that you allow me to, so to speak, steer the discussion in the direction of that theme. Let's see what happens.

What I wish us to discuss and try out is not complicated. In fact, it is very simple. It is we who are complicated. We complicate everything.

We know from the excellent research of Rosslyn McLeod (and for those of you who have not read *Up from Down Under*, I would certainly recommend it) that, in the early days of Alexander's search, he experimented with various vocal and respiratory techniques. In fact he was, at one time, a teacher of the Delsarte System of Dramatic Expression, which is, in many ways, what we might nowadays call a mind–body discipline.

Let us start by considering some aspects of Delsarte's work, because I think it is very interesting that Alexander was not, as perhaps may previously have been thought, a "blank sheet of paper" (but then if one thought about it, how could he – or anybody – have been?).

In looking at Delsarte's life and work we find some interesting parallels with Alexander's own story. Here are the words of the Abbé Delaumosne as quoted by Genevieve Stebbins in her book *The Delsarte System of Expression,* in which she describes the Abbé as "...the compiler of Delsarte's system of dramatic art."

> François Delsarte was born Nov. 11, 1811 at Solesme, France. His father, a physician, died leaving his family poor. The young Delsarte was sent to Paris, in 1822, to study with a painter on china, but his tastes carried him into other channels. He became, in 1825, a pupil of the conservatory, a government institution for instruction in dramatic art, music and the ballet. Here, for the want of proper guidance, he lost his voice. Finding himself thus incapacitated for the stage, he resigned that career for that of a teacher of singing and the dramatic art. Realising that he had been shipwrecked for want of a compass and a pilot, he determined to save others from his fate by seeking and formulating the laws of an art hitherto left to the caprice of mediocrity, or the inspiration of genius. After years of unremitting labour and study – study which took him by turns to hospitals, morgues, asylums, prisons, art galleries etc., patiently unearthing the secrets and methods of past genius – study which kept him enchained by the hour watching children at play in the great public gardens, weighing humanity everywhere and everyhow, he succeeded in discovering and formulating the laws of aesthetic science. Thanks to him, that science has now the same precision as that of mathematics. He died, without arranging his life-work for publication, July 20, 1871."[1]

(A brilliant and eloquent summary. I wish someone could write one as concise and poetic about Alexander.)

Well, the coincidence of the loss of voice is remarkable, and, if that fact was known to Alexander, would certainly have drawn him to try to discover more. Knowing his pertinacity, it is likely that he would have attempted to go into it in some depth, but given that Delsarte did not publish his own work, it is not known to what extent the so-called Delsarte System has been accurately transmitted.

Nevertheless, it would be interesting to look at some aspects of the system. Much of it, with the benefit of hindsight, could be deemed "beastly exercises", but they are exercises requiring a certain precision and, indeed, kinaesthetic awareness. I don't propose today to spend too much time on this; let those who are interested take it further, but the index to Stebbins' book (printed in the 1880s and possibly, unless Alexander came across some itinerant French Thespian who taught him, Alexander's source) makes interesting reading in itself; it includes: "Decomposing Exercises", "Harmonic Poise of Bearing", "Principle of Trinity", "The Legs", "The Walk", "The Hand", "The Arm", "The Torso", "The Head", "The Lips and Jaw", and "The Voice".

One of the principles is the "Law of Opposition": "Simultaneous movement must be made in opposition"[2]. There is a "Law of Evolution":

> Example – Lift your arm, vital force in upper arm, forearm and hand decomposed. Then unbend elbow, vital force flowing into forearm. Then expand hand, vital force flowing into fingers, – all this being a gradual unrolling or evolution of vital force through the various articulations.[3]

The idea behind "deconstruction" is a kind of relaxation seen in terms of the withdrawal of energy from parts of the body:

> I withdraw my will-power from fingers, then hand. Touch it. Do not shudder. Do you feel as if a dead thing had struck

> your living palm? Now I will show you the same phenomenon with forearm, entire arm, waist, spine, hips, knees, ankles, toes, jaw, eye-lids. Now I fall. Give me your hand and help me to rise. I did not mean to startle you so. I have not even bruised myself. I simply withdrew my vital force into the reservoir at the base of the brain.
>
> The first great thing to be acquired is flexibility of the joints. These exercises free the channels of expression, and the current of nervous force can thus rush through them as a stream of water rushes through a channel, unclogged by obstacles.[4]

There are some very interesting ideas here when we think about "direction" as a flow of force.

So, returning to Alexander, who was teaching Delsarte's method in some form or other, what is interesting is that his first attempts to solve his own problem were "physical": he tried to maintain a certain posture of his head in relation to his torso, but was unable to do so in the face of a stimulus. Despite all the subtlety of Delsarte's system (and the other methods he investigated), Alexander was not able to stop a reaction to a stimulus. He had to look elsewhere.

Well, we all know the story, but once he realized that his "thinking" was involved, it may well be the case that he took a look at what was known about "thinking" at that time. The work of William James (and I am indebted to Professor Murray for drawing attention to this in his NASTAT lecture some years ago) may or may not have been known to Alexander, but there is certainly some material there which would seem to have a bearing on Alexander's discovery. If we look at some of the chapter headings from James' most popular work, *Psychology: the Briefer Course,* we will find: "Habit", "The Self", "Attention", "Reasoning", "Consciousness and Movement", "Instinct", "Will".

From the chapter on habit we find such gems as "Habits are due to pathways through the nerve-centres," and ". . . habit diminishes the conscious attention with which our acts are performed."

The chapter on "will" has some very interesting material on volition, inhibition, and consent.

Did this work, first published in 1892, have some influence on the young Alexander as he sought to understand something about the relationship between his thoughts, muscles, habits? Perhaps we will never know.

What, then, was Alexander's contribution? Was he just a synthesizer? Indeed not. His contribution was to find a vital link between the mental and the physical; to realizethat they are part of a whole, and to devise a methodology for practical work on the self in the all important area of stimulus and response. Let's look at what James said:

> The whole neural organism, it will be remembered, is, physiologically considered, but a machine for converting stimuli into reactions; and the intellectual part of our life is knit up with but the middle or "central" part of the machine's operation. . . .
> Every impression which impinges on the incoming nerves produces some discharge down the outgoing ones, whether we be aware of it or not. Using sweeping terms and ignoring exceptions, *we might say that every possible feeling produces a movement, and that the movement is a movement of the entire organism, and of each and all its parts.*"[5]

Is there, then, the possibility of interposing "something" in between stimulus and response? If so, then the consequences (in the light of James's mechanistic view as quoted above) are enormous. There is the possibility of some "input" which is not part of the chain of stimulus and response, a window of opportunity. Where are we to look for this "window"?

Margaret Goldie would often point out that if there is a reaction *in the brain,* then it is too late. If a message has gone out of the brain (if neurons have fired, we might say in modern parlance), then there is no power on earth that can reverse that. Of course, we can send out a countermanding message to hold something in check, but that is something else, and usually creates conflict in the nervous system and tension in the body. So it is clear that the message must not go out. And this is the very interesting area of research that Alexander arrived at and describes so well in *The Use of the Self.*

So we are talking about a different state of mind. I met a very interesting gentleman some years ago who had been a pupil of Dr. D. T. Suzuki in Japan soon after World War II. He told me that Suzuki, who played a large part in introducing Zen Buddhism to the West, had been very interested in Alexander's work and wished to meet him. But it was one of those great meetings of minds which never happened. What this gentleman told me was that Suzuki tried to teach him to keep his mind in a state of "flux": never to let it fix on one thing. He wondered whether or not this related to Alexander's ideas. I rather like the term "flux", as I think it describes very well the state necessary in order to prevent the mind from firing off neurons at every stimulus. The state of "flux" needs a certain amount of attention. It will not come about without it. We have to "be here".

How, then, is this experienced? Can one just change one's thinking? We are moving towards a most enlivening area now. It is called "the unknown".

I was very stuck by something I heard Sir George Trevelyan say some years ago. He said that he had thought for a long time that, in order to be able to direct, one had to inhibit. But, in later years, he had come to think that it may be the other way round. That in order to be able to inhibit, one had to direct. What did he mean by this? My interpretation is that to "inhibit", that is to say, to prevent an incoming stimulus or impression from affecting the brain in such a way that it begins to discharge neural energy, is a very highly evolved function. It is not even possible unless there is already a degree of organization and integration within the organism. Sir George was, at the time he spoke of this, discussing "verticality", and there is something of a mystery in how that relates, but when one has the experience of an inner organization around a vertical axis, there is a sense that in such a "directed" state, there is more possibility of maintaining, or renewing, this state of flux in the mind and not reacting to every internal and external stimulus.

Then there is a certain "potential" rather than "kinaesthetic" energy available. "The readiness is all", and unless there is a certain sense of alert readiness, it is unlikely that one is in this state.

And what then? Well, then there is "choice". But the known still seductively calls one back into the deep furrows of habit. How is one to sustain oneself in this more rarefied atmosphere where significant psychic processes are going on?

Let us now try to explore some of these ideas in a practical way.

(In the practical part of the workshop, my intention is to try, with some volunteers, to first bring about a certain change of state as a result of working with their head, neck, and back relationship and their attention. Having established a certain "energetic connection" between the head and the body, I then present the volunteer with a simple stimulus and ask him or her to explore what they experience. This *résumé* being written before the presentation is given, it is unknown how the participants may respond, but from previous experience it is my hope that they will notice how quickly the brain and body react to a stimulus. We will then try to experiment with "not reacting to a stimulus", without, so to speak, shutting the whole system down (an all-too-often found deadening of one's state which is the antithesis of real "inhibition", which calls for a "quickening of the conscious mind").

We will then explore how choice becomes available, how habit tries to intervene, and how activity can be initiated merely by "giving consent", rather than "doing" it. As this is essentially experiential, I don't propose to try to describe such experiences in writing.)

References

1. Genevieve Stebbins *Delsarte System of Expression* (Werner, New York, 1891) 4th edition, pp. 4-5.
2. *Ibid.* pp. 172-3.

3. *Ibid.* p. 173.
4. *Ibid.* p. 11.
5. William James *Psychology: The Briefer Course* (Harper, 1961) p. 237.
6. Genevieve Stebbins *Delsarte System of Expression* (Werner, New York 1891) 4th edition, pp. 4-5.
7. *Ibid.* pp. 172-3.
8. *Ibid.* p. 173.
9. *Ibid.* p. 11.
10. William James *Psychology: The Briefer Course* (Harper, 1961) p. 237.

John Hunter has been studying the ideas of F. M. Alexander since 1978 and teaching them since 1984. After completing his training at the North London Teachers' Training Course, he studied extensively with several teachers qualified by F. M. Alexander. He has assisted in the training of over forty teachers at two London training courses and has taught the Technique at The Royal Academy of Music since 1985. In 1993 he opened the Westminster Alexander Centre, which offers introductory courses as well as advanced and specialist group classes. He has also taught in Australia, Brazil, France, Germany, Spain, Switzerland and the USA. From 1985 to 1996 he served on the Council of the Society of Teachers of the Alexander Technique and from 1989 to 1992 was Chairman of the Society.

8 Hop Gardens (off St. Martins Lane)
London WC2N 4EH
England
+44 20 7240 2118
e-mail: wac@alextech.demon.co.uk

Educating the Public

Elizabeth Langford

When the Congress directors asked us to put forward ideas for presentations, I wrote back as follows: "It is now more than 100 years since F. M. Alexander made discoveries so fundamental that he could justifiably speak of a 'Universal Constant in Living'. His books – like his practical teaching – had enormous impact in his lifetime. In this rapidly changing world, how can we, as a profession, ensure proper public understanding of the constant and universal importance of F. M.'s discoveries? Does our huge numerical growth guarantee that AT will increase its influence on people's lives in the next 100 years? What other factors may determine the extent of our influence? During thirty years of teaching the Alexander Technique, I have amassed a number of questions of this kind, and I should welcome an opportunity to share them with colleagues."

Then I started jotting down my thoughts, and they spread about all over the place. I find that as one gets older there's a tendency for everything to connect with everything else, which is true, it does. But since speech doesn't work like that, if you're not careful you try to say everything and find you've said nothing coherent at all. I found myself looking at the past, peering into the future, zooming in on specific present concerns. In the end, I got my thoughts into some sort of order, and I'm going to keep to it, in case they start getting untidy all over again – hence all these bits of paper.

Looking through them, it occurs to me that I've raised more questions than I've answered – I hope that won't disappoint anyone. It may not be a bad thing: the right questions sometimes lead to good answers. I'm thinking particularly of a certain young man of about 20, whose impatience with unsatisfactory answers led him to think up some entirely new questions, and to work through them with extraordinary patience. It seems strange, now, to think of F. M. as young and impatient, but he must have been, and we can all thank our lucky stars for it.

Questions: I remember an "Any Questions" evening, organized by STAT about 20 years ago. It is difficult, after such a long time, to remember very much of what was said, but something that has stuck in my mind ever since is that one of the questions was this: Would the panel say what they think will be the future of the Alexander Technique? And I remember two of the answers: Paul Collins, with whom I was running a teacher training course at the time, quoted the preface to the first edition of *Man's Supreme Inheritance.* Back in 1910, F. M. had written: "I wish to do away with such teachers as I am myself." Paul told us what he thought it might mean. I shall return to that. The other answer that I particularly remember was given by Patrick Macdonald. He said: "I don't think it has a future, really." It's all very well for us to smile, sitting here at the 6th International Congress! We're in a growth industry, I know! But I said we'd be glancing back as well as forward, and it won't hurt us to remember the ups and downs and discouragements that the earliest teachers faced not so very long ago.

It seemed terribly sad, that a man who had spent his working life in the Technique should say it had no future. It also impressed me as a bold remark to make on such an occasion. I don't forget that, either, and I have often wondered just what led him to say such a startling thing. What provoked it? Pessimism? Idealism? Perhaps it was the reaction of someone who had known Alexander well enough to realize how far short we all fall of what Alexander himself could achieve by means of the Technique he had originated and developed. I don't remember that Mr Macdonald expanded very much on his reply, and sadly we can no longer ask him just what he meant.

But I suppose we all have our own thoughts about the possible future of the Technique. If we're to discuss them, perhaps first of all we should try to be clear about what we mean by the "Alexander Technique". I have just read a thoughtful report by an AmSAT subcommittee whose task is to define it.

The subcommittee members have also added some arguments for calling it something else, which you can read in their report. What I should like to do just now is think about why it is called by its present name.

Reading from left to right, the Alexander Technique. A man's name. Why not? The names of individuals have been given to all sorts of things. Wellingtons, sandwiches, cardigans, mackintoshes, hoovers, and biros all leap to mind; also plants, birds, animals, comets, parts of the body and a whole string of diseases. Nobody can ever have been more closely linked to what was named after them than Alexander was to his discoveries, and to his practical development of those discoveries into something usable. And arguably, he was better at using them than anyone else. At least, there are still teachers who knew him, and who seem convinced that every other teacher has a long way to go to catch up with him.

All the same, as I said, some people would like to think of another name for this technique. In a way I can understand this, because I once toyed with the idea myself. One can be totally committed to the work itself and still have an impulse to change its name. The problem about that is that Alexander's discoveries have such wide implications that even a concise description is hard to find.

A Belgian directory once tried, with the best of intentions, to describe the Technique, although teachers of the Technique in Belgium were not consulted. The description contained expressions that are better avoided: "correct posture" was one. I'm sure it's best to keep clear of words like "posture", "relaxation", and "tension". Everyone thinks they understand them, and very few people indeed have ever thought about them for two minutes. "Stress" is another word that I think is due for a rest. I hope we won't get drawn into the tendency to use these words carelessly.

That directory entry really had to be corrected, so one of our teachers[1] thought up a form of words: "re-education of basic coordination patterns underlying all movement". As a condensed definition, I like that very much – though I must say, the more I teach, the more I long to say "*de*-education".

However, that would baffle people, and require a lot more explanation, whereas re-education is a widely accepted term.

Re-education of basic coordination patterns underlying all movement. It avoids all those compound words: psychophysical, psychomotor, psychosensory, psychosomatic and the rest. They are all open to the criticism that they seem to imply a dichotomy while saying there isn't one. Again, our description doesn't make any assumptions about causes, it doesn't imply conclusions that need defending. It just says what we are supposed to be able to do, without getting involved in theoretical discussions. That appeals to me. For while research gets tantalizingly nearer to what Alexander knew 100 years ago, theorizing seems almost luxurious compared with the importance of getting on with the job.

Anyway – we had a definition our members could accept. A new name would be something else. The present name does at least bring us back to basics. As long as our work bears Alexander's name, I suppose some people at least will read what he had to say about it – a strong point in its favour.

Then, what about the word "technique"? One objection was put forward at last year's STAT conference – the speaker said she'd banished the word technique from her vocabulary because "it means being very good at something, perfecting yourself in performance. There's nothing like that in Alexander. You don't get better and better at it. You think better." I can only think this was one of those off-the-cuff remarks that come out not quite as the speaker intends. Not get better and better at it? Why did F. M. do all that work? To suggest that improved thinking doesn't or shouldn't have anything to do with improved action seems to imply a total severing of ends and means, which I'm positive is not what F. M. intended. (I don't think I'm a wonderful teacher, but I seem to have been getting better during the thirty years I've been teaching – and so I jolly well ought to! Just give me another 30 years or so, then watch my smoke.)

More plausible is the objection that "technique" sounds restrictingly mechanical, mundane, specialized; that it sounds too technical, so to speak! STAT Council discussed that long ago, when some people thought that "technique" should be replaced by "principle", while others said "technique" was good enough for Alexander, and good enough for them. Certainly the word occurs repeatedly in *Constructive Conscious Control of the Individual,* and in *The Universal Constant in Living,* while in *The Use of the Self* there is the marvellous chapter actually entitled "The Evolution of a Technique".

I didn't think "technique" sounded restricting. As a violinist, I saw technique as the great liberator. You can be what is vaguely called "musical" – so what? Without a technique to put it into effect, your musicality is in chains; nobody will hear whether you are musical or not. Some ideas won't even occur to you, without reasonable technical means. Do you see where we are getting? I could hardly explain my thoughts about "technique" without saying "means" – for technique is the means whereby we gain our ends. Not only that – it is also the means whereby our "ends" themselves can evolve.

Well, that was and is my personal point of view. But terms can be a problem, though, of course, we all know what they mean. Or do we? No harm in thinking about them again. A principle, according to the dictionaries, is: a fundamental assumption, truth or law forming the basis of a chain of reasoning or action. That's a very apt description of the way F. M. went to work, don't you think? Did you know that "technique" is derived from the Ancient Greek word for art? In modern English it means mechanical skill in artistic work, and by extension, a means or method of achieving one's purpose, especially skilfully. Aren't we getting very near to Alexander's "reasoned means of gaining one's end"? We can see why he chose the word "technique". Alexander was a great one for using words accurately, you know. Also, he was an actor, a performing artist.

The principle behind the Alexander Technique, as Dr Wilfred Barlow pointed out, is the great principle that *use affects functioning.* We should never allow ourselves or our pupils to forget this for a moment. Everyone takes it for granted when they think of machinery; it was F. M. Alexander's genius to apply the idea systematically to himself. By means of this principle he groped towards his Technique – painfully, because at that time, remember, the principle was merely a hypothesis. Nobody had investigated it before.

But since the principle, the fundamental assumption, was reasonable, and since F. M. refused to be distracted from it by any difficulties, it became the basis of a chain of reasoning and of action that resulted in a means of achieving his purpose, skilfully, i.e. a technique. And his Technique, applied in practice to a variety of activities, opened the way to the further discoveries, and refinements of discoveries, that Alexander was to make during the rest of his long life.

The hypothesis was right, the principle sound; the Technique works. When you have a technique that works, the thing is to get on with using it, with applying it, with "getting better and better at it" – if you'll pardon the expression!

Why, though, is it still a battle to get people to accept what seems so clear? There are huge numbers of people who relate to themselves in the same way as to their cars. As soon as there is a problem, the cry is "I must get it fixed". 100 years on, they *still* don't understand! Yet it may be that more people than ever before are consciously seeking improved well-being. Just look at the mushroom growth of umpteen therapies, diets, exercise systems, relaxation methods. People sometimes confuse our work with those things, and they'll give us a try in the same way as they try anything else.

They still don't understand that use affects functioning; that it is often misuse that is responsible for malfunctioning; that there is a way of addressing misuse. Alexander's message hasn't got through. What about us, then, the bearers of the message? The brutal question seems unavoidable:

How and why are we failing?

I can hazard a partial guess. F. M., an artist, wanted his technique viewed as an art. He said so. To acquire real skill in any art takes time – lots of time and dedicated work, and a long, long struggle to catch up with our teachers, and – who knows? – maybe one day to surpass them, because we haven't had to find out everything for ourselves like F. M.

Now, remarkably few people have yet had an experience of teaching the Alexander Technique as long as F. M. himself, so I don't think we should get too worried about the undoubted fact that most of us are not terribly good at it yet. When I started, of course I knew I wasn't very good, but I used to take comfort in the thought that I knew the Technique itself to be sound; I knew also that I had had a good training and I was doing my best to follow it faithfully. I reasoned that what I was able to offer was better than nothing and probably I would improve with time and experience. I can't remember worrying about it.

But it seems that, as we become more numerous, some teachers do worry quite a bit. Perhaps with good reason. They ask what is being done or can be done to publicize the Alexander Technique. They complain that they don't have enough work to support themselves without other jobs. Now this is serious, not only for them but for the Technique, because it means that the teachers concerned are not getting enough experience to become as good as they might. So: how should we publicize the Technique?

Publicity, in the wide sense of placing something in the public domain, is important, and we'll talk about it presently. In the current sense of advertising and popularizing, it may be a two-edged sword. Why? The worst disaster for the Alexander Technique would be the creation of a greater demand than we can satisfy. That's when untrained people jump into the gap. We've seen it before. You know the sort of thing: someone has been to a lecture or an introductory course (some people collect them, the more the merrier) and they gaily add the Alexander Technique to the impossibly long list of things they pretend to know about. They may be trying to give themselves what they think is a bit of an edge in publicity terms, but often they are perfectly sincere – I know, because when I hear of it, I ring the person up and ask them what training they have had.

Quite often they start to tell me what the Technique is and why they think it's such a good thing! They are quite surprised to learn that it is a profession demanding a minimum three-year training – and even more surprised when I point out that listing it in their curriculum vitae along with Feldenkrais and Reiki and sophrology and god-knows-what-else detracts from their credibility. Sometimes we have quite nice chats. I resent spending time on this, but it must be done. It's a question of defending the reputation of the Technique and the livelihood of the new generation of teachers.

Which brings me back to the teachers who say they don't have enough work. I wonder why they don't, when the need everywhere is so great. Don't they tell their friends and acquaintances about the Technique? That's where publicity starts. I'd like to help new teachers, if I can. What can I say? I can suggest five pointers that worked for me.

When I began, the Technique was less well known than today. As I started my training, I promised myself I would:

1. always answer questions – even frivolous questions – as sincerely as I could. (That's publicity, too.) If anyone asked me "What are you doing these days?" I told them, which led to "Why, what's that?" if they hadn't heard of it, and to the "How do you learn it/where/how long for?" if they had. It worked rather well. Six months after qualifying, I decided I could risk giving up my orchestral job. I had some lean periods, but I survived.
2. Assume that all questions are serious. (It's better publicity.) Even some of the people I'd thought were putting me through the hoop out of idle curiosity ended by coming for lessons, or sending their friends.

When pupils do come, of course you have to be available, and sometimes at inconvenient hours, so:

3. If that's when they are free, that's when you take them, and never mind if it suits you, when you are still building your practice.

And, of course:

4. You have to be able to deliver, to be convincing, to make a difference. (That's the best publicity of all.) If I didn't think I was getting through to someone, I didn't hesitate to ask them to go and see a more experienced teacher – and accompany them if possible. I'm glad to say my own former trainees do the same thing. I found that:
5. Nobody thinks any the worse of you for not pretending to know everything. (Caring more about the pupil's progress than your own purse is also good publicity.)

In any profession where you work as a freelance, it always takes time to build a reputation and a clientele. It's normal. So it may well be that for financial reasons, new teachers can at first devote only half their time, say, to teaching. But so many people need the Alexander Technique that, to any teachers whose practice isn't growing, I'm going to be rude enough to suggest that perhaps they should be asking themselves a few searching questions. Like:

- Can I, with my hands, reliably give a convincing experience?
- Do I take the trouble to answer questions, and do I know enough to answer them?
- Not to beat about the bush, was my training adequate?

I thought a lot about whether I should put things as crudely as this. I know it's not the done thing; but it doesn't seem helpful to avoid difficult areas. Let's take them in order.

Are you giving a convincing experience? If your pupils keep on coming back, probably you are. If not, what's wrong? In either case, refresher courses, post-graduate courses, and work with other teachers can all be helpful and stimulating.

Answering questions can be tricky. I have heard of training courses where Alexander's books are not studied: it is inconvenient if you can't draw on the basic literature of your profession. I have heard of training courses where anatomy and physiology are not studied at all, and that seems such a pity. We have nothing to fear from facts, and they can make a useful bridge between teacher and pupil.

If you think your training was lacking in those respects, there are ways you can catch up. I read about a system that's been around quite a while now: a way of learning at your own speed, anywhere, any time. It's inexpensive, portable, no attachments, powered by daylight or artificial light. All the information in it is easily accessible: text, diagrams, pictures, photos, anything. You can look backwards or forwards at the flick of a finger. It's the "Built-in Orderly Organized Knowledge System", otherwise known as B.O.O.K.S. or "books" for short.

Seriously, you can't get away from the fact that Alexander's four books are fundamental. People used to be expected to have read one at least, before Alexander would even see them. The assumption was that if you were interested in something, you would be prepared to read about it. That was then. Today, it seems, people's reading habits have changed. Even some teachers find Alexander's books rather forbidding. It goes without saying that more translations are needed. But I know teachers who have learnt English so as to understand what F. M. wrote. (Hats off to them!) On the other hand, there are people who say the books are badly written. One can't discuss taste, and I won't try, because I don't see that it's relevant. F. M.'s books are required reading for our job, and that's that.

But perhaps I can say something to help the people who find them so difficult. I agree they take a bit of getting into – but so does a lot of serious writing. It's never like picking up a magazine at the hairdresser's. Long sentences occur in many other important works; they aren't peculiar to Alexander. Besides, put yourself in F. M.'s place. You've made an important and totally new discovery. How do you explain how you arrived at it?

It can be interesting to try to "translate" Alexander into the kind of writing you are comfortable with. But be careful to keep the exact meaning!

Or, try reading aloud. I once got a group of young actors to take turns at reading the "Evolution of a Technique". They started as if it were a period play with slightly pompous elderly characters. Gradually, all that dropped away: spontaneously, they were identifying with the frustrations and excitements of the discovery. Fascinating – and worth trying.

F. M.'s writing looks repetitive on the page. It's not, but it looks it. This, too, is because what he is saying is so new. He must make things clear – above all, he must not be misleading. So when he finds an adequate phrase, he sticks to it, he handles it in different ways, rather as a mathematician might use an equation. If we try to appreciate the nuances in the apparent repetition, we can follow him, we can be present as he develops his ideas.

Why isn't F. M. given more credit for being precise? Why does Lulie Westfeldt berate him for not explaining that "head forward" doesn't mean "neck forward"? On the face of it, why, when a man is explaining something quite new, *why* should he go into all the things he doesn't mean? Eggs and bacon often go together, but I can order eggs without people bringing me bacon, can't I? Well then. When F. M. said head, what he meant was: *head.* To get his meaning, we have to pay attention to things like that!

Another point: it doesn't do to take an isolated sentence from an early book and assume you've got hold of his final thoughts on the subject. He must have made his first discoveries when he was barely twenty years old. Think how many years of practical experience he had, years to think over and develop the implications of those discoveries. Nobody can get it all in a casual reading. Yet for years and years, the reprints and new editions kept pouring out, and the next book was eagerly awaited. F. M.'s books were considered so important that throughout all the shortages of World War II, paper was made available to keep them in print.

In his writing, Alexander tended to stick to a limited range of expressions, as I said. But in teaching he seems to have tried very hard to say things that would ring a bell with each particular pupil. Some of his quoted sayings are hard to understand without knowing to whom they were said, and in what circumstances – but they must have found their mark or people wouldn't have remembered them. Apart from the teaching and his books and articles, he wrote letters to the papers, to correct misunderstandings and misrepresentation. (And how I wish I could have seen those plays!)

In all these ways, Alexander himself really did a lot to educate the public. By telling what he knew, seriously and uncompromisingly, he seems to have been very good at publicity in its widest sense. In fact, I think he was much better at publicity than many of the people who have written about him recently. It's not nice to criticize; I shan't enjoy it, but I think I must give examples of where I think things are going astray.

What impresses me is how careful F. M. was *not* to say what he *did not mean*. All right, so he didn't draw a diagram of the head on the neck; but at least he didn't draw all the hopelessly *wrong* diagrams we have seen. [At this point, some slides were shown.]

The relationship of head to neck is so crucial to this Technique, that this is something we must not get wrong. I'm not saying you can't give somebody a helpful turn with your hands without knowing a lot of anatomy. I am saying what we all know: the head–neck relationship is vital to our work. It follows that we, of all people, should not propagate misinformation about it. Please, don't think I'm pointing the finger at anyone in particular. I've got a whole collection of drawings like this.

Question: Do those drawings come from books by Alexander teachers?

E.L.: Yes, I'm sorry to say they do.

Question: From which books?

E.L.: I prefer not to say. I don't want to get at anyone, and anyway, these aren't the only ones, just the easiest to see at a distance.

A lot of people imagine the atlanto-occipital joint something like this: lower than it is. So it's hard for them to be free where it really is. It won't occur to them, because they don't know they have a joint up there. Even more people believe the joint to be behind where it is. So of course they hold on tight at the back of the neck. From their point of view, it's only commonsense to stiffen the neck, to stop the head falling forward. Some unfortunate people believe both, like this. (Though I can't say I know anyone who wears their vertebrae back to front!) And, as we all know, some are convinced their head moves from the seventh cervical vertebra. So naturally, everything above is jammed.

In my experience, simple misconceptions like these are among the many reasons why people stiffen their necks, and it's difficult enough to sort out their confusion. To have that confusion added to by the books they read is truly terrible. Since we're talking "public education": don't we Alexander teachers owe it to the public to rid our own minds of that very same confusion? And since we're talking "publicity": I do think the proliferation of inaccuracies may well be a reason why the Technique is not as valued as it deserves.

It is sad that the Alexander Technique is so often seen merely as a form of treatment, one among others that "might be worth trying". Let's not forget we are entrusted with one of the most significant discoveries of recent times, perhaps of all time. In making the Technique clear to people – and even to ourselves – we all face a difficulty that belongs to the nature of our work. We mustn't get bogged down in detail, for what we are trying to offer our pupils (literally offer with both hands) is freedom from inessentials. Yet the Technique is about how we think, so if we can't think precisely about essentials, the freedom may suffer. It's a quandary that won't go away by itself, and may take at least a lifetime to resolve.

To return to the specific point we were discussing, it's true that a helpful anatomical drawing of the atlanto-occipital joint is hard to find. I'm hopeless at drawing, so I asked Enci Noro, who is an Alexander teacher and a highly competent professional artist. It was difficult, but she managed to balance a skull so that one could see the occipital condyles. And she had a brilliant idea – perhaps inspired by those packs of furniture that come with instructions for home assembly. Well anyway, this is what Enci came up with. She also did these simplified diagrams. [Slides were shown of some of Enci Noro's illustrations to *Mind and Muscle*.]

I'm sure we should not be misled by that story of Alexander meeting some leading anatomists, and saying they didn't seem to have benefited personally from their knowledge. He wasn't belittling the importance of that knowledge. He knew the difference between what he knew and what he didn't. So he avoided making a fool of himself, and a number of doctors realized he had opened an important new field of enquiry. He was also held in considerable respect among leading scientists and intellectuals and by people high up in the government.

Of course, not everybody understood or agreed with him – witness the famous libel action in South Africa. That seems to have been largely a matter of those who didn't know his work arguing against those who did; of people assuming they knew what he'd said, instead of reading his books. What an awful warning to us all!

I was glad to hear Tony Spawforth, in his opening address, mention the problem of what he called "sloppily-written" books about the Alexander Technique. As I said earlier, there are huge numbers of people who need the Technique, and who don't know about it. The sheer urgency of their need can tempt teachers to rush into print without sufficient care. A little less anxiety to communicate, a little more (dare I say?) inhibition, might have avoided some embarrassing mistakes, some bad publicity.

For instance: people assume we know something about muscles. Between ourselves, let's face it, some do, some don't. One book has a section on muscles in which almost every standard term used is used wrongly. That should not happen.

Hands are such an important part of our working tool that you'd think we must know something about hands. How embarrassing to find colleagues declaring in print that the wrist rotates! It doesn't. Other strange references to wrists have appeared recently, radial deviation being advocated, sometimes along with pronounced flexion of the *radiocarpal* joint.

It would take too long to go into all the dangers of this emphasis on what are often impractical positions (that would require a lecture to itself) but I beg everyone to read carefully the section in *Constructive Conscious Control of the Individual* called "Illustration" and to consider the implications. F. M. did know a thing or two about hands.

Another thing we're supposed to know something about is breathing. Yet in one book, there are two diagrams of the lungs, and anyone can see they cannot possibly both be right. And here and there, I have seen quoted, without disapproval, remarks that must have Alexander turning in his grave. If persistent myths about breathing are going to worm their way into Alexander teaching, then perhaps the Technique really has no future. After all, F. M. Alexander was known as "the breathing man". First and foremost, that's what he was famous for: he'd proved that it depends on general coordination, and was very definite that we should not try to breathe in specific ways. So-called "abdominal" breathing, for example, is not the same as not interfering – and I hope nobody will drag Alexander's name into it. In this, as in so much else, freedom attaches to precise attention to what F. M. says – and what he doesn't say is also significant.

Voice, of course, is where the Technique started, so there is an assumption that we know something about it. Perhaps we should, but I'm not convinced that many of us do. A reference to enabling the *larynx* to be "open so that the voice quality is true and free" may be an unfortunate misprint for *pharynx* – I hope so.

No doubt we all sound very knowledgeable as we quote F. M. about problems associated with "depressing the larynx". A description of the larynx as "the cavity in the throat containing the vocal cords" is one that depresses me. I mean, how would you set about depressing a cavity? To be fair, I've seen those very words in a dictionary – the one that describes F. M. Alexander as "an Australian-born physiotherapist"(!). But in this case, why rely on the dictionary? What are anatomy books for?

The larynx is fascinating. It's an organ of phonation, an air passage, an essential sphincter (to stop food and other unsuitable things getting into the windpipe) and a blockade to build up pressure for coughing. It consists of nine cartilages, plus ligaments, membranes, arteries, lymph vessels, and nerves; it has moveable joints and 17 intrinsic muscles (eight paired and one single). Its extrinsic muscles are very interesting from an Alexander point of view – but let's not get into that just now. The larynx extends from the root of the tongue to the top of the windpipe. *Gray's Anatomy*, which needs ten pages to describe it, says: "its primitive phonational potentiality . . . would seem to be a fundamental factor in the evolution of human intelligence." (That sounds like quite a "cavity"!)

I have some worries about descriptions and depictions of our practice of lying down with the knees bent and the head on some books. Some people call it "semi-supine" – which to me seems illogical. But what matters a great deal more than what you call it is how it is shown in our literature. That's what worries me. As we all know, this lying down procedure is enormously useful, if only people will do it regularly – and correctly. But we have seen it illustrated with books shoved right in as far as the shoulders, people with their heads so low they seem to be pulling them back, people with their legs stretched out on the floor. There isn't time to show you, but I'm not making this up. I daresay pupils do get up to all these things when we're not there – but encouraging mistakes in print is something else.

It seems such a shame, when this is something people can do for themselves, so easily and with so much benefit – with or without lessons. If more people did it as a matter of course, the back pain statistics that are crippling health services everywhere would drop dramatically. It is something that really should be in the public domain, and it's a serious matter when we, who are supposed to know, don't explain it properly. Of course, if we disagree about how it should be done, we've a responsibility to discuss it, as some of us have been doing this week. (Believe me, I'm not being provocative for the sake of it. Words are difficult – but they are what we talk with! This Congress is a good opportunity to use them, to share our concerns.)

I think how we deal with these things must often depend on context. For instance, this drawing once appeared on a publicity leaflet – though I believe it is no longer used. [Here, a slide was shown in which movements between sitting and standing appear to occur without any forward movement from the hipjoint.] I'm sure it makes a useful teaching aid, to convince pupils that standing up doesn't work like that. The trouble is that so many people believe it does! If they were to see this outside the context of a lesson, there would be a risk of reinforcing that belief. So I think it was wise to withdraw it from the public eye. We can all miscalculate, and it's reassuring to see a mistake being corrected.

But may I tell you when I do seriously worry about the future of the Alexander Technique? I worry when we behave as though we understood everything on God's green earth. I worry when we are so keen to get things right, that we try to control everything (for ourselves or our pupils) and therefore slow movements down unnaturally, forgetting F. M.'s saying: "The right thing does itself." I worry when sometimes it looks as though we've forgotten why we do things, as though our procedures were just rituals, attempts to call forth some forgotten magic. We're not concerned with magic. Walter Carrington says the Technique is "systematized common sense". I think he was quoting Dewey – anyway, I like it. Systematized common sense.

Common sense, systematized or not, has always been a rare commodity, in the Alexander world and outside it. I think a lot of our current problems have their roots in the long period when Alexander's books were out of print because of copyright difficulties. It became highly necessary for teachers to make themselves heard, for there was a spate of quite shockingly ill-informed books: books that made false claims; books full of contradictions; books that never mentioned inhibition by its own or any other name; a book that promised to tell us, believe it or not, "the secret exercises of Alexander" – with a frightful photo of the author trying to pull her own head upwards; a really horrid book by someone who thought the Alexander Technique was about posture, and told us "be your own sergeant-major"!

I knew a man who insisted on reading that one aloud to his family, despite protests. His own daughter was training to become an Alexander teacher, but he put his trust in the printed word. A lot of people do – that's why I'm going on about it. And now we have *Teach Yourself the Alexander Technique*!

Even so, I'm inclined to think that our main publicity problem today is not so much the misrepresentation of our work by unqualified people. What's worrying is that teachers themselves sometimes let slip things that an intelligent schoolboy might question – and thus they undermine the exciting work that is going on in all sorts of fields, and the possibilities it is opening up.

Take music, for example. Musicians benefit a lot from the Technique. The presentations given at last year's conference of Alexander teachers who work in music colleges are really worth reading. But what the public is more likely to see are nice-looking books that can give the unfortunate impression that Alexander teachers are ready to barge in where angels fear to tread. I'm thinking in particular of one where a child who seemed to be playing the violin quite happily has her posture "corrected" until she obviously can't play at all. And then, to crown it all, her photo appears again, printed in reverse, so the instrument appears to be held in the wrong hand. (Very poor publicity!) In another book, you can see obvious mistakes in the use of musical clefs – so embarrassing! And so unnecessary, when you think how many musicians we have amongst us, whose professional advice could have been asked.

Question: What can we do about this sort of thing?

E.L.: It's tricky: you can't ban books just because they're inaccurate. STAT Books appears to have a policy of distributing virtually everything on the subject, without discriminating – at least we can all know what's going on! – and its Teachers' Catalogue does offer a certain amount of guidance. And we must remember that STAT Books itself has published some really important books.

Question: But isn't there a risk that people will think that any book from STAT Books has some sort of official approval?

E.L.: Perhaps. But of course bookshops will continue to sell the careless books. And I suppose that the profits from selling so many books have helped STAT Books to publish some significant books we should otherwise be without.

Question: Can nothing be done to improve the general quality of books?

E.L.: I was coming to that. I have just one suggestion. I referred just now to the fact that we have many musicians among us. The same is true for a number of other disciplines: I think it would be a good idea to publish, for our own use, a list of teachers with different sorts of expertise, to whom anyone planning books or articles could refer for criticism, advice on sources, avoidance of silly mistakes, etc. Perhaps STAT's panel of "moderators" might give this matter some thought, in what is laughingly know as their spare time.

One more howler (the last of this collection, I promise): you may have seen a photo of Paul Collins under the absurd heading: "Olympic marathon record holder". I do hope Paul himself never saw that. I can just imagine his reaction. He would have said, "That makes us look like a bunch of phoneys who don't care about the accuracy of our claims". What's more, it detracts from Paul's real achievements. I think I owe it to his memory to place the facts on record here.

The truth is that Paul represented Canada in the Olympic marathon of 1952, and came 19th, having injured both knees badly, and, as it seemed, permanently. After a long struggle, and thanks entirely to the Alexander Technique, he recovered from his injuries, became interested in ultra-distance running, which means longer distances than the marathon. And in a six-day race I saw him break all the recognized world records in his veterans' class: 100 miles, 200 miles, 300 miles, 400 miles, 24 hours, 48 hours . . . ten official records altogether. I forget exactly what the others were. What I do remember is the compulsory medical check at the end of the six days: the doctor remarked that Paul was the only athlete who hadn't needed his help during the race. Whether or not this sort of thing grabs you, it was a remarkable achievement for Paul and for the Technique. Accurately reported, it might interest athletes more than has been the case till now. That was why Paul wanted to do it.

If you happen to tell this story, please don't refer to Paul as "the record holder" – there must be a new record by now. If you don't get your facts right, someone will notice – and you'll be left with egg on your face. (Not only you – more bad publicity for us all.)

An accumulation of small errors of fact can undermine our credibility in the eyes of people who are experts in their own field. I'm afraid I do get a bit worked up about these things. I should remember what Walter Carrington once told me, when I was going on about something: "Well, Betty, you know, if you do potty work, you meet potty people." [Potty: slang word meaning "crazy".]

Well, perhaps we are all a bit crazy at times. And of course I realize I've stuck my own neck out a long way, since I too must plead guilty to having written a book.[2] I have done my best to check its accuracy, but if you spot any factual errors, please tell me. I mean it. For one thing, I've always liked that saying of Alexander's: "The man who can tell me where I am wrong is my friend for life."

For another, this is a time when our role in the domain of health education is recognized and likely to be under increasing official scrutiny, whether we like it or not. Anyone who doubts this, please study the Report of Committee A to this year's STAT Conference. I understand that similar developments are afoot in a number of countries. Like it or not, we have to be professional.

Which raises the interesting question, professional at what? Long ago, when F. M.'s books were out of print and we couldn't afford the copyright, I heard of an association of "alternative therapies", and was wondering tentatively if a connection with it might have advantages in terms of funding. I still remember Peter Scott saying roundly, "Rather than come under that umbrella, I prefer to get wet." I think he was right, and I hope we can avoid becoming classed as "one of the alternative therapies". Sometimes, even to ourselves, we may appear to be just that. Naturally, when we can teach someone this technique that works, and they begin to use it for themselves, the "therapeutic" effect can be startlingly successful. I've had pupils who were in pain – haven't we all? – and some who were severely handicapped. But it always seemed to me that I was teaching them – learning from them, too. And how!

Briefly then, I can sum up my attitude to this question: therapy, no; health education, yes, indeed. The distinction may not be immediately apparent to anyone but ourselves, but I do think we should strenuously defend it. We know the Technique goes beyond health education, but our contribution to health education is vital. And we may find ourselves less able to make it if the distinction becomes blurred.

Perhaps, however, a certain blurring of outlines is inevitable, given the universal character of the Technique. And perhaps that is why I always read people's ideas about how we might improve the way we present ourselves, or explain things to our pupils. I often long to discuss them. Whether I agree or disagree, they always stimulate a reassessment of my own understanding of basic concepts.

I think that anyone who has been as outspoken as I have today ought to indicate, however briefly, how she understands the fundamentals of the Technique. So here goes:

Inhibition: The story goes that Dewey foresaw the linguistic confusion that might ensue from the popularization of Freud's work, and begged Alexander to avoid the word "inhibition". F. M. said, "Am I using it incorrectly?" Dewey said, "No." Alexander said, "Well then" – or words to that effect. And indeed he was right. But Dewey was right in thinking people would misunderstand. Inhibition is so important that if a pupil is likely to misunderstand the word, we must avoid it, but get the idea across somehow. Yet the precise physiological term is precious: by inhibition we mean the arrest of the functions of a structure or organ, by the action upon it of another, while its power to execute those functions is still retained.[3] Sherrington's explanation is also precious: to refrain from an act is no less an act than to commit one, because inhibition is co-equally with excitation a nervous activity.[4] Obviously nobody can get along without inhibition: without it, everything would seize up.

Alexander introduced a new dimension with his *conscious* inhibition – and we discovered greater powers of choice than we thought we had, and at a level more fundamental than we realized. "Saying no" doesn't quite sum it up – but it's a necessary start. As we learn to use it, inhibition comes to mean choice, as in "When? How?" Inhibition often means "Not yet!" and sometimes it means "Now!". Inhibition is selective, and progressively so in complex activities. F. M. found it to be the logical route from failure to success. The "no" of inhibition became an integral part of his total "yes" in gaining the end he longed for.

Direction for me has all its usual meanings: where to, how to, and taking responsibility for how things go. Giving a lesson could be summed up in the words of the old song: "I know where I'm going, and I know who's going with me."

End-gaining, means-whereby: this is professional jargon – why not? Nobody else uses these terms, but they are useful abbreviations. Ends and means: ordinary English. Everybody speaks of a means to an end, wonders whether the end justifies the means, and so forth. (Incidentally, isn't our discussion of education and publicity really about ends and means?)

Paradoxically, "end-gaining" is pejorative. Yet, if Alexander hadn't had in view an end he desperately wanted to gain, he would never have taken the trouble to make his discoveries and develop his technique. Every time I read *The Use of the Self*, I'm always stunned by F. M.'s determination to reach his "end", and by the roundabout route he was willing to take. He coined the term "end-gaining" to mean rushing thoughtlessly at an end without first considering the best means of attaining it. That hadn't worked for him, so like the practical man he was, he stopped beating his head against a brick wall, and experimented with other ways of going about things. He never lost sight of his end, throughout all his long search for a means whereby he could gain that end. Ends and means belong together and F. M. clarified their relationship for us.

Other key notions for me are: balance; lightness; moving at natural speeds; trust that "the right thing does itself"; the paramount importance of F. M.'s instructions for hands on back of chair.[5] (Those instructions are very clear in *CCC*, and F. M. said that if we can carry them out properly, we have what is needed for using our hands in teaching. Yet I find that many people are not clear about them.)

When I started planning this talk, I expected it to be largely about how to educate the public about our work. . . but it seems to have been more about how *not* to. I suppose that won't shock Alexander teachers too much: we always stress the importance of not doing the wrong thing. Some of this talk has been about educating ourselves. Well, we're all used to the idea of working on ourselves, so probably I don't need to apologize for that, either.

After all this looking backwards and forwards in time, at what I see around me, and at my own attitudes, I wonder if I'm any nearer being able to guess at what Patrick Macdonald may have feared, that evening so long ago, as we were all trying to peer into the future. I think I discern a sequence, at least.

First, as I said, for a long time Alexander's books were out of print. When we had them again, some people found the language "dated" and difficult. At the same time, it was necessary to let people know that Alexander teachers can help them in all sorts of ways. So people within the Alexander world and outside it start writing articles and books. At first this is exciting; then, in some ways, worrying. The teachers of a new generation make sincere attempts to think things out in their own way. There are disagreements, along with a felt need to preserve unity – at least in public. Discussion of teaching becomes more about the *how* than the *what*. Teachers drift apart in this way. Then come the moves to mingle with other holistic disciplines; the suggestions that we should avoid stressing what is special about Alexander's Technique; the appeals to stop being insular, to up-date ourselves, to change the terminology, to change the name. And then what? Do we all pack up and go home and forget about Alexander and his "dated language"? *No way!*

How did Alexander himself see the future? Let's look again at the preface to *MSI*: "I wish to do away with such teachers as I am myself." If you remember, F. M. continues:

> My place in the present economy is due to a misunderstanding of the causes of our present physical disability, and when this disability is finally eliminated the specialized practitioner will have no place, no uses. This may be a dream of the future, but in its beginnings it is now capable of realisation.

He ends by stressing that "it rests with each of us to attain it by personal understanding and effort."

Alexander wrote those words about 90 years ago. How do we imagine that "dream of the future" being realised? What "personal understanding and effort" is required of each of us? About 20 years ago we were discussing it during the meeting I mentioned earlier. Paul Collins said he thought there would come a time when anybody teaching anything would be doing so in the light of the Alexander Technique. Specialized knowledge would obviously not cease to exist, but each speciality would be illuminated by the insights that belong particularly to the Alexander Technique. Paul thought that there would also be a need for what he called "Alexander specialists". They would protect the very core of the Technique, they would be the people to whom we would turn when reviewing the soundness of different approaches.

I think that may very well be so. Ideally, the Alexander Technique should be a required study for anyone proposing to teach any subject. (Rather as in England in my young days you couldn't study any subject at university level without passing with credit an examination in English language, and for some subjects, a credit in Latin, too.) In most countries there are all sorts of prerequisites for the teaching of any subject. I think the Alexander Technique ought to be an educational requirement. Teaching small children, teaching an instrument, or voice, or drama, teaching dance, or sports, or physical education, medicine, nursing, psychology, social studies – wouldn't all these specialities and many others benefit from being studied in the light of Alexander's discoveries?

We have a long way to go before we get anywhere near that ideal. So, although in a way I agree with Paul, I think he was looking a bit too far ahead when he said there would be specialist teachers in all these things and, at the core of the Alexander Technique, specialist Alexander teachers. As we evolve, that may indeed happen at some stage. But if we are ever going to get that far, first we shall all have to be specialist teachers of the Alexander Technique, whatever else we are!

As Dewey said, "of the intermediate acts, the most important is the next one". I think we should now aim at becoming: people who know their subject inside out; people who have got a grasp of both practice and theory; people who can express themselves clearly and accurately; people who are prepared to think and experiment and argue with each other in the interest of getting things right; people who can use words vividly to present the images that are often so useful in teaching; who can use them also to express humdrum facts in the most literal way possible; and who are clear about which way of using words is which!

Above all, we shall need constantly to come back to source, back to basics, back to what people can still tell us at first hand about Alexander, back to what he taught in his life, in his books, and in that tiny film footage of him, which can tell us a lot. F. M. valued thoughtful observation as much as he despised superficial imitation. His parting words to his first assistant, as she left for her first job were, "Good luck, and don't do anything you've seen me do." He had given her the means whereby *she* could do *her* best. That, surely, is why we should still return to Alexander, to learn more about the technique that bears his name. That is central.

Certainly we shall radiate out from that centre in as many directions as our own interests suggest, as many as will be dictated by time and opportunities and demands for what we can do. Just as certainly, we shall need to remain clear where the centre is. A difficulty we shall have to face is the tendency of different strands of learning to fly apart – through circumstances of time, place, personality, individual experience, all those unavoidable conditions of life. We are all aware that there are already different traditions within the Technique. I am glad the Congress directors have encouraged us to face it, for only that could encourage the frank exchanges that will, I hope, help us towards what we all most want: a deepening understanding of F. M.'s discoveries, at the core of all our work.

The summing up of these reflections I leave to a Belgian colleague who is also a psychologist. The other day, she said to me: "You know what I like about our work? It's precise. Also, I like the fact that we don't work *on* our pupils, but *with* them; we don't impose on people, they're free to be themselves. I am always hearing about other approaches that fundamentally are about doing things to people. I don't much care for that – besides, they all seem so terribly vague. Yes, that's what I love most about the Alexander Technique: precision."

Yes, so do I. To explore the freedom and the precision, the precision and the freedom, and their fusion in the Alexander Technique . . . that sounds like a good project for the next hundred years. I'd love to be around to see how it all turns out!

References

1. Malcolm King, who did his Alexander training in Belgium and now lives in Italy.
2. Langford, Elizabeth *Mind and Muscle* (Garant, 1999).
3. *Oxford English Dictionary*
4. Sherrington, C. *The Brain and its Mechanism*, Rede Lecture (Cambridge University Press, 1933).
5. Alexander, F. M. *Constructive Conscious Control of the Individual* (STAT Books,1997), pp. 126-27.

Elizabeth Langford studied at the Royal College of Music and became a professional violinist. She trained in the Alexander Technique at the Constructive Teaching Centre 1966–69. She is former chairman of the Society of Teachers of the Alexander Technique and current chairman of the Belgian Society of Alexander Teachers (AEFMAT).

Rue des Fonds 4
1380 Lasne
Belgium
Tel/fax + 32 2 633 30 59

Inhibition

> Inhibition is a human potentiality of the utmost value in any attempt to make changes in the human self and my experience has convinced me that it is the potentiality most in need of development. My technique is based on inhibition, the inhibition of undesirable, unwanted responses to stimuli.
>
> F. Matthias Alexander, *The Universal Constant in Living*, 1941, p. 114.

Alexander's discovery illuminates our humanity – body, mind, and spirit, visible or invisible, conscious or unconscious – and the self in relation to the world. Drawing on their different lives and research Katja Cavagnac, Ulrich Funke, Marie Françoise Le Foll, Santiago Sempere, with Richard M. Gummere, Jr., will explore the heart of Alexander's philosophy and practice: the principle of inhibition.

Part One
Marie Françoise Le Foll

F. M. Alexander's work and teaching – now our work and teaching – bear upon our ways of being and *our responsibility to shed layers of* conditioned responses to make way for more creativity and authenticity.

From him we have come to see the value of inhibition as a key to choice, verticality, and freedom in the important couple "stimulus/response" and their interactions. He has taught us the "undoing approach" which allows the energy fields of the brain to interact more naturally.

As a young Victorian progressive the idea of evolution galvanized him, and he later realized that in his discovery of a new manner of response he had chosen a path towards the advanced consciousness which posterity must develop lest civilization perish. He knew he had only begun a work for others to continue.

As an actor, Alexander had been steeped in Shakespeare, from whom he often quoted passages to reflect his own burning love of life.

> To thine own self be true and it must follow as the night the day Thou canst not then be false to any man.
>
> Hamlet, quoted in *The Universal Constant in Living*

Here is the first of five short stories giving evidence of *our faculty of inhibition* as a marvellous key to freedom and responsibility of choice and to consciousness.

Through my first encounter with the work of F. M. Alexander in 1972, I discovered the existence of that force and I want to specify that *it does not belong exclusively to teachers and students of the Alexander Technique,* but that they, better than others, should know its nature and function, as well as how to use and how to transmit it.

It took me years to realize that under the word "inhibition" – so often understood as an enemy to life – was hidden an extraordinary faculty, provided we go on searching its properties, again and again, because on that key depends the shape, the meaning, the life we give to it. And if one day it becomes a magic key, it will have the prints of all our movements, our questions, our encounters and solitudes, our doubts and joys, our wanderings and dreams, *and our inadequacy with our verticality; that is our consciousness in relation to our essential and existential life, and there we have the choice to be passive or creative.*

I mention today only a few doors I could close or open thanks to "inhibition" *as a process of undoing our conditioning and increasing our authenticity* in areas we already know and value or those we have yet to discover. Should such a journey interest you, then you need to create your own key for the particular doors you will close and open; that means you need to work on your own verticality, on your movements, at yourself here and now between heaven and earth.

My husband Michel, a Parisian architect, enjoys discussing these subjects with me, and likes to quote other great personalities of the century who are related in similar ways of thinking: for example Le Corbusier, the Swiss architect. In talking to his students, Le Corbusier said,

> . . . I have already mentioned that precious event born out of the forces present, the ones belonging to our rational world, a technicality that can be learnt, and the others emanating from our consciousness, which can only grow through our own inner work. Those of you, lovers of architecture ... may encounter that event you yearn for, the emergence of spirituality, and that only can bring transcendence to our work.

Coming back to F. M. Alexander: he represents for me a man – among others – who took great interest in the qualities of our thoughts, of our actions and reactions, that is, of our movements – maybe because both his personal history and events at the start of the 20th century were for him sources of trouble and of questions about human evolution. We know he searched a lot and he recognized in his own superb manner a "human potentiality most in need of development"... in such fields as education, medicine, society, environment, consciousness ... that he could more or less teach and transmit to a few people and expose in his four books.

Let me now insist at this point that it is not his personal aspects that we must copy or repeat (with the danger of creating meaningless formulae) but his universal value that we should comprehend and develop with respect. Especially as he himself wished that others would continue a work that he could only begin.

Any person willing to read or re-read with interest and attention what F. M. Alexander wrote about our faculty or process of inhibition, will realize that he describes a science of living or an art of living – a way of living which is "against stupidity in living." He writes about our choices and qualities of responses and relations to stimuli, that is, our actions and reactions, our exchanges and our movements at every level of our being; *as if everything could be an action, a movement, qualities or colours of movements*; everything: our steps, our emotions, our feelings; our thoughts; our silences; our presences; our words; our dreams; our memories; our physical-emotional-mental-spiritual attitudes; our language; our ways of thinking, of sensing, and of communicating; they are our movements: unconscious/conscious movements, invisible/visible rhythms, essential/existential exchanges, etc. *Movements and qualities of our lives*; these can be more or less flexible, stiff, collapsed, conditioned, or free and creative, as so many colours in their ever-changing interactions: *simplicity and diversity, at the same time! Now, the process of inhibition becomes more clear to perceive: to apply and transmit – under the strict condition of working with movements and their qualities* and of not "being touched and touching" by our projections and delusions; not confusing thinking and thinking with our emotions only.

To summarize, we could say there are stimuli and there are responses (our qualities of movements, and relations to stimuli; these are often a question or a problem). As to those responses we create and intend to change, it is a process of inhibiting or undoing poisonous conditionings and of activating, allowing, or opening freer responses and interactions, and new expressions of our potentialities.

With children (not only) we sweep undesirable clouds away and sometimes meet the eternal blue sky. It is so nice to be a cloudsweeper and to see how a key of resonance has a magic which a key of reason does not have.

If we accept that we touch not only with our hands, but also with our words and silences and in so many other ways, then it is easy to imagine that a lesson can be a privileged situation for "undoing work": a moment and a place of active attention, receptivity, and decisions. It is also easy to imagine that our life offers us the best opportunities to teach and learn about an "*undoing approach*" in a concrete sense of readiness, creativity, authenticity, etc., where, for example, readiness to lead or to follow, to give or to receive can have a non-doing quality. It does not have to consist of opposing and separated qualities, but of complementary forces such as no/yes, spirit/matter, verticality/gravity, and receptivity/activity.

We can also see how the process of inhibition involves the

duality "closing/opening" as a whole movement, and the time–space we need is not so much a quantity as a quality of our inner space–time. Of course "thinking in activity", even at moments of greatest stress or when we need speed or strength, can be an undoing activity. Let me point out that when we use the verb "doing", we should be precise about its quality, the *how* we are doing, and when we use the verbs "inhibiting "or "undoing"; we should also be precise about what we are inhibiting or undoing: is it our prison or our freedom? Is not our faculty of inhibition, our space of verticality , our autonomy so much in need of recognition or development, because it has so often been ignored, manipulated, and perverted? Do we really have a choice between a thought that imprisons and one that liberates us? Do we recognize where our movements, our conditionings, or our authenticity come from? Do we know to which world we belong, between heaven and earth, and under the law of cosmic resonance? Do we situate our verticality in a world of materialistic values and fear of death, or in a creative and transcendent world where death does not exist? Because we actually touch as we are, c*onsider the importance of what verticality means for us* and how we express it in our being, thinking, and doing. In fact it is not long since I first heard that F. M. Alexander did use his hands, "his non-doing touch", only later in his practical teaching, and then because his students did not understand what he wanted.

In our teaching and training, are we still truly concerned with and working with our innate faculty of inhibition – when it has not been too damaged? Has not that touch sometimes become a support of the teacher's power rather than the student's autonomy in exploring new ways of thinking? What is the purpose of that "non-doing touch"? I hope F. M. wanted it to be a support, a guidance, a direction, sometimes very precise indeed, but from being a precious means-whereby, has it not become too much an endgaining, and sometimes a routine? Do we always differentiate working on somebody from working with somebody? And how do students become autonomous from "hands-on-work"?

These questions lead to this so important one: *What is the reality of our work and of our teaching today, one century later?*

As I meet more and more people who need to work with their spines and verticalities, in fact with their approaches and apprehensions of life and death, shall I begin to apprehend transcendence?

F. M. Alexander was obviously concerned about us being actors of our lives on a stage called the universe, maybe eternity.

Of all his teachings, I value the faculty of inhibition most. Today I can present it to you as concretely and simply as

stimuli
responses I create
the intention to change
the act of undoing my prisons
the opening of my true self.

As phrased above, the key is analytical and inert, but you can learn to make it alive and efficient, you can practise it, it is yours, it is you. You can make it a key of matter and necessity, or a key of spirit and freedom depending on who you are and what you value and want, depending on the reality and verticality you apprehend, depending on what *Man between Heaven and Earth* means to you.

These words are the title of the last book written by Etienne Guillé, a French Doctor of Science, a professor who teaches in universities in Paris that each human being has within himself the hidden treasure of a universal alphabet, carried along by the DNA molecule, affecting every level of life. In other words, everyone is a unity of spirit, soul, and body.

Those were usual words, but became new realities in 1989 when I first encountered his work. I had to accept "faulty sensory guidance and deceptive appreciation", as far as the level of reality of my work was concerned: I thought it could be essential, now it was existential. Most important concepts had to be reconsidered, with a different attention, and a new exigency. Should I continue to mention that our fears, preconceptions, and inertia were our main conditionings to undo, or could I move towards a new apprehension of the human self as a unity (spirit, soul, body); this unity having to rediscover his potential, his symbolic verticality – his transcendent authenticity?

How can I indicate that our "undoing approach" should not deal exclusively with the negative side of our unconscious, but should reach and include the positive side as well, illuminating our conscious life, without our true potentialities being reduced or distorted? Can our faculty of inhibition be a key of reason, a key of resonance, or a key of transcendence? In other words, do we have a choice to adapt to the "having" mode of "producing-consuming-dying" (to become its slave and its property) or to participate in the "being" mode of "creating-resonating" with the world, and in eternity? Different realities correspond to different potential or active structures and receptors in us – in our bodies, our brains, etc., that can resonate with different modes of thinking and acting.

We now can study them. Etienne Guillé's teaching, including both science and tradition, offers a thrilling new ground and exigency for further practical study of our *consciousness.*

I do not say more today but *inhibition* and *alchemy* – a reality? Who knows?

Bibliography

Articles by Etienne Guillé from 1982 to 1985 in *Troisieme Millenaire,* Paris:

L'alchimie de la vie (*The Alchemy of Life*) Edition du Rocher, Paris, 1983.

"Symphonie du vivant: Pour une médecine de l'être," Ouvrage Collectif, Edition Miexon, Paris, 1989.

L'energie des pyramides et l'homme (*The Energy of Pyramids and Man*) Edition l'Originel, Paris, 1989.

Le langage vibratoire de la vie (*The Vibratory Language of Life: Body, Soul and Spirit*) Edition du Rocher, 1991.

L''Homme entre Ciel et Terre (Man Between Heaven and Earth), Edition L'Originel, Paris, 1996.

Le Corbusier: *Entretiens avec les étudiants des écoles d'architecture,* Les cahier forces vives aux Editions de Minuit.

M. F. Le Foll first encountered F. M. Alexander's work in 1972 with Elke de Vries in London, later on was trained by P. J. Macdonald and has been practising since 1976 in France. She has been directing a training course in Paris (1984–95), where she still teaches and lives. She encountered Etienne Guillé's work in 1989 and is becoming increasingly involved in it

99 Rue de Vaugirard
75006 Paris
France
Tel/fax +33 1 42 22 99 90
e-mail: fonde@club-internet.fr

Part Two
Ulrich Funke

I would first like to say how, from my own experience, I have been able to use my faculty of inhibition.

When I speak of inhibition, I refer to our movements in response to stimuli, especially (but not exclusively) those responses we want or we need to change, like closing-in, stiffening, tension, passivity, etc.

In my lessons, I often replace the phrase "to inhibit" with "say *no* to" and "say *yes* to", knowing that in our work everything is an activity.

At one point I wanted to work on a kind of situation which I found difficult to experience and to put up with: situations of conflict. Here is an example:

> One day, I wanted to take part in a dance workshop. I tried to register by leaving a message on an answering machine, asking whether or not I was accepted. Having had no answer, I turned up on the first day of the workshop. As soon as I arrived, I went to see the organiser to explain the situation and to ask him if it was possible to join. The person cut me short, and answered in a very aggressive tone that there were already many people taking part in the workshop, but that as I had come, he didn't really have a choice, and that I might as well join in. Such an aggressive answer immediately affected me and I could feel my temper rising and, at the same

time, I was riveted to the spot, as if paralysed, and didn't say anything.

I knew very well this kind of response (a sort of closing-in, a very strong emotion, and a sensation of powerlessness), having often been through these kind of situations, but I had not been able to change it. I used to consider that it was "beyond my control". On the basis of the exact words used in relating this situation, I defined what, in that case, was the stimulus, and what was my answer to the stimulus:

Stimulus: "The person answered me in a very aggressive tone"

Answer to the stimulus: "I could feel my temper rising, but was riveted to the spot, as if paralysed, and didn't say anything."

Like F. M. Alexander who had noticed that he himself created his own problem ("... it was what I did that caused the trouble," *The Use of the Self*, Centerline Press, 1986, page 8), I started off on the principle that it was me reacting or responding in a certain way to the stimulus that created the problem. (The trouble was about my response to the stimulus and not the stimulus or the situation, as I might think.)

I created my response, and then translated it to reflect my action in that situation:

"I could feel my temper rising" became "I got angry."

"I was riveted to the spot, as if paralysed" became "I riveted myself to the spot" and "I paralysed myself."

But how did I do it, and what closing-up movements could I inhibit or undo? What closing-up movements would I agree to inhibit or undo? I found out what I was doing and could avoid doing in the situation described above, and also in other, similar, situations:

"I look down."

"I keep my eyes down."

"I don't say anything."

This was my first result.

Later I was in disagreement with someone and, after some discussion, I thought that the person started to make me feel guilty. I then realized that I had already adopted my pattern of response in this kind of situation: I had gotten angry, I had riveted myself to the spot, I had paralysed myself, I was looking down, I didn't say anything, and I continued in this manner.

At that moment, I found myself facing a huge conflict, because I not only felt overwhelmed by the situation, but I could also see the closing-up movements with which I was responding; and I couldn't stand it.

So I managed to inhibit and undo the: *"I keep my eyes down."*

After a while I looked up; this has been very important for me.

I want to stress the fact that the act of looking up was an indirect result of the act of inhibition; I had not chosen to look up and face the person and I would not have been able to do that. (The "no" and the "yes" are very close, and we are above all interested in the quality of transformation and opening-up in which the "yes" appears. For this reason this has been so important for me.)

Suddenly, I found myself on totally unknown ground. It was like a leap into the unknown, because the new response to the situation did not at all fit with the image with which I had defined myself, and through which I was limiting myself.

This new response, to look up, was not a totally free answer, but it meant a wide opening-up.

Later on, I have had other occasions of continuing the same work, and little by little I have become able to respond more freely in such situations.

I would like to tell you about a book which I discovered some time ago and which became very important to me. This book is *To Have Or To Be* by Erich Fromm (Abacus, London, 1976). In the passage of this book I will quote now, Fromm talks about "the meaning, of having and being":

> By being or having I refer to two fundamental modes of existence, to two different kinds of orientation towards self and the world, to two different kinds of character structure the respective predominance of which determines the totality of a person's thinking, feeling, and acting.

> In the having mode of existence my relationship to the world is one of possessing and owning, one in which I want to make everybody and everything, including myself, my property.
>
> In the being-mode of existence, we must identify two forms of being. One is in contrast to having . . . and means aliveness and authentic relatedness to the world. The other form of being is in contrast to appearing and refers to the true nature, the true reality, of a person or a thing in contrast to deceptive appearances. . . (page 33).

Then he talks about "the concept of process, activity, and movement as an element of being":

> Living structures can be only if they become; they can exist only if they change. Change and growth are inherent qualities of the life process (page 34).

The distinction made by Fromm between these two modes of existence helped me to think about my work, the sense I give to it (and perhaps to my life), my values, the place and the meaning I give to others, etc. I like his concept of man actively and creatively participating in all processes of life, man being in movement and being movement.

Do I have the choice between these two modes of existence?

Now I come to the research I have been sharing with other people for two years. It is about the relationship between inhibition and the arts on stage, in our case especially dance and theatre.

In improvisations we work on the recognition of our movements of closing-up, tension, stiffening, etc., and our capacity to inhibit them. For example, we realize that very often the trouble is with our ways of thinking, which then express themselves in certain attitudes (emotions, fears, tension, etc.).

We work in an atmosphere of confidence and complicity where the exchange between the person who improvises and the person who observes is of great importance.

This work is above all a training in which we can figure out how to use it well in all situations of life; but it changes – as does our approach of movement and our understanding of the meaning of representation and performance.

It touches important subjects like

quality of presence
quality of interpretation
emotions
difficulty of creating a lively moment out of a concept;
the relationship between "the role we have" and "the person we are"
the meaning given to the act of being on stage.

Inhibition is the tool which helps us to come back, every time, to the present moment. This is very important. Inhibition is our "magic key" to develop our qualities of presence.

But it is a long work which is only at its beginning.

Ulrich Funke has been trained by M. F. Le Foll and is a teacher of F. M. Alexander's Technique since 1997. He now lives and teaches in Toulouse and he continues to work as an actor and dancer. He has been researching the relationship between inhibition and the arts of the stage for two years.

26, rue Montarely
31000 Toulouse
France
tel/fax +33 5 61 290148

Part Three
Katja Cavagnac

The story that I'm going to tell you (which is one that I have lived) can be divided into two parts as far as inhibition is concerned. In the first part, I would like to talk about a form of inhibition which did not take into account the F. M. Alexander Technique. In this case, everything went and had to go quickly; there was no choice. On the other hand, in the second part, I deliberately achieved reflective inhibition. After telling you my story, I would like to share with you my analysis of inhibition.

During my career as choreographer and dance teacher, a moment came when I felt immense fatigue wash over me. From then on I was out of touch with myself. This was particularly evident in the way in which I took on as much work as possible in order to prove to others (and, first of all, to myself) that I was someone full of courage.

My longing did not come from an inner fire which would have made me delve more deeply into myself; I just wanted to prove something. In reality, the form was taking on greater importance than my true inner source.

There was only one way out of the problem and that was to take action quickly, which is what I did.

I gave up everything accompanying a complete and well-filled professional life in order to take a two-year degree course in "the analysis of the body in dance movements." Once I had gotten my diploma, I enrolled in the teacher's school in the F. M. Alexander Technique, directed by M. F. Le Foll. This was an absolute revelation for me.

I thus discovered a method which offered the possibility of managing oneself while at the same time remaining autonomous. My body came alive in its entirety. I came to realize that the "means" used to carry out a movement were more important than the result itself. I became aware that not just my movement but also my whole being were changing.

Yet I knew that I had lost something within myself, and it was at that moment that the real problem began. The question was, what did I really want? Having eliminated the old longing, I had nothing left, and I fell into a black hole. Everything I had done to find a new line of work was failing. I had to persist in accepting the idea that, with time, I would find both an outlet and my equilibrium.

It was very painful to go through this period without taking action, but I realized that the notion of time was indispensable for me. Strangely enough, I began to join together all these new movements within myself in order to construct

– creatively – a really personal manner of transmission. And, luck being with me, work knocked at my door, and I blossomed, happy and full of desire.

If we were to look at this in outline form, it would be like this:

A. Inhibition

1. Dead end.
2. Reaction: acting quickly and nervously.
3. Awareness of a disarray which, in fact, I created myself.
4. Saying no to the form.
5. Saying yes to getting rid of form and accepting the need to analyse the body in movement.
6. Transformation, learning.

B. Reflective inhibition

1. Losing my desire.
2. Responding; first by rebelling, then by letting myself slip into a kind of depression.
3. Painful awareness.
4. Saying "no" to my rebellion and my depression.
5. Accepting the necessity of letting time do its work; accepting long, empty months.
6. Ideas, desires, longings beginning to emerge.
7. Saying "yes" to a re-awakening of desires. At last I am able to choose.
8. Transformation in my verticality, in my proper movement.

Now I pass to the second part of my talk.

Verticality is a movement that is specific to each individual. The basis of my work consists in having each student discover his or her own verticality with all its attendant tensions, whether good or bad, *both physical and mental.*

I help students by encouraging them to achieve self-perception, to remove any notion related to ego, wanting to do "too much" (overly wilful intentions), in order for them to discover their own verticality. Through this method I observed that each one could discover his or her own authenticity.

We were lucky enough to be able to work together over a period of time that allowed these young people to acquire a method of applying the F. M. Alexander Technique. I was deeply moved in observing that they were gradually finding their innocence, as if they were bit by bit taking off cumbersome clothing, and rediscovering their true sources. By getting rid of their awkward and harmful tensions they were able to find greater liberty in the movement of their verticality and also a broader freedom in their mode of being towards the world and themselves.

I'll explain myself with an example:

I ask a student-actor to say a brief text out loud in front of the director.

Stimulus: say a text.

Reaction: panic, trembling, need to perform well, a strong sense of ego.

The student-actor's awareness of his state of tension. He understands that he's creating it himself.

Say "no" to his ego, rather than to the trembling which is the result of his tension.

I help the student-actor to perceive his own verticality, his own movement. Not by touching him, but in speaking, by suggesting that he think actively and rapidly.

This time of active thinking allowed him to discover (to perceive) his proper verticality.

He says yes: he accepts his stage-fright and agrees to adopt his acceptance in his professional practice.

There was transformation in the sense that his body became a living space in relation with the world.

In the end, he could say his text in a very simple way despite a little bit of stage-fright.

As a result of Le Foll's teachings, I am deeply attached to the process of inhibition. My life has been completely changed by those years of apprenticeship and my personal experience as a teacher. They have really enriched my relationship with the world and with myself. Nevertheless, I know that inhibition is a process and a movement and that one is always in a constant state of imbalance; this imbalance is constantly necessary in order to bring about movement, a process which is, as we know, endless.

To summarize, having worked with all kinds of people (and not just with artists), I could say that our work is effective with anyone who desires it and is seeking to be autonomous in his or her own behaviour.

Katja Cavagnac is a former dancer with the Netherlands Danse Theater and the Dirk Sanders Company. Founder and choreographer of the Centre Chorégraphique du Rouergue. Double laureate of the Bagnolet Choreography Contest (1980). Founder of the Emma Calvé Children's Company (second national prize in 1989). First national formation and first pedagogical experience in France of "Danse à l'école." Professor of contemporary and classical dance. Analyst of the body in dance movement (diploma 1995). Certified teacher of the F. M. Alexander Technique (member of the ATI, 1996).

La Galinie
12220 Galgan
France
+33 5 65 80 43 22
fax +33 5 65 80 44 66

Part Four
Santiago Sempere

Form and creative will

My experience as a dancer and choreographer showed me that behind the image of "free choice", behind the phrase "I like – I dislike", even behind the guarantee of aesthetic, moral, and conceptual choices, there lurked a whole stock of conditionings, preconceptions, and habits that were interfering with the act of creation. We therefore tend to prefer known and comfortable emotions to unfamiliar and strange discoveries. We generally admit as "beautiful" something our perception can recognize. That's why certain laws of perspective that we have mentally integrated prevent us from appreciating and enjoying the perspectives born out of other laws (such as cubism, and so on). In the same way, academism or orthodoxy may bar us from entering the aesthetic and personal world of an author. We often have to practise active conscious awareness, and show an open mind in order to live with others: to share, to be tolerant (which means a will to explore the realm of the senses – reality – instead of being satisfied with our falsifying projections of images). In the history of art, there are many instances of discoveries which have been rejected, turned into ridicule, and even strongly fought. Gustave Flaubert thought that the worst enemy of art was good taste. I think this might have been part of F. M. Alexander's experience – in his own particular context of living – which paradoxically might have led him to elaborate the basics of his technique.

His work does not concern a particular concept or an idea but a whole way of thinking. His discovery cannot be imposed; it belongs to a world where *convincing* matters more than *winning*, where the "coming out", the obvious, can only become manifest when the emitting and receiving partners (as in the exchange between teacher and student) are equalled and become an operating whole.

Einstein used to say something like, "undoing a fixed idea is more difficult than disintegrating an atom."

In the "alchemical act of creation", we sometimes stop the process of "letting come out" an image or a form because we are afraid of the unknown, afraid of being watched, of being judged, or of other unutterable fears. We should let something free which has always been there. We should not interfere, we should not separate the imaginative work in process from the awareness we have of our body, from the present context, and from our own thinking. Nevertheless, I think, in the field of individual creativity, whether one is an artist or not, that we do have the possibility to help our students (and if we are choreographers, to help the dancers) to become more aware of those attitudes that impoverish the mind and sometimes make us more censors and judges of good taste than true lovers of art and life. I have noticed that when a work is being created – one could say "is coming out" – our eagerness to get it accomplished, or our excessive emotion may interrupt the process of coming out. The arms and legs of a dancer may sometimes get blocked, the choreographer himself may find many good reasons to limit himself to areas of his psychism that are more reassuring, even if painful, or to rush into conventional forms rather than to visit new and uncertain parts of his unknown creativity. As if we were afraid of starting off from our planet, afraid of wandering into space, with no ground nor identity, with no evidence of our own reality. We think that we are making our own choices, whereas very often our fears are making the choices for us.

Being an artist and a creator myself, I accept that this free creative process is not always a positive movement. All movements of the self and within the self, including trials and errors, are bound to happen. (The concept of inhibition as recognized by F. M. Alexander is the result of such a creative approach). Many discoveries were brought out by error or by chance. A philosopher from Andalusia[1] used to compare movement to changes of state, like the water of a stream which flows from one place to another, like the rain falling down, like ice melting into liquid or into invisible stream, like the metal turned from red to white by fire.

Actually, what takes place in space is "movement": not only spatial movement but also the movement from a state of potentiality to a state of activity, which happens progressively, such as a black item which turns into dark grey, then into light grey, and then into white. We should beware of our own projections, and only be there to help and to allow the movement to find its way and means.

The relationship choreographer/interpreter

We can also recognize certain interrelations when a choreographer persists in working with the qualities he perceives (or guesses to be) in a dancer while still ignoring the potentialities, the richness, and the various possible discoveries which they could both work with – if only he could be more open to his "interpreter". How many artists are left frustrated and broken because of such errors! We should always be aware of such responsibilities in our work.

For his part, the interpreter sometimes persists in offering resistance to his director or to other partners, often because of affective or psychological reasons, more or less under the cover of physical limitations. Very often it is an expression of a psychophysical complex. People can hardly give enough attention and respect to their own body on a stage, which is a place for practice and performance and not for trials. Nevertheless we have to keep in mind that this is a reality which is part of our work, a work of relation. Otherwise we may encounter unhappy surprises, injuries, or come to unfortunate deadlocks.

In my case, through the teachings of Alexander, I progressively changed my own ways of working, as well as the requirements of my choreographic purposes, my own movements, games, methods, and conditions of work. What I previously considered to be of the highest importance, I could now see as a rigid attitude, and what I thought was of humanistic or universal scope seemed rather the inheritance of my own personal history. The "show" must not always "go on" at any cost. A moment of skill, of particular beauty, or emotion should not be gained at the cost of wounds, whether physical or moral ones.

I even say to the dancers that they also should audition the choreographers, and not let the choreographers only audition them. Yet they should also meet the work with a quality of readiness for true adventure, and be free from preconceptions.

Life, creation, death, inhibition

I do not pretend to bring any new enlightenment upon these vast subjects which are for some people mere imagination –

yet who knows? I do want, however, to talk about being with the dying.

Too often in situations near death I saw people frightened, running away from the sick, rejecting them, sometimes with violence, or abandoning them more or less consciously, with more or less guilt or sense of responsibility. Yet other persons have lived those moments as real moments of life, of their own life. They feel that these moments really belong to them, and are not, as is often said, mere "experiences".

I believe that the death of other persons is as much part of ourselves as that which we call life, although we often consider it as opposite.

I would like to talk about what happens when we are assisting a dying person, when we are touching that person with our hands, when we perceive the body of that dying person just at the moment of passing away.

These are, for those who have experienced them, among the most beautiful moments of life, where we feel the closest to creation in its fullest sense.

Provided we are in a state of readiness, have a quality of readiness and openess, we may bring to the dying person some relief, some peace, help his or her love find its expression, or we may simply help him or her breathe a little better, or merely remain there watching time passing – probably the most difficult thing for us to do.

These encounters were the best teachings I had about life. The process of inhibition becomes clear at those moments and there I could learn that this work has very little to do with knowledge or compassion, and nothing at all to do with money.

Some things are hardly taught or even shared:

- to be able to endure time; duration is not a matter of technicality but a quality of consciousness, a quality of responsibility and choice which we all have.
- to be able to let flow, not to allow one's own anxiety in front of death to meddle with the wish to conceal a probable deadline, to refrain from giving false certainties

urged on by some sort of so-called compassion. Up to the very last moment when we can no longer perceive their signals and their self, the dying persons are as alive as we are. This means that they own a gift as we do, this gift being made of perceptions, thoughts, affects and concepts. A single moment includes in itself the past and the future as well as space, whether small or large – a matter of very little significance.

- to be able to let go of our obsession of quantitative measurement is perhaps one of the many "presents" we can receive from the dying persons at the very moment of their death. Our responsibility is very simple: to accept; to be present, wholly, consciously, allowing things to happen; to be ready to answer, and to realize as much as we can that the other person shares with us and with all that surrounds us the same universal nature.

I shall conclude with an invitation to read again F. M. Alexander who gave us the present of his life and work as he aroused in us the desire to transmit and continue his discoveries into an unlimited present; especially pages 242–43 from *The Universal Constant In Living* (Centerline Press): "The improvement and control of man's reaction . . ." and ending with ". . . that sense of his personal responsibility which includes being true to himself, and equally so to his fellow men."

1. Abraham Ibn Daouda (1110–1180) in *The Jewish philosophy of the Middle Age in Islamic land* by Colette Sirat.

Santiago Sempere was born in 1954 in Valencia, Spain. He has been living in France since October 1968. He studied dance with Wes Howard at the Sainte Baume monastery; Alfredo Pietri, the Besso sisters, classical dance, in Toulouse; and Anna Maleras, jazz dance, in Barcelona. He started as a professional dancer in Madrid in 1977 and was part of dance companies in France. In 1985, he created his own company. He has continued as a dancer, both in solos and in duets; a choreographer in residence; a director of his company, giving workshops in dance and in composition; and lecturer at conferences in Europe, Asia and South America. Since 1987 he has studied with Le Foll. He received his Certificate of the Alexander Technique in 1996 and has been a member of ATI since 1997. His activity as an Alexander teacher ranges from individual lessons to group workshops, mostly in France, Italy, Spain, and in Japan, where he had the pleasure of being an assistant to Le Foll at the Kappa school.

4 rue Androuët
75018 Paris
France
+33 1 42 55 32 30

Part Five
Richard M. Gummere, Jr.

Blink of the eye, tremor of the soul

"You can study anatomy and physiology until you are black in the face – it all comes down to this: sticking to a decision against your habit of life." And yet Alexander craved recognition from scientists. The most distinguished scientist to endorse his ideas was the engaging Sir Charles Sherrington. Early this century Sherrington's bold physiological research, which began with the knee-jerk reflex, earned him a Nobel Prize. The research led him, at the expense of a small army of laboratory monkeys, to several epic discoveries, one of them the crucial importance of inhibition in vertebrates.

When I raise my arm, the excitatory nerves take over. But I cannot lower it until my inhibitors resume their role in the democratic government of my whole organism. The political key to the organism's working is the contribution of the inhibitors to the harmony of my two-party nervous system. During the hurly-burly of daily life, the excitors appear to rule the system but they do so only with permission of the inhibitors. If I may continue the political metaphor, when the excitors are the "Ins," the inhibitors are the "Outs," and as in any legislature, a party which is out becomes a loyal opposition. F. M. Alexander and his brother A. R., told by their medical friends of this neurological politics, mistook the present general human malcoordination for civil war. They used to pronounce, pugnaciously, "The excitahs have got the better of the inhibitahs."

Sir Charles knew how to make the most of both excitation and inhibition. When bored with the laboratory at the hospital where he worked, he would let his excitors drive him to the top of its tower for parachute jumps. During World War I, on the other hand, his inhibitors took over one day and he disappeared, leaving no address or phone, even for his wife. He did come home to replace a lost collar stud – you couldn't buy them in wartime – but disappeared again. He'd taken a factory job to study worker fatigue – *incognito.*

Today, another biologist, Benjamin Libet, attached to the medical school of the University of California at San Francisco, has stepped up to join Sherrington in support of F. M. Alexander's concept of inhibition. In his research he had relied, not on the torment of animals, but on the patience of human volunteers. Some of you may have heard Dr Libet at the 1989 annual meeting of NASTAT where he summarized a scholarly article: "Unconscious cerebral initiative and the role of conscious will in voluntary action." In this study, Libet goes farther than Sherrington by even clocking precisely the time we are offered to inhibit.

Let's imagine a millisecond. A thousand milliseconds make one second. Now, would *you* say these three little words, quickly: "one one-thousand." That took us one second. Libet found that a typical human response to a stimulus takes half of a second, or five hundred milliseconds. The phone rings and the first 350 milliseconds of our response are preparation for the action we'll take. But these 350 are unconscious. So are the last 50 milliseconds, the action itself, which goes off like a gun after you've pulled the trigger. You recently bought a lottery ticket and they may be calling to tell you you've won. More likely it's dear old Aunt Polly, who is a champion talker. No matter: in between the unconscious preparation and action, 100 milliseconds whizz by in a flash of consciousness – less than a blink of the eye. Now please stare ahead for a moment and then allow a quick natural blink. Call one quarter of that blink – *inhibition time.*

That's an incredibly small window of opportunity for deciding whether to try something new and creative or to protect the old and familiar. Sherrington proved that, in its watch over our behaviour, inhibition is not excitation's fool. In other words, as he told the bustling Edwardians, not doing something is just as much an act as doing it. Indeed, in his tome *The Integrative Action of the Nervous System*, Sherrington glorifies inhibition for its subtle but irresistible command over our whole person. In how many studios of Alexander teachers, however, have you seen our stately human skeleton or our gory musculature set off by another wall chart? Where is the exquisite filigree of our nervous system, the servant of the brain? Doesn't this omission reflect a dangerous bias in the rhetoric of today's promotion of the Alexander Work? And doesn't that habit suggest a general departure from the founder's attention to the whole self?

What does happen in that 100 milliseconds, which is given to us for change? Does our will nudge some flow of energy into a new channel? Or do our born reflexes see and seize the opportunity? Or can we count on the creativity some physicists say will come to each of us from the quantum world? None of these wonders could happen without Benjamin Libet's little window opening up for us. And now – what's that voice I hear coming down from the ziggurat? Everybody listen. It's a British accent. There it is again: *"inhibition time."*

Richard M. Gummere, Jr., studied with F. M. and A. R. Alexander and qualified as a teacher in 1944. He graduated from Harvard in 1934 with a B. A. and in 1951 from Haverford with an M. A., both degrees in Latin and English. In the early 1960s, he did a doctoral study in Guidance at Teachers College of Columbia University. He is author of *How to Survive Education* (1971), a characterization of American colleges and universities.

2 Station Hill Road
Barrytown
N.Y. 12507
USA
+1 914 7585 088

Using the Arms:

The ancestry of the human arm

Jamie McDowell

In this talk I will review the evidence that the human arm derives from the arm of an antecedent climbing primate. I will make practical suggestions about using the arm in a way which takes account of this heritage. I will propose some clarification as to what the human arm is *not.*

First, I wish to remind you of our general evolutionary context. The significant starting point here is that we are vertebrates. That is to say, the vertebral column is a distinctive feature of our anatomy, and is fundamental to our physical form. We are not insects, nor are we molluscs. The directions for insects would surely be very different. Probably the directions as we know them would work for all vertebrates.

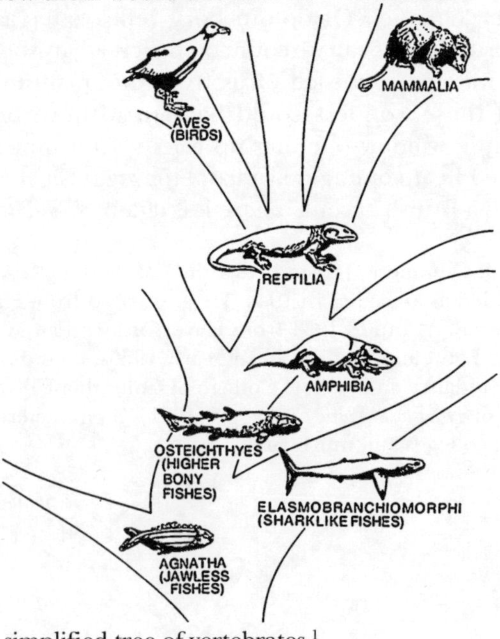

Fig. 1. A simplified tree of vertebrates.[1]

Vertebrates are all descendents of an ancient segmented sea-worm. Although the group is generally drawn with fish at the bottom and mammals at the top, we can remember that this is an arbitrary arrangement, and we have the privilege, rather than the right, of being placed at the top (Fig. 1).

If we want to draw the diagram another way, we could put the fish at the centre, the trunk of the evolutionary tree, with the herring, the most numerous vertebrate, at the top. Mammals are then a side shoot, and primates a small twig off one branch.

I want to make two points about fish:

1. They move by flexing first one side, then the other, a movement pattern which pulls the tail from side to side. They do not move by rowing with their fins. The fins are there to give stability to the creature as it moves through water; they keep the top uppermost and enable the fish to go in the chosen direction (Fig. 2), which is what they do most of the time. Fish spend most of their time swimming around looking for something to eat, usually other fish.

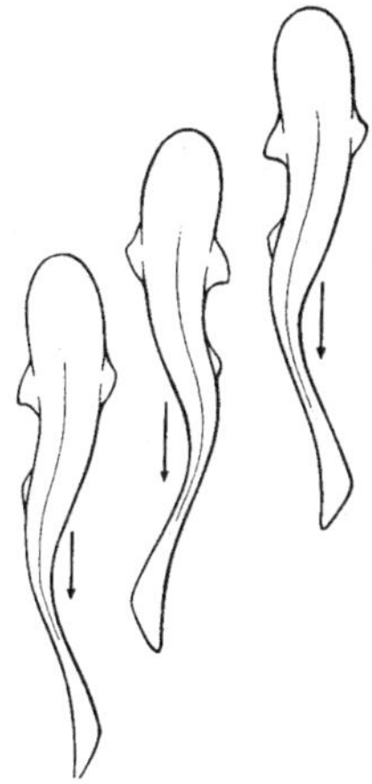

Fig. 2. Fish movement pattern.

Fig. 3. Salamander movement pattern.

2. What gives modern fish an advantage is their bony jaw. When you have a bony, articulated jaw, you can close your mouth while eating. This enables you to consider a larger menu. This is the unsavoury basis of our success in the past.

The progression from sea to land in the evolutionary story is probably familiar to most of us Some fish lived in tidal muddy regions. In order to remain on the spot, neither swept out to sea nor stranded by an incoming tide, the *stabilising* fins became capable of exerting a little leverage in the mud, holding the animal against the pull of the moving water. When conditions changed, and the sea receded, leaving muddy banks, the survivors were the ones who were able to use these strengthened fins to move around across the mud. These creatures developed to become the amphibians, which still need wet skin in order to breathe successfully, and they developed to become reptiles, whose leathery scales give them access to drier regions inland. Note that these move in the fish-like way, flexing each side in turn in order to fling the limbs forward (Fig. 3).

It's an inefficient mode of locomotion, and crocodiles tire easily when in motion. They prefer to support the body weight on the ground and not on their limbs. When they are walking, they are doing constant press-ups.

The reptiles were tremendously successful for about 200 million years, from about 300 million to 100 million years ago. After the decline of the big reptiles – dinosaurs – the ancestral mammal appears. The modern mammal most similar to that ancestor is the tree shrew (Fig. 4).

It is small. As the name suggests it lives in a tree, and it is *insectivorous*; our ancestors ate insects. The significance of this is that, in order to catch insects when you live in a tree, you need:

1. good binocular vision
2. a rotating forearm and a grasping hand

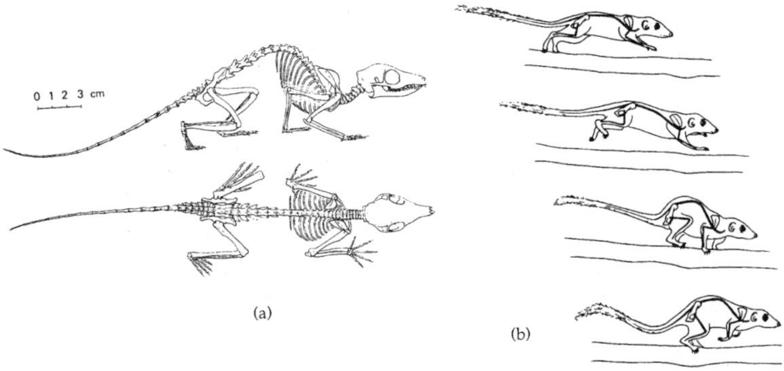

Fig. 4. Skeleton and movement pattern of a tree shrew.[2]

3. a more than usually flexible spine, so that you can reach around the back of branches.

All of these attributes are identifiable in the modern human.

Look at this series of pictures of a boy walking (Fig. 5). Notice that his upper torso can rotate by about 45 degrees in relation to his pelvis and the direction of travel.

We do not often see this rotational flexibility in adults. Try this for yourself:

Place one hand on your sternum, at the top; place the other hand at the arch of your ribs. Now move the top hand away from the lower as you look over the shoulder of your upper hand.

Your ribs have the capacity to rotate in this way. The anatomical detail helps to make this clear: the joints between successive vertebrae, called "facet joints", in the thoracic (rib) region, permit this axial rotation. Interestingly, no such rotation is possible in the lumbar region of the spine, although it does bend forward rather well.

It is at this point that we can divest ourselves of the first misconception about arms: that we were brachiators, like the

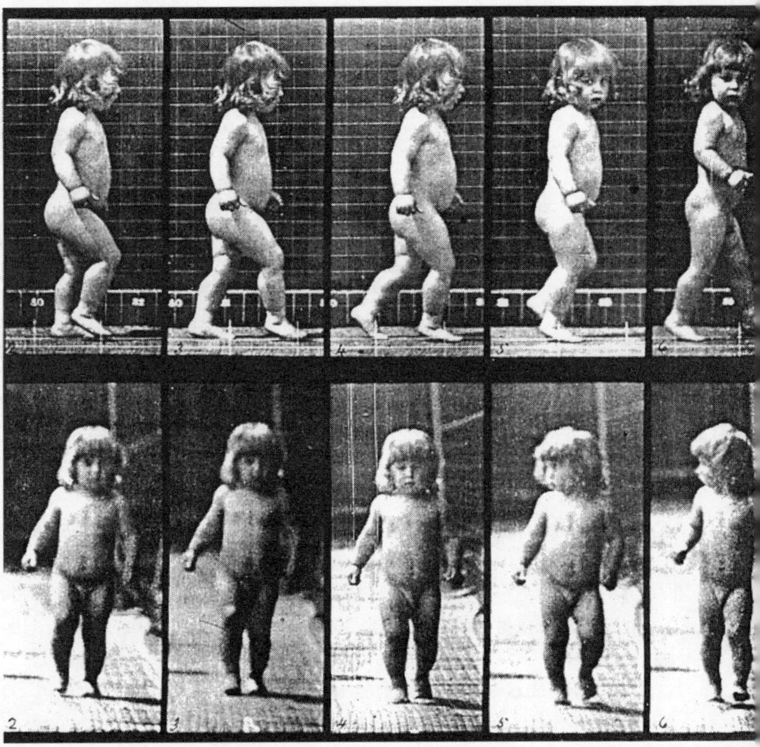

Fig. 5. Boy walking.[3]

gibbon, swinging gracefully from branch to branch using our arms as the primary support for the body weight (Fig.6). It probably wasn't so. The rotating (door-handle opening) forearm, which we have, was developed for picking up insects. Try the gibbon movement. You'll see that you don't have enough rotation at the elbow. 180 degrees is not enough. The gibbon has 270 degrees.

It is probably the legacy of the Tarzan films that so many of us imagine that brachiation is possible for us. It is not – we would fall out of the trees.

The human arm is not a brachiating arm. What is it then?

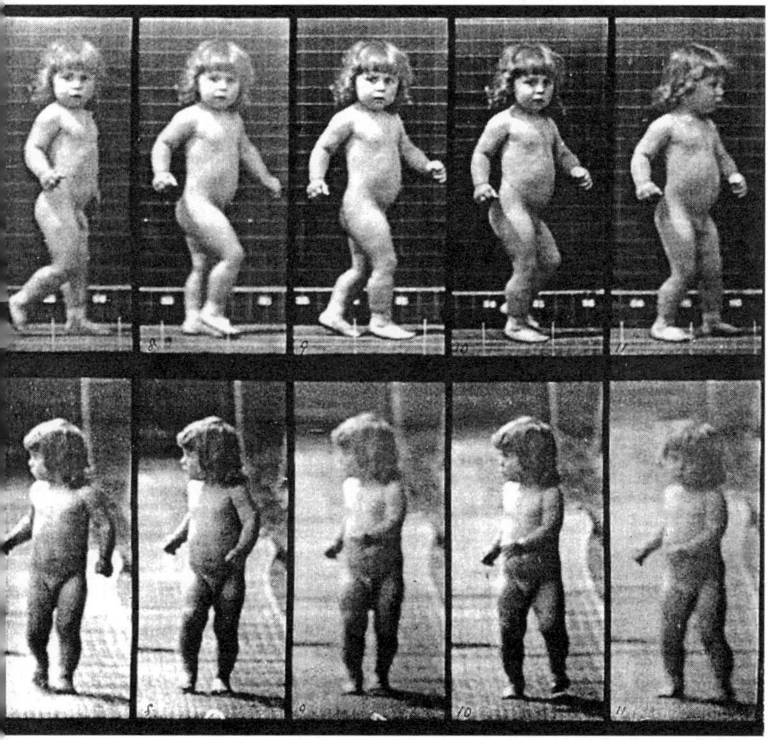

The following quotations from a recent book[5] on evolutionary anatomy cast some light on this:

> [Studies] have shown that vertical climbing in primates is much more similar to human bipedal locomotion in joint excursion and muscle usage, and may have been the precursor form of locomotion to human bipedalism.[6]

> and

> . . . there is no skeletal evidence for humans having passed through a knuckle walking stage of locomotion.[7]

Fig. 6. Brachiating gibbon.[4]

In other words, bipedalism may not be an ascent from the ground but may have occurred thus: as a direct descent from the trees into the upright stance. Bipedal walking uses the same groups of muscles as are used in climbing. The weight travels through the joints in similar angles. Knuckle walking is the sort of scampering on two, three, and four legs that chimpanzees are seen to do. It involves a different overall pattern of muscle usage than bipedal walking (Fig. 7).

Our arms belong above the shoulder girdle when used for efficient support, not below, and the support is suspension and not compression.

No fossil wrist bones which show the sort of thickening that occurs when the wrist is habitually load-bearing (as it is in knuckle walking) have been found in any hominid (human ancestors) remains.

There was no quadrupedal phase after arboreal life. There was a quadrupedal phase much earlier, in the amphibian and reptilian phases of our development; and, of course, it's important not to confuse individual development with evolutionary development.

The infant human does indeed go through an ascent from quadrupedal to bipedal; climbing is involved too. Perhaps

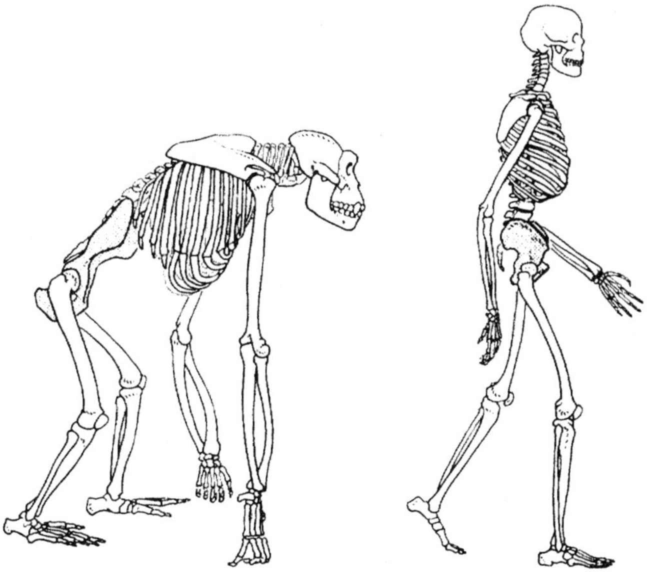

Fig. 7. Knuckle walking and bipedal walking.[8]

climbing is an aspect of child development which is somewhat overlooked, or at least not well explored, mostly for want of a suitable environment.

The great ape which is most similar in this respect is the orang-utang. Too heavy to swing freely, it climbs through the canopy of branches. Climbing is a form of locomotion in which (mainly) one limb out of four is moved at a time, in a planned manner. The body is supported by the three other limbs. The arms, in turn, take a portion of the body weight, and only rarely do they support the whole body weight, trapeze style.

I have found it interesting, in talking to rock climbers, who move in a similar fashion, to discover that the key to greater success is not increased strength but greater intelligence. Difficult rock climbs are achieved by solving a complex three-dimensional puzzle, called "the key" to the climb. Note, that rock climbing is a sport where both men and women can excel.

The use of the arm can be practically explored in a situation where it is possible to take part, *but only part*, of the body weight on the arms.

Fig. 8. Arrangement for encouraging upper torso mobility.

The arrangement in Fig. 8 offers this. Inhibition is most important here because there is a compulsion to play on this by swinging on the bar straight away. This leads only to more misuse. The task is to first stand, and then go smoothly into monkey, leaving the arms and the shoulder girdle free, both in ascent and in descent.

The little bench (about 30 cm high) increases the sense of height by changing the line of sight to the ground. The pole (about 5 cm in diameter) needs to be adjustable to be slightly above head height. It is an assisted exploration of the sort that most Alexander Teachers are familiar with. Can the pupil inhibit the impulse to grab? Can direction be maintained in this novel environment?

One of the results of working in this way is an enhanced mobility in the upper torso. Of course, we're not strictly concerned with outcome as such, but the pole arrangement provides a supporting context for working with the Alexander Technique.

References and sources for illustrations

1. Romer & Parsons *The Vertebrate Body* (Saunders College Publishing, 1986).
2. Pough, Heiser & McFarland *Vertebrate Life* (Prentice Hall International, 1996).
3. Muybridge *The Human Figure in Motion* (Dover, 1955)
4. Aiello, L. & Dean, C. *An Introduction to Human Evolutionary Anatomy* (Academic Press, 1990).
5. *Ibid.*
6. *Ibid*, p. 272.
7. *Ibid*, p. 347.
8. Pough, Heiser & McFarland *Vertebrate Life* (Prentice Hall International, 1996).

Jamie McDowell MSTAT trained with Don Burton at ATA, London, 1980–83. He works in Manchester and in Kendal, and is Head of Training at Cumbria Alexander Training (formerly Fellside Alexander School).

Fellside Centre
Low Fellside
Kendal
Cumbria LA9 4NH
England
+44 1539 733 045
e-mail: jamie@fellside.f9.co.uk

How do you feel about being an Alexander Teacher?

Robin Möckli-Cowper

When I had my first Alexander lessons I was mystified, intrigued, and sometimes sceptical and frustrated. The concepts my teacher was presenting to me, fascinating as they were, did not seem very connected to what I was actually experiencing in the lesson. I had great difficulty finding any means of expressing to my first teachers what I felt during my lessons and what I felt about the self who was having these lessons and the whole expanding situation in which she was attempting to find herself. I felt myself becoming more and more confused and less and less articulate, which was not a comfortable situation.

The decision to continue with lessons and, eventually, to become a teacher did not spring from what I would have called at the time the "rational" part of me. It was a real gut urge which kept on goading me forwards, aware that some numbed part of me was being coaxed awake by my teacher's insistent hands. Part of my personality which had been swept under the carpet at a young age (enabling me thus crippled to appear sweet, good, and placidly happy to my family) was coming to life again and trying to find a voice. This awakening felt wrong, and it was good to gradually understand that it was okay to feel wrong. It felt painful, like a limb which has gone to sleep, prickling with pins and needles, but there was a hope of more life to come. Years later, after giving birth to my children, I was able to recognize this as a birth process. I think we may go through several "births" in one lifetime if we are so blessed or so cursed (as it sometimes may seem), each time bringing to life new facets of ourselves. The Alexander Technique is excellent training for this process of birth, and the Alexander teacher a very skilled midwife.

I had difficult times while training, as well as wonderful ones, as well as strange and funny ones, all of which remain with me, as they do with most of us, and help and sometimes hinder the ongoing process of teaching this work. There were times when the intensity of the work brought up immense waves of feeling, and seemed to uncover a deep well of unacceptable stuff which I didn't much want to look at, and I was sure no one else did either. There were mornings when I would remain in bed in a deep depression, unable even to call in sick, and no amount of directing seemed to help. The patience of my trainers with the state I was in, and the acceptance I felt from my fellow students, were immensely helpful. It was non-interference all round.

We have, in learning this wonderful accepting touch, one of our greatest and most important tools. It gradually calmed me down and showed me, time and time again, that I was not as unacceptable as I felt myself to be.

So, my feelings were not reliable, the screwed-up map I had was not the territory, but remember, these feelings were still there. I still had to go out into the unknown, knowing that I could not rely on my map, with all these feelings screaming at me. I'm talking about myself, which is difficult, and feels quite frightening, but I have seen enough similar cases to believe that I am a useful example.

I think it does require a lot of courage to train as an Alexander teacher. I'm often surprised that people keep going on training courses, even knowing better than I did that they're going into the unknown without a map. Yet I suppose we know that what we are looking for is not to be found anywhere else.

On our training course, we somehow got the message that we shouldn't get too emotional in the actual training course room (remember, this was 25 years ago) and fellow-trainee Dominique Jacques and I often escaped into the kitchen or one of the other rooms in the house to sob or let off steam. A lot of important work gets done in the kitchens and hallways of training courses, and the talks with colleagues at lunchtime or after class are often part of the training process. I am very grateful to Dominique for introducing me to the principles of re-evaluation co-counselling, which were an invaluable aid to me during my training. I became a co-counselling teacher before I finished my Alexander training, and parts of my twisted map unsnarled themselves a little bit with the help of co-counselling theory.[1] Co-counselling looks at the mental and emotional blocks we create for ourselves, and how these can be released.

Beginning to teach is the start of another learning process. We are challenged by the students who come to us, and stimulated by their difficulties and questions. I taught first in Glasgow and then in Paris before settling down in Zürich for eight years (the longest I've lived anywhere in my life). I felt very privileged to have so many interesting students in these different places, and I think I never questioned that I wanted to earn my living teaching this work. Perhaps it was a help not to have any other profession to fall back on, although it certainly didn't always feel like it.

In Zürich, I realized that it was time to look more closely at that well of difficult feelings I mentioned before. I began Jungian psychotherapy and started a training program in bioenergetics with Gerda Boyesen. Both approaches were extremely helpful in deepening and strengthening my work on myself, and for becoming more aware of what was going on with my students. That Pandora's box of emotion I'd clamped shut in my early childhood turned out to have a lot of treasures hidden away along with the pain, and sources of creativity and energy waiting to be unleashed. Gradually I found a language for putting into words those feelings which had seemed so difficult to express in my early lessons and which had threatened to engulf me during my training. I began to dance and sing more, to write poetry, and to keep a journal. It seems to me that taking the trouble to express a feeling, be it in words, music, form, or colour, often results in a release of muscle tension as well as an enrichment of neural connections in the brain.

I think that an interdisciplinary outlook is essential to the development of our profession, whether we choose to follow up other methods in depth for our personal benefit or not. There is a wealth of information in parallel fields, which clarifies and enlightens our own, as well as pointing out what questions we may need to ask ourselves.

Alexander is supposed to have said, "As a matter of fact, feeling is much more use than what they call mind, when it's right."[3] Dewey tells us, "Emotions become sophisticated unless they become enlightened, and the manifestation of sophisticated emotion is in no sense genuine self-expression."[4] We are challenged not to allow ourselves to become fixed emotionally, and to keep on exploring and filling out our emotional maps of the world. Our feelings often determine whether life is heaven or hell for us; they can be so powerful and pervasive.

In this workshop, we've tried to look at how we feel about the Alexander teaching situation [participants took time for an exchange with a partner discussing their best and worst feelings about teaching] and what this may link up to in their lives. It is always possible for us to intellectualize our feelings almost out of existence, or to always try to put them in second place. We owe it to ourselves not to do this, to notice what we feel in different situations and not to let unconstructive mental habits get the upper hand. In the workshop, we also spoke about times when students' emotional difficulties can become difficult for us to handle as teachers. It is important to acknowledge this, and to find support for dealing with the feelings that can be stirred up in us by a student's emotional turmoil; for example, supervision in a peer group.

1. Harvey Jackins et al. *Fundamentals of Co-counseling Manual* Revised Edition (Seattle, Washington, 1970).
2. For an explanation of what is meant by this see Gitte Fjordbo "An Interdisciplinary Approach to the Alexander Technique" in the *Congress Papers* (Jerusalem, 1996).
3. Quoted in "Notes of Instruction" in *The Resurrection of the Body*, (USA, 1969) ed. Edward Maisel.
4. John Dewey's "Introductory Word" in *Man's Supreme Inheritance* by F. M. Alexander (Methuen, 1918).

Robin Möckli was born in the USA and has lived in Europe since the age of fourteen. She studied singing, the violin, and medicine, before training as an Alexander teacher at the Constructive Teaching Centre in London. She now lives in Fribourg, Switzerland, where she and her husband, Erwin Möckli direct a teacher training programme, and she also teaches privately in Zürich and Berne.

Rue de la Gd-Foutaine 11
1700 Fribourg
Switzerland
+41 26 322 1180

Alexander Technique in movement and dance improvisation

Elisabeth Molle & Renate Wehner

Many of us dancers have trained in the Alexander Technique and, within the dance community, many are working in the field of movement improvisation. This forum offered a space for dancers/movers to share their experiences, both verbally and in movement: how do the principles of the Technique influence or change thinking and moving in our approach to improvisation?

Because of the number and diversity of the participants, we first gave guidance to move together, and we then discussed the experiences. The need to move was great after so much talking during the day, and we enjoyed meeting quietly lying down, or rolling on the floor, or running through the space.

We can look at improvisation as an exploration of our own movement, with its many facets and variations.

Whether we are aware of it or not, each of us has her/his own movement, or own song, which is always part of the movement of life:

sometimes we go with it;
and sometimes against it;
sometimes we ignore;
and sometime we celebrate.

Using the principles of the Alexander Technique, we can take time to stop and to listen, to allow and to respond, making decisions that affect the necessity, the playfulness, and the freedom of our own movement.

Elisabeth Molle studied dance in France and in New York. After her qualification as a teacher of the Alexander Technique from ACAT in New York she moved to Berlin. She teachers both privately and in training courses. She continues to explore movement under different forms and is inspired at the moment by the work of Suprapto Suryodarmo. She has two sons, who take care of reminding her about inhibition. . . .

Lehrterstr. 57
Berlin 10557
Germany
+49 39789499
e-mail: elisabeth.molle@t-online.de

Renate Wehner studied new dance at Bewedgungsart Freiburg and with many teachers. For over ten years she has been teaching dance classes (technique, contact improvisation, Alexander Technique and improvisation), mainly in the course and training program at Bewegungsart. She qualified as a teacher of the Alexander Technique in 1992 and is now an assisting teacher on the training course run by Elisa Ruschmann in Freiburg.

Rahel-Varnhagenstr. 35
79100 Freiburg
Germany

The Use of the Self: doing and non-doing

Peter Ribeaux

This workshop explores in a very practical manner some of the central concepts of the Alexander Technique including *the use of the self, the primary control, inhibition, direction* and *non-doing.*

Most teachers of the Alexander Technique will not object seriously to the following description of the Technique.

1. Most of us distort the manner in which we respond to the stimuli we face in life. We pull our heads back and down on our necks in response to the stimulus to act: to speak, etc. When repeated sufficiently often this tendency brings about distortions throughout ourselves, creating faulty habits in the *use of ourselves.* In order to reverse these distortions we must start to
2. *inhibit* our distorted reaction to the stimuli of life, and
3. give ourselves *directions* for an improved use of ourselves and, only then, whilst maintaining these directions, respond to the stimulus in question.

The benefits of such a procedure will be not only an improved manner of responding to a stimulus but also a progressive removal of the overall distortion in the use of the self (which arises from a history of such individual distorted responses).

The purpose of this workshop is to explore some of the consequences which follow from this relatively uncontroversial statement of the Technique.

First a word about the concept of *inhibition.* If an action is distorted by misuse of the self, the task is to remove the element of misuse (undoing or non-doing).

Here, arguably, begin many of the disagreements in the Alexander Technique, disagreements of technique.

What is this non-doing? Is it a sense of effortlessness? Or is it something different?

What is it that is being inhibited? Is it possible that inhibition, the non-doing of the misuse, might involve an effort of some kind?

In the case of a stiff neck or tight wrists there is not too much controversy. Do less of it and the misuse is less. But what about the case of that all too common misuse – collapse? How does one not do a collapse? As Alexander says, any change to a new and unfamiliar use of the self is likely to feel wrong or uncomfortable. Not collapsing is likely to feel like an effort, not at all like any popular idea of "non-doing".

This brings us to the title of this workshop, which is an exploration of the role of non-doing in the re-direction of the use of the self.

Issues covered are those of the comfort zone of the pupil (when is a new experience too much?), the use of words (e.g. "relaxation") and personal space.

In the course of an Alexander lesson the pupil is likely to experience feelings (emotions, sensations) which are not in accordance with what he or she is used to. Remember the whole thing about *faulty sensory appreciation*? The question now is, "What kind of new experiences are appropriate?" This will clearly depend on the conditions present in the pupil. But here lies a burden on the teacher. Does the teacher remain simply a catalyst for whatever is going to take place in the pupil? Or does the teacher actually engineer new experiences for the pupil? If the former, might the teacher be neglecting the good of the pupil? If the latter, might the personal space of the pupil not be invaded and the pupil's right to their own rate of progress be infringed?

A related issue is that of the use of words. Words carry connotations. "Relaxation" and "doing" are two important examples. It follows from what has been said above that the teacher might have to use words in non-conventional senses in order to convey to the pupil what is required. Back to the old question of how to "not do" a collapse. . . .

All this is not just about words. It is a crucial element in a major issue. What actually happens in an Alexander lesson?

Peter Ribeaux is an Alexander Technique teacher of over 30 years standing. He is co-director of the Centre for the Alexander Technique, London. He has been a guest trainer in the USA, Switzerland, and Israel. He has taught the Technique in a number of different settings in various countries to people from many walks of life including the performance arts and industry. He is also a psychologist and works in the Business School of Middlesex University in London, where his particular interest is in the encouragement of individuals to manage their working lives.

Centre for the Alexander Technique
46 Stevenage Road
London SW6 6HA
England
e-mail: p.ribeaux@mdx.ac.uk

The Dart Procedures

Robin Simmons

Dart work

There is a danger that the very valuable material Dart has presented in four papers comes to be seen by Alexander teachers merely as a set of procedures, i.e. a set of interesting movements to do. This would be rather like reducing the Alexander Technique to "getting in and out of chairs" and "monkey", to merely physical ways of "doing things right". The subtlety and immense potentiality of Dart work extends very far beyond such a superficial assessment. It is obviously not essential for Alexander teachers to learn and practise the Dart procedures. But, rather like looking into the experimental work of Dr Barlow or Professor Frank Jones, Dart has much to reveal to us that both enhances, enriches, and even explains what we are up to in our Alexander work. Dart's insights and suggestions link our work to that of scientific investigation, to the worlds of embryology, human growth and development, to what might be called wholistic anatomy, and to an ancestral evolutionary perspective. Not everyone will be interested in these matters but, like many unique experiences, once you've had a taste of it, it tends to invite further interest and enquiry.

The presentation, 13th August

Given the limited amount of time, I decided to prepare a short paper to give an overview of where Dart and his work originates, functions, and fits in with our Alexander work. Copies of this paper are readily obtainable from me at £3 + p&p. The purpose of the paper was to obviate, to some extent, the need to spend time during the workshop explaining the background and wide perspective of the significance and value of Dart work to us. I am in the process of preparing a larger document to fill out what I see as a gap in the literature on Dart to date.

We went through what was but a very small beginning in the possible adventure Dart opens up for us. Beginning in semi-supine (Dart's term for lying down) we explored how to continue to give our Alexander preventive directions as, taking great care to be aware of our psychophysical unity, we explored some variations of vision. Then we extended slowly into supine and over into "edging" where we paused somewhat, before finally rolling into prone. After remaining in prone for a short while, we rather cursorily looked at some parts of the anti-gravity sequence to bring us back and up onto the feet. We then paused to evaluate our experience.

At this point I demonstrated some implications and extensions of what we had looked at, and I introduced the possibilities of "flippering" in prone. To keep all the preventive directions continually alive whilst investigating in an attentive yet leisurely way, a range of movement possibilities in prone took up the remainder of the class. As is so often the case, the class I had prepared in my introductory brochure was too extensive a programme for what was actually possible within our time constraints.

Dart work is mainly self-help work. I hope from even the little we began to look at in this class, the participants gained awareness of some value to themselves personally in trying out some of Dart's suggestions. Naturally, I hope they will be encouraged to explore this rich area of work further in the future.

Robin Simmons, STAT Cert., trained with Walter Carrington 1969-71. He has a private teaching practice in London and, with his wife Béatrice, runs a STAT approved teacher training course, having qualified over 50 trainees to date. He began working with the Dart procedures in 1970 when they were introduced to him during his training. His main concern in imparting these procedures is to help Alexander teachers deepen their individual work on themselves and improve their own functioning, range and possibility of movement stemming from the security and safety of the floor. Robin and Béatrice travel regularly to Switzerland to give workshops on Dart work.

4 Marty's Yard
Hampstead High Street
London NW3 1QW
England
+44 20 7435 4940
robinsimmons@bitinternet.com

Unreliable Sensory Appreciation

Ken Thompson

> Surely if it is possible for feeling to become untrustworthy as a means of direction, it should be possible to make it trustworthy again.
>
> F. M. Alexander, *The Use of the Self*

A learned automatic response to a stimulus is developed in most activities. These learned responses are however not fixed, they have a certain amount of flexibility and adaptability built in. For example, a jazz musician can improvise with others whilst playing, a tennis player, reacting to a quick volley at the net, can rely on the automatic learned responses to hit the ball cleanly, but in that split second can also consciously decide where to hit it.

When people begin to learn new skills, there is a great tendency to look for a feeling tone in their muscle groups that reflects their idea of the movement. This invariably leads the person astray, because it is very difficult for a person to know accurately, without the guidance of a competent teacher, if the movement is being performed in the manner required.

We all tend to trust our feelings, and at a basic sensory level that is OK. For example, we all know when we are standing up, or sitting down, whether we are hot or cold, etc. But if we start to go a little deeper into our make-up, then things tend to be less clear.

As an example, if you normally write with your right hand, put the pen in the other hand and write something, and notice how much energy you put into the task. Now, put the pen back in your right hand and write; do you notice that less energy is required then before?

Or have you noticed that when you go to climb a flight of stairs you always tend to step off with the same foot? If you try with the other foot it feels all wrong.

Reversing the normal way we do things gives us a great opportunity find out more about how we are using ourselves, particularly in the expansion of energy.

That is because our habitual use tends to be "overdoing", producing excessive use of muscles, including muscles unrelated to the task, particularly in our neck.

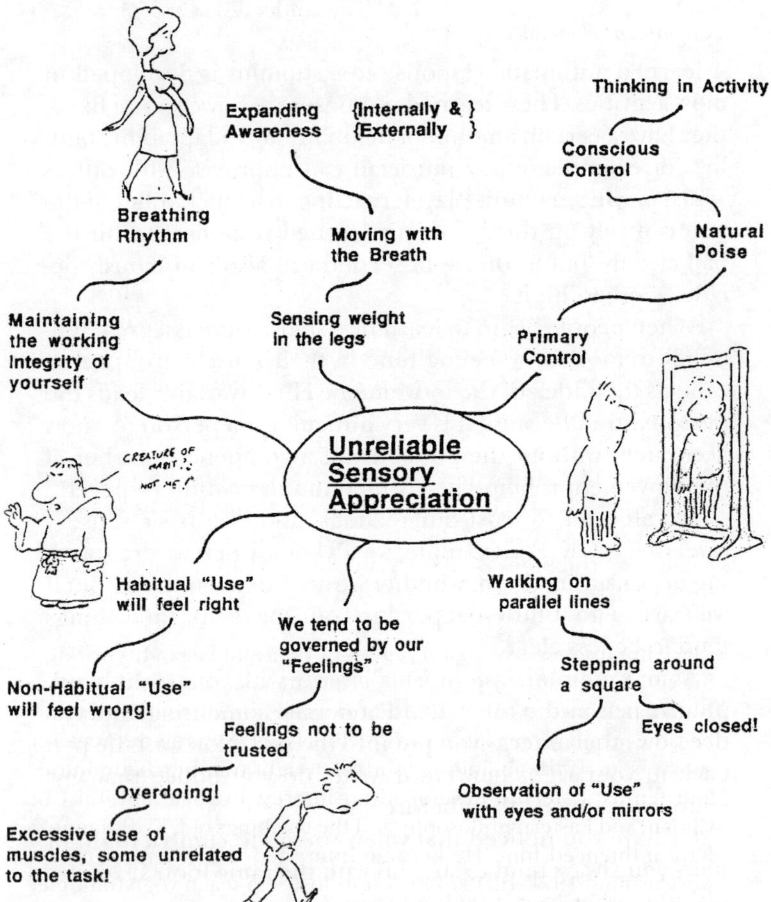

The basic walking procedures of the Chinese Tai Chi Chuan are done slowly and in harmony with the breath, and are ideal for maintaining the working integrity of yourself in motion. Learning to walk along parallel lines, in a way that is definitely unfamiliar to most people, proves a great way to experience something that at first feels "wrong", but turns out to be right when you observe your feet.

Co-ordination movements

By expanding one's awareness to include sensory appreciation together with an observation of yourself in action, it is possible to begin to bring about a change in your response pattern at that moment in time.

This can be achieved by doing some simple coordination movements from a lying down position. These are not exercises in the normal sense of the word, but slow movement patterns, where you have the opportunity to follow the movement closely, observing which muscles groups are in action, what range of movement is possible in the joints, and how much energy is being used, etc.

Because of the limited time available it was only possible to execute a small number of the coordination movements. For the full hour sequence, there is an audio tape and *The Movement Book* by Ken Thompson (Bibliotek Books) which is available from Angela's Books 65 Norfolk Road, Seven Kings, Ilford, Essex, IG3 8LJ.

Ken Thompson was born in London in 1935 and began his working life as an apprentice surgical instrument maker. After two years National Service in the R.A.F., he returned in 1955 to industry and became an electronic laboratory technician. He was always keen on sports from youth, including football, weight training, badminton, and tennis. Later he developed an interest in yoga and Tai Chi Chuan, and Eastern philosophy and the teachings of J. Krishnamurti have influenced him. He became interested in F. M. Alexander's work around 1971. In 1973 he left industry to teach yoga full-time. He trained with Walter Carrington (1976-79), started a private practice in London, and worked on a number of training courses, including ATA in London, and the course in Aalborg, Denmark. He visited Australia and New Zealand in 1982 in order to promote Alexander's work among yoga students. In 1988 he opened the Essex Alexander School and has graduated 31 teachers to date. He has attended the congresses in Brighton, Engelberg, Sydney, and Jerusalem.

65 Norfolk Road
Seven Kings, Ilford
Essex IG3 8LJ
England
+44 20 8220 1630
e-mail: ken_thompson@lineone.net

Sun and Moon

Tommy Thompson

Birds ceased to fly, the wind ceased to blow and the temperature dropped; the planet appeared stilled in the non-ordinary. In the absence of primary light, secondary reflection illumined the earth – casting light and shadow in such a way that the depth of field and colour were more delineated than ever before. Stillness permeated both earth and atmosphere. While looking out over the valley of the Rhine two days ago, this is how I experienced the solar eclipse. Because of the immediacy of this past event in our experience, I shall use the metaphor of sun and moon to illustrate my views and thinking about direction and inhibition in our work.

Recall for a moment your own personal experience of the eclipse, when for a brief period of time the reflective light of the moon gave the appearance of being primary, the true and primary light having been shadowed by the moon's passage between the sun and the earth. My personal experience of that passage, when secondary reflection gave the semblance of being primary, was how quickly all that was cast in the reflective light pre-empted what I remembered as being primary.

Similarly, when I consider my body (that is to say that aspect of myself which provides me with a sense of place, boundary, and context from which to respond to all I am in relation to), I do not think of the physical me as my primary expression of self. More primary is the quality of my being, my awareness and my intention reflected in the expression of my body. To the untrained eye, however, whether it's my own or an observer's, the patterns of movement expressed in my body are far more tangible than the initial movement of energy, which originates in my awareness and my intention.

Now, let's consider the body in relation to the solar eclipse. While the body is tangibly available for view to an observer, and kinaesthetically available for sensing to the person embodied, less tangible is a person's intention. Not unlike the moon reflecting light from the primary source, the body reflects the fact that I am up to something, but physical patterns of movement are not the cause of whatever I am up to. Which of the two, then, the body's patterns or the attention patterns, needs to be addressed to effect real and lasting change?

By way of analogy, during the solar eclipse when the sun could no longer be seen, did you believe for a moment that our primary source of light would not return? The reflective light of the moon was far more tangible given the moon's pre-eminence. If you doubted that the sun's light would return, you might have been tempted to accept the conditions of light caused by the moon's passage between the sun and the earth as primary. Otherwise, you'd probably just allow the experience of the change in light, and would wait for things to return to the integrative state of the natural order of things.

Is there something we can learn from this solar eclipse? It might very well be the degree to which, in our thinking about habit and change, we are prey to paradoxical inferences of primary and secondary sources similar to the eclipse. In other words, when changing habitual patterns that manifest themselves physically, if our "attention self" is the primary source of interference, then our focus on changing the way we use our bodies, however apparent the habitual patterns appear, is secondary. When we give direction, to some extent are we not working with the reflection of the problem rather than with the true and primary source of the problem? If so, how then do we use the kinaesthetic messages sent by the body in a constructive way, not deluding ourselves into thinking that if we change the body, we'll rid ourselves of the problem that in itself governs the body's response? Essentially, which do we hold accountable – the reflection of our interference, or the primary source of interference?

Let me offer by way of example a recent experience that speaks to this conundrum.

As a boy, my home environment was not all that it might have been had my parents' own childhoods been different.

Life at home was unpredictable, prone to emotional and physical violence. To avoid experiencing that which was unpleasant and threatening, and in order to protect myself from the overwhelming nature of a given experience, I distanced myself from my actual experience. This helped me manage the present, in anticipation of the future. (Ask me about something "close to home" today, and I know quite well what I feel in reaction, but I don't have the same clarity of feeling or clarity of thinking about my actual experience.)

Is something missing here?

A part of me is missing.

Unfortunately, it is the part that usually helps one to make decisions that enrich one's life. However, when you only know what you think and feel in reaction, or more specifically what you think and feel having reacted to yourself having experiences, you miss valuable information about how life encounters have really affected you and, because of this, what really matters to you. You end up making decisions based upon your attachment to a series of experiences you never knew you were avoiding, and which, as a result, were partially lived.

This dilemma has become clearer to me than ever. During this past year my wife and I sold our home of 12 years in a neighbourhood we truly loved, to buy a home in a neighbouring town better suited to our children's education. When we placed a bid to purchase a new home, the circumstances around the sale required the purchaser – me – to know much more in that immediate moment what the experience of home was. However, historically, my favoured reactive response was to make things work, even when clearly they did not. As previously suggested, this distances one from one's true feelings. So, distanced, and with my wife's blessings, and under great pressure from the realtors, I placed a bid on the house – fearing I would lose the purchase if I didn't act quickly. The bid was accepted; then, when I saw the house for the first time in the light of day, I regretted my decision, and was baffled and distraught as to how I could have made such a decision in the first place.

I was in despair. To console me, a friend offered an Irish saying: when you move into a new house, the first year you invite your enemies, the second your friends, and the third you move in. I took this to heart but was hardly consoled. The realtor who sold us the house was exasperated over my angst. She claimed that I knew nothing was wrong with the house. "A house is," she said, "after all just a house." She said I was upset about the circumstances in which I had to make the decision: having viewed the house at night and having been under pressure to find the right house for my family.

In fact, I was more upset about the process by which I had made my decision. In hindsight, at the moment I placed the bid to buy the home I wasn't present in my feelings, except in reaction to my past. I had learned, as a boy, rather than to live through what I actually felt, to distance myself from what I was in the process of experiencing. Unconsciously, I taught myself how to avoid feelings and thoughts which were associated with unpleasant experiences in order to manage situations and make them work. I favoured reactive responses which circumvented the actual experience first presented.

Alexander suggested his method would preclude a person having to make good what was entered into wrongly. In using his method of learning, a person could reason the better way before the wrong way was taken. I have no doubt that the inhibitive thought and the inhibitive emotional response do provide a space between the stimulus and response necessary to reason the better way. However, I am not entirely convinced that any method of reasoning which places at the helm the very part of me that keeps the other missing, can ever make the appropriate selection of the information necessary to right the wrong. I am more interested than ever, after this house episode, in knowing when I am allowing myself to experience what I am experiencing, and when I am reacting to myself having an experience.

In other words, at what step along my path of awareness do I inhibit – moreover, who is doing the inhibiting: the part of me who is missing, or the part of me who, although more present is, nonetheless, present in reaction? First, I will offer a tale which, I hope, will shed light on this dilemma, and second, we will explore this issue in practical ways: as teachers in the traditional sense we will inhibit and give direction, through using our hands and verbal instruction, to dissuade our students from reinforcing habitual patterns of reactive behaviour; then secondly (somewhat untraditionally), we will encourage our students to allow their awareness to expand to include not just what they experience but to take in as well that moment when they distance themselves from the immediacy of the experience, and move towards reaction. At that moment the teacher, through using his or her hands and verbal instruction, continues to provide the integrative support of primary control, without, however, guiding the student away from the direct nature of their experience. In this manner, one is asked to reorganize one's awareness but not to reorganize the body. Since intention is the principle around which the body organizes itself, one has been encouraged to inhibit reaction, and to let direction co-ordinate around one's clarity of intention.

Believe me, they are two different worlds. In the former, the teacher works with his or her student as if the primary source of interference resides in the student's body. The teacher subsequently directs the student's attention to the habitual patterns in the body, attempting to make the changes in that context. In the latter, the teacher sees the body as a reflection of interference and works more directly with the student's attention self as the primary source of interference.

Let me offer a tale which illustrates both approaches. Suspend time for a moment. Imagine that we are in Switzerland, in May of 1997. Watch with me as I arrive by car at the retreat where I will lead a workshop for Swiss teachers. During the next five days, we will live together, work together, take meals together, and walk in the hills together, while studying the principles of Alexander's teaching.

There is an incredibly soft, mostly misty rain. The hills surrounding the inn are covered with vineyards and dotted with small, Swiss-designed homes. In front of the inn there is a freshly ploughed field, in the midst of which there is a farmer, and two young boys about the ages of nine or ten, whom I make out to be his sons. The two boys are standing apart from each other, watching silently as their father kneels on one knee, and holds his arm at shoulder height, stretched out – poised. I wonder what exactly is he doing. Then as he continues his movement, I see what he is up to.

Between his thumb and index finger he holds a seed. Kneeling, he lets the seed drop from shoulder height to the earth. The farmer repeats this process with three seeds, each time allowing the seed to fall and find its place in the soil. The farmer is strong in his appearance, yet his fingers pull apart from the seed gently, albeit with great certainty. The boys watch. The farmer, still kneeling, scratches some dirt around the seeds, rises, then he and his sons walk away from the field. Maya, the driver of my car, pulls to a stop at the side of the inn. The spell is broken.

With no interpretation, I step from the car, having taken in this tableau of the hills surrounding me, the homes scattered about the vineyards and the misty rain I can barely see, and now feel. My experience is impressionistic, a mutual exchange of information and impression of which I am a part. I attach no meaning to this unusual way of planting seeds. I am simply in the experience of what I see.

The next day, the Swiss teachers are interested in, among other things, the value of Alexander's directions, taken in context with his concept of inhibition. Alexander himself argued both ways. He was for the directions because the instructions to free the neck, etc., provided the necessary means whereby, in that space between stimulus and the habitual response, habit might give way to the neutrality associated with primary control. On the other hand, he bemoaned ever coming up with the directions because he never felt people knew how to give them without "doing" them.

Personally, I believe, like Frank Jones, that, while directions do help to supplant personal identification with habitual patterns, the conscious giving of the instructions often substitutes for the real learning that comes from simply meeting yourself at that moment of inhibition. What lasting value is there in changing patterns by avoiding patterns, without seeing yourself being yourself? Once you give directions, rather than consciously experiencing yourself being yourself at the moment of interference, which is who you really are in that moment, you run the risk of turning yourself into someone you're not for the sake of good use. My response to the Swiss teachers went something along these lines. However, to my mind, I still didn't give them a satisfactory answer.

We break for lunch. Then after lunch, we have three hours to process our morning, to do whatever comes to mind. Like most, I take a solitary walk in the hills. This day, unlike the previous one, is bright and sunny, no rain. Springlike, all newly alive. After my hike, walking back towards the inn, I come upon the field that had, on the previous day, belonged to the farmer and his two sons. Today, the field is empty. There is no misty, enchanting rain, just the field, freshly tilled, fertile. Without the rain and without the farmer and his sons there is only the field to view, a broad and fertile expanse of earth.

In that moment the meaning and place of directions becomes clear to me. This field, I thought at the time, had to have been tilled before he planted his seeds. I realize that the farmer had only planted his three seeds in the manner he had done because he trusted that the field was fertile. There was no question, no doubt as to whether or not the seeds would take hold in the soil. The field was fertile. His raising his arm, poised to plant one seed, simply allowing it to fall into a random place was, to my mind, his way of acknowledging the relationship between soil and seed. And, for me, between inhibition and directions. His dropping the seed was more of an offering in celebration of the way he had come to view things in his life. His sons had come to watch. They, like him, had come to celebrate the mystery they depended upon. Perhaps? Who knows? It is what I took from the experience because of the questions the Swiss teachers had posed. Today, as the field stands empty in the sunlight, the impressions of the previous day have meaning because of the Swiss teachers' questions.

Why had I not experienced this interpretive view before? I believe it was because I was captivated by the dropping of the seeds. The farmer, in his arresting, stilled poise, was filled with such certainty and grace that he completely captivated my attention. My entire impression was that of the farmer planting and his sons observing. I took for granted the fertility of the soil. However, at some point previously, the farmer certainly must have ploughed the earth, for that must be done in preparation for planting. Sounds simple, but let's look at this for a moment in terms of direction and inhibition. Let us say that the seeds are Alexander's directions, the planting of which he wishes to take root, to grow apart from the habitual seeds which seed themselves, moment by moment in habitual response. Now, where are *we* in this analogy of soil and seed? Certainly, we are not the directions. Rather, we are the soil, either barren without the space to receive that which is new, different and unknown, or fertile, without attachment to the habit of identity.

First and foremost, our bodies provide us with our experience of ourselves. The nature of the integrity of our design allow us to function without having to do much about it. We do not have to work at being us to make ourselves work, especially since we are designed to function even apart from our desires. Essentially, with so many seeds blowing in the wind, we don't really have to select which seeds we feel are right to plant (certainly not if the soil is prepared, sifted clean from interference). Similarly, from an Alexander point of view, we don't need to determine which directions need to be selected and given at a specific moment. There are no receptors in our make-up designed to tell us when things are right; rather the receptors let us know when we interfere.

Astonishingly, when all is working right – and this is important – we tend to feel little apart from the experience we are having. When we are working right, we have the luxury of being more directly involved in the experience at hand with no reaction to it. I repeat, when all is working in the manner in which we are designed to function, we are more available for the experience, free from preconceived notions, and less inclined to retreat into reaction – which is to manage the experience. One either informs the experience, thus fitting all information into one's own paradigm, or else one allows the experience to inform oneself.

Since our design is self-contained, and without the need of our personal assistance, this raises an interesting question: what's in it for us? What's left when we are not in reaction? We, of course, are not the we whom we are constantly grooming, but rather the we who allow our experience to inform us anew, over and over, of who we might potentially be. Yet this, as we know, is not the way it usually happens. Seldom do we allow ourselves to experience directly what we are engaged in experiencing.

Almost immediately, we move away from the direct nature of the experience and into managing that experience, making certain it fits into our paradigm. Rather than allowing the experience to inform us, we inform the experience. This is reaction. It is the field onto which we usually toss our seeds.

Is not our task, however, simply to prepare the soil of ourselves first, before we plant the seeds: to inhibit reinforcing old patterns of reactive behaviour and perception, allowing new information to flood our senses (apart from the information we feel we must have in order to respond)? For many, directions are the manner of preparing the soil. But the priorities appear to be wrongly placed. If Alexander truly meant that his technique was only doing what nature was already doing anyway, of what real value is this constant attention to directions? This presupposes that the experience you are having is ill suited, ill placed, and not worthwhile. It is what it is, however faulty one's sensory impression.

How, then do we prepare our soil except by inhibiting our continual pattern: to react, reinforcing our same perceptions? What if the soil were simply our experience of things; simply us experiencing something. My way of preparing my own soil to receive this analogy of the soil and seed, the day following the original series of impressions, was to allow myself simply to take in information apart from what I customarily see, and not try to fit it in anywhere. This led me to experience more directly the experience I was actually having, moved by the impression of it all. What if I had been so inclined at that critical moment "close to home"? Drawn by the direct nature of the experience, might I have met myself being myself at my weakest moment, and backed off from the decision to buy the house? And, which of the two – the body's patterns or the attention patterns – needed to be addressed to affect my awareness and insight sufficiently to make a choice apart from reaction? I'm not certain. I still believe that my learned and patterned behaviour in that instance was so deeply ingrained that today I can only live with myself having made the decision, awaiting the opportunity to make a better one.

Remember, when changing habitual patterns that manifest physically, and yet occur "attentionally", if our "attentional self" is the primary source of interference then our focus on changing the way we use our body is secondary. When we give direction, might we not be working with the reflection of the problem instead of with the primary source of the problem? If so, which do we hold accountable – the reflection of our interference, or the primary source of interference? I offer this question simply as territory to explore.

Historically, our approaches to making changes when learning the Alexander Technique are based on kinaesthetic recognition of habitual patterns. However, because kinaesthetic recognition necessarily involves bodily sensations, we often reflect inward, drawing away from active participation in what we are up to, and behaving as if those patterns we perceive kinaesthetically are primary, when in fact they are really more of a reflection of the quality of our attention and awareness. My daughter once said to me, "If you want me to change, change my mind, not my body."

What I'd like to explore with you now are patterns of interference, given a person's involvement in an activity. Let's see what happens when you make changes in the primary source (i.e., "attentional" recognition) as against making changes in what is reflected in the body (i.e. kinaesthetic recognition), and how working with the primary source of interference will guide you through the experience you usually avoid, thereby informing you of what you actually think and feel. The retreat into reaction is obviated because, indirectly, you've inhibited through direct experience.

This concludes the paper; now, let's explore the sun and the moon.

Tommy Thompson was involved in theatre productions as a professional and university actor and director prior to teaching the Technique. In 1982, he was a co-founder of Alexander Technique Association of New England and the Frank Pierce Jones Archives, and the F. Matthias Alexander Archives, and was the organizations' director for six years. In 1992, he was a charter and founding member of Alexander Technique International, and was Chair of ATI's Executive Board 1993–98. He has been running a teacher training school since 1983 in Cambridge.

1692 Massachussets Avenue
Cambridge
MA 01238
USA
+1 617 497 2242
e-mail: TTATInt@aol.com

Sun Eclipse

11 August 1999

Carol Levin

Shadows go berserk
    as the tumbling temperature shivers
us into silence.
    It is highnoon, hummingbirds hibernate,
crickets sing night songs.

Cathedral bells are subdued
where women and men sit in friendly clumps
on wet grass in a Black Forest mountain meadow
    above yam coloured
roofs of Freiburg.

Looks like a meadow full of sci-fi villains
wearing cartoon cardboard glasses
with polarized pinprick eye holes.
    Everyone inspects

    the sun,

disappearing, nibbled away
by the moon savouring its time,
leisurely as a heron glides in air
or the way the Tai Chi master moves on breath,
as tenderly as we will melt

    Herr Hermann's perfect
praline cheesecake on our tongues
at dinner, tonight.

Carol Levin is a poet and translator. She is currently studying with Cathy Madden to become a teacher of the Technique.

7315 34th Ave. NW
Seattle, WA 98117, USA
e-mail: clevin@televar.com